# Acclaim for *But G*



"A young cinephile meets an America
Tafoya explores every Ford film, mak
influenced the master (e.g.Murnau) an
lessly between past and present, [citing Ford's visual echoes in so many
directors]. Tafoya addresses performances, politics, and social context, but what grabs the reader is his own unique style—rambunctious, lyrical, conversational, but deeply knowledgeable. This is a wizardly book of first-class scholarship"

*- Molly Haskell, pioneering film critic and author of From Reverence to Rape: The Treatment of Women in the Movies, Steven Spielberg: A Life in Films, and Love and Other Infectious Diseases: A Memoir*

"Scout Tafoya revisits the movies of John Ford neither to praise nor bury him, but to show how alive his movies are 60 years after his death. To paraphrase Tafoya, reading about Ford's films in chronological order has rewards far beyond the poetry with which the filmmaker used his camera and with which Tafoya uses his words."

*- Carrie Rickey, award winning feminist art critic for The New York Times, San Francisco Chronicle, The Village Voice, The Boston Herald, and Artforum*

"Scout Tafoya takes a deep dive into Ford's psyche, pinpointing both why the director is so significant to American cinema, and why he's so easily dismissed by modern audiences. He doesn't shy away from the full history and injects his own feelings on Ford's work, with full awareness that his subject is a complicated and eccentric one. He sheds light on innuendo and masked themes, reminding us that Ford may've even had a biting sense of humor. Required reading for any student of the great American story."

*- Joel Potrykus, Director of Relaxer and The Alchemist Cookbook*

"When some folks are ready to say, "So long, ya bastard!" to John Ford, Tafoya instead marshals his work into the present, wrestling with the sociopolitical complexities and lasting influence of the American master. Tafoya's casual, contemplative prose guides readers on a voyage through the complete Ford oeuvre as he draws connections to filmmakers as disparate as Robert Bresson, Jacques Tati, and Roland Emmerich. God Made Him a Poet is not only a personal reflection on a complicated artist but a timely reminder that great art should continue to challenge us."

*- Jared Gores, Reel Fanatics*

ISBN 979-8-9874787-1-4



www.withanxbooks.com

Cover Design by Tony Stella

Layout by Jon Nix

Assistant Editor Traci Hlafka

WAX004

# BUT GOD MADE HIM A POET

*Watching John Ford in the 21st Century*

Scout Tafoya

MMXXIII

*We have a right to rejoice when a true seer comes at last, some man in whom is an excellent spirit, to whom have been given light, wisdom, and understanding; who can accurately read the 'Mene, Mene, Tekel, Upharsin' of an original mind (however unripe, however inefficiently cultured and partially expanded that mind may be); and who can say with confidence, 'This is the interpretation thereof.*

- Charlotte Brontë

*The function of the critic is to make clear, not to obfuscate; to interpret rather than to judge. John Ford had an original mind - "Vision" perhaps would be a better word- and it is for us who dare to play his critic to offer the interpretation thereof.*

- Lindsay Anderson

*Once our empires glorious but now the empire's gone, the dead gave us the time to live and now our time is done. Now we are victorious, we've become our slaves. A land of hope and glory, building graveyards for the brave. Have you seen the writing on the wall? ...from Hollywood to Babylon, holy war to kingdom come. On a trail of dust and ashes, when the burning sky is done...*

- Iron Maiden

# Table of Contents

# ADJUSTING THE HORIZON

ADAM PIRON

If memory serves me right, it happened again around a year ago. A much-cited, non-Indigenous expert on the history of Hollywood's Native American representations called me out on Twitter to state that I was incorrect in interpreting John Ford's *The Searchers* as racist. Their argument was that the film should not be seen as such because it was itself a look at bigotry and in effect questioning who was the more "savage" in the end. I countered that, although that might have been part of Ford's intent, the film actively engages in the very bigotry it aims to tackle through the tropes it employs specifically in its depictions of Native Americans, which prompted said scholar to block me. Being a Native American working in film, seeing non-Natives rush to defend Ford's work as I saw it was nothing new. The nuance around what could be considered racist versus an act of racism, especially when reflecting on a 60+ year old film and the era it was formed from, is something that can be easily buried in any critique, let alone an online discourse via a social media platform designed to inflame passions. More so, it points to something distinct about interpreting Ford's work as a whole and the continued dialogue, reassessment, and reaffirmation of its ongoing legacies today. What becomes evident are the refractive qualities of the acclaimed director's filmography on various audiences and the reflection it embodies of an America that it both imagines, celebrates, and scrutinizes.

When Scout reached out to me to provide a word before this book, I was both flattered and somewhat stumped as to how to kick off this look at Ford's work. For some time, I've followed Scout's work and have long admired the strength of his critical analyses, as well as the thoughtful consideration that informs his approach. Seeing how this book is meant to approach Ford's work, specifically from a vantage point rooted in the present and our knowledge of both film and American history, I understood why I was being asked. Admittedly I have my own bias about Ford's work in ways that I would assume are somewhat expected for a Native American viewer, as well as those that might not be as obvious. Ford undeniably created both the peak and a valley of Native American representation in Hollywood. One need only look at his films with Will Rogers, arguably the best studio films headlined by the only Native American to ever reach such heights in the industry, and compare them to the cringeworthy images in *The Searchers, Drums Along the Mohawk, Fort Apache*, or in the case of *Stagecoach*, the dehumanizing obfuscation and absence of them. With this in mind, it's also important to point out that Ford himself had a certain level of awareness of his own work and its effects and tried to make a corrective measure with *Cheyenne Autumn*, his self-admitted apology piece to this land's original people. While that film could never undo the damage done, I think the spirit of that work within the larger trajectory of his career is something this book aims to inspire. If Ford himself was able to meaningfully reconsider fundamental elements of his own work and their effects some 138 films in, why shouldn't we?

As with any work from any artists of their time, there is as much to wrestle with as there is to embrace. The beauty within Ford's work is undeniable and its aesthetic and technical achievements continue to shape the seventh art. Woven throughout his oeuvre is a distinct sympathy for the plight of the underrepresented, a championing of the everyman against an increasingly corrupt and oppressive world. *The Grapes of Wrath, How Green Was My Valley*, and *The Quiet Man* are all emblematic of this sentiment as a driving force behind his own filmmaking voice. Being a second generation American and an Irish Catholic, marginalization and struggle were part of Ford's roots. He understood the pain and the poetry of the lives of those deemed unworthy, and even more so knew how to tell it through images that would burn themselves into the psyche of a nation, many of whom saw themselves in his pictures. He not only created visions of an America as it wanted to see itself, but also ones that it hoped to aspire to.

That being said, it's easy to get lost in that dream. As much as beauty lies in the eye of the beholder, it's important to ask whose sight it was designed for in the first place and when. Similar to the thematic line from *Stagecoach* to *Cheyenne Autumn*, we'd be remiss not to consider and weigh the implications of Ford's involvement, however peripheral, in D.W. Griffith's *The Birth of a Nation*, in which he appeared as a klansman. It makes his later use of Stepin Fetchit's (the film comedian born Lincoln Perry) racially-charged "Laziest Man in the World" routine in *Judge Priest*, *Steamboat Round the Bend*, and *The Sun Shines Bright* all the more egregious and troubling. When one arrives at *Sergeant Rutledge*, one of the first studio films to give the starring role to an African American actor and to openly address racism, it bears questioning what got him to that point. Ford undoubtedly saw the impact that Griffith's work had on culture at large, notably the resurgence of the Ku Klux Klan, as well as the turning tide of the incoming Civil Rights Era had on Fetchit's career. If one were to run with the notion that *Sergeant Rutledge* could have been something like the director's attempt to make amends for his own complicity within a larger legacy of this nation's historical distortions fueling the worst of itself, it again hints at Ford's willingness to admit, in his own way, however imperfect and unsatisfactory, that he was wrong. More importantly, it indicates that he was open to adjusting to changing times, new ways of thought, and recontextualized history. If anything, audiences of Ford's films shouldn't be averse to doing the same when it comes to engaging with his own work.

Looking at Ford's work and reconsidering it presently, as this book does, is not a light lift. While there's no shortage of allure, poetry, and cinematic pleasure to be savored in his filmography, there's equally if not more to weigh, especially within the era in which we occupy. In considering all of this, I also wondered how viewers experienced his films as they were released, more specifically Native American audiences. How did these images of Indigenous bodies piling up on screen affect them? I thought of one of my uncles, who holds a culturally prominent position in our community, who grew up on John Wayne films and regularly has images from his films as his profile picture on Facebook. He seemed fine. I also considered my grandmother, who regularly watched westerns with her family at her local theater growing up in rural Oklahoma. She said she had her fill of them, but only on account of them being the only things her brothers would watch. Lastly, I reflected back on my late grandfather. Some of my fondest recollections of him toward the end of his life was him enjoying an afternoon in his chair watching westerns by Ford, Wyler, Wellman, and reruns of shows like *Bonanza*. One night I had dinner with him and he was telling me about his day and how a friend of his, a non-Native man from Ohio close in age, had given him a call earlier. This old pal had watched some western recently and had really been affected by a scene that reenacted a massacre by cavalry troops against a tribe. I had met this man quite a few times growing up; he was about as unapologetically red, white, and blue as one would expect from The Greatest Generation in Middle America which made the purpose of his call all the more unprecedented. He had phoned my grandfather to apologize for not knowing about this side of American history and how truly awful he felt about it. My grandfather chuckled it off and told him not to worry about it. History was what it was, they couldn't change that. Moreover, they were friends. What he saw, he consoled his old time friend, was just a movie after all. All of us at the table had a well-meaning laugh about the incident, but then I remember asking my grandfather what he thought about westerns and how Natives were always the villains. As clear as day, I can still hear his voice when he told me, "They were just trying to survive."

Adam Piron (Kiowa/Mohawk) is a filmmaker, writer, and programmer based in Southern California. He currently serves as director of Sundance Institute's Indigenous Program and is a cofounder of COUSIN, a collective supporting Indigenous artists expanding the form of film.

# INTRODUCTION

What you're about to read is a study of the films of John Ford specifically from the vantage point of this moment in time, November of 2022 when the first draft was completed. I attempt to look at the necessary and thorny work of unpacking a conflicting and frustrating political worldview as reflected in movies made by one man across five decades that also saw two World Wars and 10 presidents. There will be an argument made up top about the need to look political anachronism and dissent of every stripe in the eye and understand, to not pretend things were better and that our looks back should be as good as we *want* life in America to have been, or that we should only hope to have uncomplicated art. Then a look at every movie Ford made that is currently available to watch (something like a quarter of them are lost forever). Finally a look at the practical influence Ford's films have had on the half century of cinema that has followed since his death. I want to thank Jon Nix for taking a chance on my potentially unpopular work and for being such a good friend to me these years. I want to thank the genius Tony Stella for his truly beautiful artwork. I want to thank my dad for showing me *The Searchers* when I was too young to understand it but just old enough to be transfixed by it. And I want to thank my mom for teaching me very young that sometimes it's just fun to watch John Wayne walk. That, too, is cinema.

PART 1

# RETURN TO FORDLAND

"Oh so you're writing the book no one wants to read." Mused Ty Burr when I explained to him why I thought now was the best time to write a book about John Ford. In truth the world likely didn't need another but I was heartened when, speaking with some of the first critics who sat and watched *The Searchers* when it was new, told me they were excited to hear that someone younger was still interested in discussing Ford. My reasoning had little to do with the admiration of people I already admired, though as always for a cussed narcissist who subsists on the endorphin rush of a compliment it didn't hurt, my inspiration was two-fold. First my friend the critic Willow Catelyn Maclay asked me if I had written anything about John Ford as she was also thinking about his movies and it occurred to me I hadn't. This was a missed opportunity, of course, Ford and Hitchcock are the pre-modernist names that are associated with cinema. Their names and "cinema" are synonyms. Or they were before Steven Spielberg dethroned them, combining as he does one's all-American poetry and the other's yen for vulgar suspense. A crucial difference between the three men is that Spielberg's cinema of spectacle was criticized as it was created, in essence always creating its own negative image as it continued. The receptions to *Raiders of the Lost Ark, E.T. The Extra-terrestrial, Indiana Jones and the Temple of Doom, The Color Purple, Amistad, Saving Private Ryan, Minority Report, War of the Worlds, Munich, Lincoln, The Post*, and *Ready Player One* were made by people whose political beliefs and aesthetic preferences are still recognizable to audiences today, a score of years after the turn of the century. The overwhelming liberal critique of *The Color Purple*, that a white man should not have made it, is still something that can be understood today and reflected a changing surface of the cultural machinery. If Spielberg made *The Color Purple* today, the same criticism would be levied, and it would be just as valid.

And yet...something has shifted in the culture.

I need to say right now that most conservative attempts to explain the behavior of the left or the "left" are nonsensical polemics based on phobias, bedtime stories, and bad dreams. There is never any logic, fact or reasoning behind republican ghouls and the websites who draw their headlines from the worst people in our country, no smart people give them credence. What, I suppose, concerns me, is the new American left's knee jerk impulse to toss things out that don't align with the dominant political perspective. Just so you know where your author stands. And yet there are very real discussions happening about the political content of movies, and there doesn't look to be any easy way to sort them out. No one has ever successfully been cancelled (except maybe Armie Hammer, who once starred as a Fonda-in-Ford western Lawyer). You get cancelled when you die.

Some idea to what I'm referring can be found in the response to Paul Thomas Anderson's *Licorice Pizza*. The movie has a scene where a clueless white man speaks in a terrible, exaggerated Asian accent while his asian business partner rolls her eyes at his truly insane attempts to sound like he understands or has mastered the Japanese language. Anderson's film is very clearly both a recollection of his upbringing in 70s Los Angeles and his recollection of the movies being made at the same time, the things he saw, and the things he knew at the time. Part and parcel with this is the absurd racism of the local entrepreneurs. Indeed It's difficult to imagine living through the 70s in LA without running into horrible racists like those depicted in the film (specifically John Michael Higgins' character Jerry Frick, based on a real man who did keep marrying and divorcing Asian women). And so the question becomes; should Anderson have excised the character? If so, why? Does it make LA in the 70s, a place stalked by deranged pussy hound Jon Peters (Bradley Cooper), a place beset by obviously racist districting policies, a city that produced both Clint Eastwood's *Breezy* and Roman Polanski's *Chinatown*, seem more realistic to exclude jackasses like Frick (played by Higgins, famous for playing overbearing dumbasses in studio comedies, chosen, one suspects because the audience knows his characters are people we're ok laughing at, not with) from the tapestry?

When the movie was first released the trade reviews were mixed but skewed positive. A few weeks later after more and more of the public and culture writers had seen it, the pieces started flowing. Wilson Wong, writing for NBC News, wrote on November 25th, shortly after the film's initial release, that people were starting to loudly call out the scene's implications. Wong quotes sociologist Nancy Wang Yuen, who says the movie "depict[s] racism "unfiltered." "If there are no consequences, scenes like this can almost glorify this behavior," she said. "You're not laughing at [Higgins' character] because he's making fun of someone else; you're either laughing with him at the expense of Asians, or you're going to be upset as a viewer." On December 18, 2021 the Media Action Network for Asian Americans called for a boycott of the movie from awards and voting bodies. On the 28th the New York Post reported on their boycott under the headline "Asian activist group demands boycott of 'Licorice Pizza' over 'racist' scenes." On the 31st Rebecca Sun wrote an extended analysis of the decision to include the scene for The Hollywood Reporter. Randy Boyagoda wrote the tellingly titled "Are audiences smart enough to handle ambiguity" in the Atlantic on January 19th, 2022. "The moral judgment here depends on why they laugh..." at *racism or depictions of it* in American movies directed by white men. Later Boyagoda says, "With apologies to Plato and the good folks over at MANAA, I want *Licorice Pizza* playing everywhere, exactly as it is, to limited laughter and viral outrage and critical disagreement." Buzzfeed, Time Magazine, and the Daily Mail variously recapped the controversy when it was nominated for three academy awards. A website called Media Diversity gave the film an F grade for its politics on February 22nd, 2022. On March 23rd Jen Yamamoto writing for the Los Angeles Times took a look at the many arguments, once more quoting Yuen: "The argument is that those [offended] are just people who were not reading it right," said Yuen. "But ... there's no context. There's no repercussions. There's no discussion. You don't even understand what the women are saying. They might be saying, 'F— you,' but we don't even understand that. It's too subtle for people to say, 'Oh, well, he's racist and it's terrible, and that's what's happening in this scene.'" This, I must say, doesn't speak very highly of Americans but I also must admit she's right. We seem to be quickly losing our collective ability and will to want to parse the meanings of something like that scene.

A hundred questions emerge from this debate. What is the moral function, if indeed there is any, of a film critic? *Should* there be one? Maybe that's *all* it should be? Can a critic divorce a movie from its intended or unintended moral dimension? The answer to that last one, anyway, is no. Not if you're meant to keep up with the film industry in a militarized America or in countries producing anti-government movies (which is near to all of them with any kind of infrastructure) as the last kind of dissenting missive allowed to escape into the world. You cannot view the movies of Jia Zhangke without a comprehensive understanding of what he is and isn't saying about life in China. Well perhaps that's not true but you'd have to go to great pains to not be able to see it. Anderson, when asked about *Licorice Pizza*, he said we shouldn't attempt to make period pieces using the lens of modernity. I don't even necessarily think that's true or a realistic rubric for every single director or moviegoer but Anderson's movie is about what happens when, as in the Los Angeles of his boyhood, there are no "adults" around. No one to tell you to go to school, to stop hustling, to go to bed, and no one to tell the many supposed adults to not be a xenophobic horse's ass. Anderson's movie is a portrait of Los Angeles without a single, trustworthy voice of reason. This, I thought, would ring true to people.

Very few movies made before today meet the ever-evolving standards of a good portion of modern audiences, which puts us in a curious position. More movies are being produced than ever for American audiences in a host of union-defeating new streaming platforms, the bulk of the product that hits the box office already have built-in streaming homes because audiences are hungrier than ever for the same stories and characters, and all of them are designed to meet the zeitgeist. What makes that dubious is the zeitgeist changes faster than ever. This isn't a problem for people - these changes (which include a louder mouthpiece for non-white, non-straight people in America and on the world stage) are long overdue. For the first time in American history the victims of its worst crimes are having their say. The trouble comes when the entertainment machine, which has historically been unable to match the demands of the times, tries to give the culture what it imagines it wants. Such "timely" movies as Carrie Cracknell's modernized *Persuasion* (2022), Rachel Lee Goldenberg's *Unpregnant* (2020), Emerald Fennell's *Promising Young Woman* (2021), Halina Reijn's *Bodies Bodies Bodies* (2022), Sam Levinson's double feature of *Assassination Nation* (2018) & *Malcolm and Marie* (2021), Maria Schrader's *She Said* (2022) and Rian Johnson's *Knives Out* movies using modern reference points, newly minted language, and a softness of delivery to feed a youthful audience without too much difficulty. The trouble is that audience will grow up and change its habits as the world keeps changing and the demands of people change with it. Furthermore the references will age, because thanks in part to the twin traumatic events of a Trump presidency and its crass headline-everyday style and then a global pandemic that killed millions, the capacity of our brain to retain information relevant to our political landscape changed. We didn't *want* to remember. We didn't want to live in this purgatorial space with no changes to our immediate surroundings and cataclysmic, unimaginable changes to the world happening at so rapid a clip you'd fill the walls of your apartment if you tried to collect every headline. We changed, and the movies tried to change with us, but we didn't change the way art can. We won't know how we processed this until we've actually survived it. Right now Covid-19 is still happening and another Trump presidential bid is just over the horizon. This dates the book, but I have to admit that was the point of the book in the first place. To take stock of a group of facts and art works in one *second* of my life.

It was unthinkable for there to be cuddly teenage pro-choice movies a short while ago. In another short while it's going to make America look rather backward that we needed them. Similarly, embarrassing references in the dialogue of some of the aforementioned movies to the website "Indiewire," the musical *Hamilton*, or Edgar Wright's *Baby Driver* were dated the second they left the mouthpieces who recite them. Movies about the world we live in now cannot survive thirty seconds in this desperate attention economy and as the American cinema becomes the province of streaming content designed to be forgotten (and directed with no thought given to depth of field to accommodate viewers who want easy, painless pictures that don't need to be considered in the estimation of a work's impact or ideas) and movies directed by underpaid CGI studios that shove everything else out of theaters, the goal is no longer entertainment, let alone to provoke thought. It is numbness. A calming, unchallenging sense of familiarly nice pictures floating by while you focus on other things, like your phone which has *yet another* stream of familiar images, though they may be designed by contrast to outrage. An uncomplicated binary of good values versus bad ones. Binaries are useful in personal relationships but they don't tend to work in discussing art history. Most of the great artists of the last 500 years were "problematic" for one reason or another, and yet we keep the Rodin Museum open. Do Céline's Nazi politics invalidate his poetry? Leni Riefenstahl is still taught in schools (thanks in part to George Lucas, of course, who took Nazi imagery and made candy colored war propaganda out of it, then had *that* taken by capitalists who cut it into fifty million pieces and shoved it back like fast food at a stomach that will simply never become full), what does that say about the education we're receiving? Is it fair to assume… *anything*?

Part of the issue as well can be explained by the lack of a coherent political threat to the creatives working in Hollywood now. In the1950s you could lose your job and go broke if you were blacklisted by the House

Un-American Activities Committee, spearheaded by senator Joseph McCarthy, who ended his career in disgrace, a laughingstock. In the 1980s and 1990s American artists were fighting against the censorship of the United States senate once more as art in response to the AIDS epidemic and the millions dead because of malicious government inaction became a national conversation. Today there is no equivalent challenge to the mettle of the artistic class or the working directors in Hollywood. Conservatives who complain that Hollywood is too gay are too obviously clowns in cheap suits to be taken seriously, and furthermore their arguments don't hold water. Our cinema has never been less carnal or less meaningfully violent. Conservatives were right that this would desensitize children, but what they couldn't predict is what happened next: nothing. Now they have no enemy because the kinda-sorta liberal version of Hollywood we have now produces nothing worth getting angry *about*. Most contemporary American artists, even *great ones*, have no public political affiliations. This goes some of the way towards explaining our perennial nostalgia for the 1980s and 1950s. Those were the last times artists and *people* had the strength of conviction to fight enemies of free expression, great and small. It was clearer in the Reagan years who the enemy was, and so all of our movies and TV look backwards to that "simpler" time. Now there's no way to even sell out because everyone taking part in financing structures has already sold out. To work is to be part of the system, whether through social media pages run by oligarchs or studios run by billionaires in bed with the Israeli government or the United States defense department. We still get great movies about the plights of the working class but it's not as though there are many American directors who make it clear at rallies, in interviews, or with their general comportment, that they are Marxists working on behalf of the oppressed. "Politics" became a dirty word in America after the blacklist and dirty it remains.

Of course, all the same, It costs nothing to *vouchsafe* a political ideology without official affiliation. Even when former Mixed Martial Artist Gina Carano was fired from her cushy gig on a Star Wars brand program after embarrassing herself by saying that trans youths were coddled and that she wouldn't be bullied into respecting their pronouns or the way they choose to live, she found work the next month on the threadbare productions of the crackpot entertainment network The Daily Wire. There is too much money at stake for producers to lose your number, no matter how transparently cruel and nonsensically virulent you are. The matter of a political class in Hollywood is all up to the deductions of the audience who look to art to have their politics mirrored back at them. When a movie like *Licorice Pizza* puts the power in the hands of its audience to determine how they feel about scenes of lovers with significant age gaps, powerful men chasing women around the streets of Los Angeles like loose dogs, politicians hiding their homosexuality to gain power, or a racist entrepreneur getting away with his dreadful behavior, that is a less comfortable position than it is to be told by the movie explicitly that all of this is bad and that the filmmakers condemn it (something The Daily Wire has no trouble doing in their movies). The culture no longer wants ugliness from the people on its side, and maybe they're right to demand it after a century of art made in the shadow of colonial powers and their genocidal designs on the future. It's not like the same six kinds of people aren't still in charge. Fred Trump the 1st ran brothels out of the Klondike for gold miners. Everything changes while nothing changes. Should our art?

What troubles me about the need for less difficult and less toxic images and ideas in our movies is that that makes for an easier narrative for future generations to look back on *this* time. Our movies will answer questions with no complication, which suggests something false about how we lived. Was getting an abortion a challenge in 2020? Yes, but with enough go-get-em attitude and a good friend by your side you can get one safely and get back to living your life in your repressive hometown (or escape to the safe haven of a big city college). Were there awful sexists like Harvey Weinstein running the movie business? Sure but we got him! He's in jail now thanks to two plucky reporters. These movies aren't meant to touch the third rail of the reality of their situations, they're meant to take a thorny truth and reduce it to its most easily digested components so that viewers leave feeling better about life in America. My question is why do we want that when things seem to somehow get worse every day? Of course if that isn't the goal behind this new type of movie, more of them would have unhappy endings. Giving into what the writer John Banville called "creeping infantilism", the world is allowed to be thorny for the first and second acts but all is right with the order of things in the end. If the films have unhappy endings, as in *Bodies Bodies Bodies* (I confess it feels ridiculous writing about this movie full stop as it careens towards oblivion), it's the fault of a degenerate culture and the kids and all their pronouns, social media accounts, and fake problems. If the kids in that movie had a few more old fashioned values, maybe they wouldn't have all killed each other! The movie doesn't intend to be a conservative call for a retreat from the new kind of identity kids can possess now, but it has no idea how else to relate to the shifts in culture other than to paint 'X's on all the changes to point them out to people. Those people will, in turn, either recognize the behavior on screen or recoil from it in revulsion, feeling alienated and superior for not taking part in the changing of the cultural landscape that allows for such ungoverned behavior. I would argue that these movies will if they haven't already all age into misshapen postures the same as John Wayne's movie of the battle of The Alamo, where the heroic suicide of hundreds of brave soldiers served to protect American values and her too vulnerable borders. Sometimes some people just *have* to die, right? The same exact split in viewer reactions is to be expected: the people who watch *The Alamo* because they respond to the values it espouses and the people who shrink from its hopeless political perspective. Those values are not my values, or they are. What other function does a movie like *The Alamo* provide? What other function do movies like *Knives Out* or *Bodies Bodies Bodies* provide as cultural texts?

It should be much more self-evident when considering the possibilities of a work's reception with the public that any rhyme with the works of John Wayne, director, really ought to be discouraged. After all the impression that a younger generation has of the swaggering cowboy actor are mostly defined by the morals gleaned from his body of work and his infamous 70s interviews, specifically the one he gave for Playboy in 1971. The interview took place on Wayne's yacht, a converted World War 2 minesweeper, which is a handy metaphor for the actor's persona. The hard-nosed leading man hadn't seen any combat but played soldiers as often as he could and developed an unrelenting conservative streak to overcompensate for his feeling of having missed out on the chance to really prove himself. In the interview he throws homophobic slurs around, rails against screen violence and sex, says black people complain too much, that the Black Panthers are a danger to society, that Native Americans shouldn't be given reparations, that welfare is helping people stay lazy, and many, many more crotchety, bigoted notions all from the comfort of his Burbank pleasure vessel. The other Wayne story that people never tire of telling is the legend of the six security guards. Supposedly Wayne had to be restrained by as many when Sacheen Littlefeather came to the stage to accept Marlon Brando's Oscar. I guess he was supposed to be thinking he'd beat a woman to death on live television. The great critic Farran Smith Nehme debunked the story pretty thoroughly on her website, The Self Styled Siren, in 2022, and it was further complicated by Littlefeather's family calling her native ancestry into question after her death, but the people who tell the story as evidence of Wayne's bloodlust miss the point of John Wayne's image, something he worked long and hard to cultivate. He only ever pretended to fight, whether in classics like Howard Hawks' *Rio Bravo* (1959), ungodly kitsch like *The Green Berets* (1968), or in real life getting mad about a symbolic victory for Native Americans or Black Panthers.

In his exhaustive 2000 biography *Searching for John Ford* (one of the most important references for this book, along with Lindsay Anderson's *About John Ford*, published in 1981 but written long before then, and Tag Gallager's 1986 work *John Ford: The Man and his Movies*), author Joseph McBride mentions that the people who were most shaken up by Wayne's comments were the First Nations tribes with whom he'd grown friendly over the course of his long career. He and John Ford had made great friends with the tribes they filmed with and employed for decades so much so that they had names given to them by the tribe. McBride spoke to some of the tribe for the book and they were shocked by Wayne's heel turn. I'm not sure whether it was naive of them to not just assume that an American movie cowboy could be friendly to their face and cruel when turned away. Wayne's sociopathic bluster in his private life is as much a part of his image as his cowboy roles because they together form a coherent picture of the 20th century and its he-man heroes. Wayne was a crucial figure in the creation of the craven perversion of the western icon; his life was part of the text as much as his art. In books and tall tales, the cowboy became a hero with tales of bravery and cunning helping them "tame" the west, an inherently racist construction from a time when only white men got to construct our reality. Then those books were turned into movies, the first feature films, with actors like Hoot Gibson, Tom Mix, and Harry Carey (who found his most adventurous collaborator in Ford). Then, at long last, the real histories were allowed to become texts as prominent as the mythic versions of events, like the Alamo, Wounded Knee, or Custer's Last Stand. The old ways of telling the stories of the founding of America were not allowed to go unchallenged. Wayne's image being complicated by his horrific views of his fellow man was a part of the undoing of the damage done by some of his movies to the idea of the white man's place at the top of the food chain in the west. That white men were *needed* to tame the land and cull the people who lived there for thousands of years undisturbed. This is a necessarily reductive view to get at the heart of the Wayne image; an uncommonly talented artist who walked tall with guns on his hip who was at heart a draft dodging racist coward, venomous towards any liberal cause. Ignoring one for the other is no way forward. All of these men are

John Wayne and thank god there was only one of him.

Ford, maybe even more so than Wayne, has become the lodestar for the argument about the horrific and simplistic view of the Western as an American genre and the people who believe in it. Currently there's a plaque at the Academy Museum in Los Angeles, CA that reads, in part: "Drawing from dime novels and Wild West shows, the western was the first US movie genre, helping to build both the domestic film industry and a national identity. Though an integral part of cinematic history, these fantasies of wilderness conquest by Euro-Americans are inextricably linked with stereotyping and the promotion of violence against indigenous populations." Below the plaque is a clip of the 2009 documentary *Reel Injun*, directed by Neil Diamond, Catherine Bainbridge, and Jeremiah Hayes which features a clip from Ford's 1939 western *Stagecoach*. In 2012 Quentin Tarantino, in conversation with Harvard professor and author Henry Louis Gates, had this to say about Ford: "One of my American Western heroes is not John Ford, obviously. To say the least, I hate him. Forget about faceless Indians he killed like zombies. It really is people like that that kept alive this idea of Anglo-Saxon humanity compared to everybody else's humanity — and the idea that that's hogwash is a very new idea in relative terms. And you can see it in the cinema in the '30s and '40s — it's still there. And even in the '50s." In 2019 he returned to the well, noting in a blogpost on the website for his theatre, the New Beverly "Now [Ford's] White Supremacy is cloaked under different names… Americanism… Esprit De Corps… Civilized Society… (i.e. White Society), but in the context of Ford's 'Fort Apache that's just a bramble bush by a different name…" He cast aspersions on Ford's character by bringing up that he was a stuntman in a Klan robe in D.W. Griffith's 1915 movie *Birth of a Nation*, still a bracing watch over a hundred years later - a movie Griffith tried most desperately to atone for with the following year's *Intolerance*. As with Ford, it's the ugliness that largely gets remembered in public discourse. Which isn't to say either man didn't earn it with frequently ugly art. Griffith finally ended his career with a biography of Abraham Lincoln in 1930, unfortunately one of the director's worst films. Ford picked up where Griffith left off, making his own Lincoln-centric movie in 1939, and starting conversations about American art and racism he couldn't control after his heyday.

Morality is not an aesthetic value, it can't be measured in foot candles or hues and try as we might to grade it, who's got that particular answer book, exactly? Thus viewing Ford's films from the vantage point of 2022, over a hundred years after he started making silent movies, can be a whiplash inducing experience.

He was not bound by his own morals or the era's. He made it up anew every time he directed. Few directors ever possessed such a poetic quality as Ford, which means that even a movie as bankrupt as his dreary 1941 comedy *Tobacco Road* contains more moving visual splendor than the text can reasonably support. When he was lionizing the US cavalry's mission to kill Apaches in 1950's *Rio Grande* or whether he was supporting the cause of the Irish Republican Army in 1957's *The Rising of the Moon* or 1935's *The Informer*, the same splendor touches everything. Does that luster diminish when pointed at scenes of manifest destiny, of casual domestic abuse, of the everyday racism that so defined American life? Are the form and content easily separated? If Ford had been born in Ireland instead of in Maine as he not so privately wished, would he have made movies about the English killing the Irish the way he did the cavalry killing the natives? Would he have still made his westerns? He grew up transfixed by pictures of "cowboys and Indians," per McBride. In 1968 in an interview with the BBC, Ford compared the treatment of native Americans by whites to the treatment of the Irish by the English, which made his interviewer very uncomfortable. This was four years after he made the first "anti-western" with the elegiac if creaky *Cheyenne Autumn* in 1964. A few of Ford's movies turn native characters into a faceless, marauding throng, an evil force to be dispatched, but in his private life, he paid millions of dollars over the years to Native Americans, giving them steady work whenever he was in town, and shared countless meals and returned the respect they gave to him. As programmer/critic/filmmaker Adam Piron points out in his article for The Criterion Collection entitled The Uncharted Frontier: Will Rogers in John Ford's America, he also was one of the handful of directors in the early sound era to give a Native American a leading role. Comedian, author, and occasional Democratic politician Will Rogers was a citizen of the Cherokee Nation and he appeared in dozens of silent movies but only a handful of surviving sound films before his death in 1935, three of them directed by Ford.

Piron: "There's an irony brought forth by the Ford-Rogers films. They add an often-overlooked dimension to a long-debated critical powder keg of Ford's work: the representation of Indigenous people in his oeuvre. Among his detractors, the accusation is that the director was a central culprit in cementing subhuman imagery of Indigeneity in Hollywood and relegating it to antiquity. Whether the Native Americans in question are the faceless, human targets in *Stagecoach* (1939), the marauding heathens of

*Drums Along the Mohawk* (1939), or the grunting rapists of *The Searchers* (1956), their slaughter is, according Ford's accusers, depicted as cause for celebration, or at the very least as an inevitable necessity to make way for the prevailing American spirit. Ford's defenders prefer to rationalize these examples as poorly aged narrative traditions of their era, counter-weighed by his quasi-sympathetic portrayals of this land's first people and their plight in *Fort Apache* (1948), *Wagon Master* (1950), and *Cheyenne Autumn* (1964). To say that Ford's approach to matters of race was inconsistent is to put it mildly."

Later in that same piece: "Against all odds, Ford's films with Rogers revolve around a Native American actor given top billing in his most dimensional roles, free of having to "play Indian" for white audiences. They're rarities in that, nearly a century later, no other Native American actor has been afforded the same opportunity in major studio films. Within cinema's first four decades, Native Americans went from being depicted as on-screen cannon fodder to having one of their own earn half a million dollars a year as the top-paid star of the industry; both phenomena that Ford had a hand in shaping. To Ford's detractors and defenders alike, Will Rogers again represents not only the unexpected Indian, but an inconvenient one at that."

Tag Gallagher said in his study of Ford's books that Ford the man was inscrutable, a charge McBride rejects in his later work. I agree with McBride, but I also take umbrage with McBride's own charge that some of Ford's decisions (to say nothing of his appallingly abusive behavior and language to his closest friends, frequently used to wrench performances out of his actors) should be chalked up to an "Evil Twin." This to me carries the same trouble as either ignoring one side of John Wayne's personality to appreciate his talent. The point is they were all of these things and part of the reason is because America and Hollywood conspired to allow them to be. To me it's perfectly clear that Ford suffered most of his life from an identity crisis and an inferiority complex - that at any moment someone would look at him the wrong way and his confidence and unpleasantness and his command of his little world would all vanish. The harsh words, the "jokey" racism he exhibited towards close friends like Woody Strode, the constantly needling Wayne about his lack of service and his failure as an athlete, his merciless sexism towards some of his female stars, the terribly shabby way he treated his own children; all of this was target practice for the day he was dethroned by someone who could not be felled by Ford's trickery and bravura. This explains why, despite having given thousands of dollars (personally, under cover) to the IRA to help them fight during the rebellion in the 1920s, he eventually buckled and stopped standing his ground against the blacklist for a few years in the 1950s. It explains why, despite giving money and work to Native Americans and saying in interviews things like "My sympathy is all with the Indians," being invited into the Paiute tribe while filming *The Iron Horse* in the 20s, being so close to the Navajo that they started calling him Natani Nez, or Tall Leader, why he frequently filmed his natives speaking the wrong dialects, cast white and Latin actors to play Cheyenne or Comanche, and also implied that they were brutal savages in his texts. It's why he gave a black man the first starring role in a major studio western after years of giving work to Stepin Fetchit, the famously loathed black comedian who would steal scenes by giving exaggerated, stereotypical performances that conform to the worst of white expectations. It explains why he could call Woody Strode horrible names on set in front of the other actors and Strode still loved the man so much that he lived with him for four months to help with his health and was quite literally *holding* Ford in a loving half-embrace when he died. The public pervert with a Catholic's outward propriety, the man Richard Nixon called a friend and a hero, the socialist union man who helped create the Directors Guild of America, the man who was so tender to Katharine Hepburn and so awful to his own wife, Mary. His jock days of school yard brawls and football glory, and his eager excitement at memorizing dialogue from the wings of a theatre he staffed as an usher, they both built the greatest poet of the cinema. To study John Ford, to know John Ford, is to keep at least two ideas in your head at once because they happen to be about the same man. What worries me just enough is we're losing the will to do that.

Ford told Peter Bogdanovich "It's good for the country to have heroes to look up to," when discussing the controversial ending of the movie *Fort Apache*. In that the racist savage Lieutenant Colonel Owen Thursday, played by Henry Fonda, marches to his death with a number of his soldiers by his side. John Wayne's Captain Yorke, who is friendly with the Apache, tries to talk him out of it, but ultimately lets him go to his death. When asked about Thursday in an interview (Ford may have been a terse interview, but he had much use for journalists in his movies), Kirby lies and says he died valiantly, that the mission is worth it. It's a disorienting pull of the rug, an ugly button on a tense story, but it's the lie on which the West, America itself, was built (just as Ford's film grammar built the American cinema – without him, as we'll see in the epilogue, there would *be* no American cinema). Looking back at a culture and only seeing perfect art with perfect values won't teach us anything. America never had a moment where it rose to *good*, let alone perfect. Why shouldn't our movies look headlong into the abyss of violence? That's honest, isn't it? If we lose our picture of the past, we'll paint it again with new lies.

Culture must (necessarily) be a reflection of our times and America has never once had a minute where the times have afforded us the luxury of uncomplicated art. That's true now and it was true when Ford made *Fort Apache* and starred in *Birth of a Nation*. It is less exciting for me personally to watch a movie like *Django Unchained* (2012), Tarantino's riposte to Ford and Griffith, and see the uncomfortable compromise between wanting to admit the country was a living hell during the pre-civil war years and still needing to insert a kindly white German man who teaches his black companion to be civilized enough that he won't be mistaken for a slave anymore. There is a reason, after all, that director and writer Terence Nance called the movie "Peak White Supremacy" at a round-table at the Black Star Film Festival in 2018. Tarantino may be able to call out, without hemming and hawing, how racist his country was and remains, but he also can't help but insert himself, the savant dramaturg, into the movie in the form of the character of Christoph Waltz' Dr. King Schultz (the name a bizarre play on Martin Luther King, Jr.). Tarantino presented a vision of the West that is as ugly as anything in Ford's oeuvre, but he made sure to explicitly condemn racism and slavery as he was wallowing in its violence in his images. All he left out was a place for the audience to do any work. If a movie ends with a freed slave killing his wife's captors and the vicious Uncle Tom-styled head of the household, it has said everything it needs to and left no political purpose in its wake. The sight of Jamie Foxx's Django killing bad men is cathartic and exciting (Tarantino is one of the American cinema's best image makers), but his movie refuses to indict the audience in even the way Ford does at the end of *Fort Apache*. You leave comfortable, knowing the bad men were dispatched, and then America continues to uphold the work of those same bad men.

Ford's politics, which ricocheted like a stray bullet from the time he gave aid to his Irish cousins during the War of Independence to the time he produced a pro-Vietnam War documentary, is hard to put into words because Ford didn't think in binaries. The Irish were fighting the English, so he hated the English, until he was working with them. Nixon was the president of the United States, the country he'd proudly gone to war for in the 1940s, so he liked Nixon, even though they had nothing in common and the Ford of the 20s would have loathed him. Nixon famously bought into the images of America that Ford painted without questioning them, which is of course to Ford's discredit that it was possible for him to do so. To make a movie that a man like Nixon could unquestioningly enjoy doesn't speak very highly of the nuance he may have brought to his own movies, but then a movie cannot be blamed for its fans unless it was courting them ideologically (as Griffith was when he lobbied so hard to get *Birth of a Nation* shown to whites-only movie theatre audiences).

Making things more complicated was that Ford spent his life on movie sets, drinking and gambling with his friends on his yacht, The Araner, on vacation with his wife or actors, and finally at war. He was never a man of the people. He didn't know how "the people" reacted to his movies. When your life is one long bender (the good and the bad, the parties and the hangovers) in a little world you created populated by the people you hand chose for the roles of your friends and admirers, you get very little sense of how the world outside is meant to operate. In short: there were no "adults" in Ford's world, just the people who loved him and the people who tolerated him. Thus his continued use of narrative devices and implicitly racist ideas that worked in critically acclaimed box office successes (like *Stagecoach* or *Rio Grande*) continues even when they have outlived their usefulness. Even in his anti-westerns, which include *Sergeant Rutledge*, *Cheyenne Autumn*, and even, I would argue, the Chinese-set *7 Women* (1966), the use of othered enemy hordes remains in place from his earlier films. The Cheyenne are not humanized so much as idly and dumbly worshipped (until he needs them for the occasional bit of terrible comedy) in *Cheyenne Autumn*, the black buffalo soldiers of *Rutledge* are heroic figures but only in opposition to the dehumanized Apache out in the darkness, and the Mongolian hordes (played by Asian extras but led by Woody Strode and Mike Mazurki in inexcusable yellowface) in *7 Women* are the challenge that forces our heroes' true nature to emerge from the visions of themselves they wear in better times. Each film rejects the attitudes of some earlier work of his, but neither one is a full about face because some habits likely wouldn't have occurred to Ford as too problematic to be ignored. Movies need villains after all, by any studio director of the time's reckoning and just as Ford the liberal was always hiding inside of Ford the Rear Admiral and Ford the anti-communist, he was not a man who evolved. He was always the kid drawing cowboys and indians instead of paying attention in class, and so even when he went out of his way to make *Rutledge, Autumn*, and *7 Women*, his ideas about movies hadn't evolved any more than his ideas about chivalry or bullying. Not for nothing, we need to keep revisiting movies with horrifying racial casting ideas because otherwise we'll take it for granted how far and how long it took the film industry to cease feeding the white mainstream ideas it thought it could handle. Kenji Mizoguchi died at age 58 in 1956, leaving behind one of the most transcendent bodies of work, replete with high class melodrama and emotionally disturbing fables, an original, a director unparalleled. Five years later Blake Edwards cast Mickey Rooney as a Japanese landlord in *Breakfast at Tiffany's*, still a beloved film with images widely proliferated in material reproduction (Warhol didn't use Audrey Hepburn's image in that film for nothing). America deserves to have these decisions remembered. *This* is what America was, and *this* is how hard some people fought to change it. Without the effort needed to wipe yellowface off of our screens it would not have evolved because it kept making money (frankly we still occasionally excuse it in our cartoons). What we can never do is pretend America didn't make these egregious calculations (to call them errors is even wrong, it implies that back then they *could have* come to the decision it was a bad idea, that this was an unfortunate accident instead of a million dollar industry making decisions that kept the cash machines printing). We did and if we forget it we'll do it again.

I've felt a couple of times during the writing of this book that it may be ridiculous and futile to try and have this discussion, but cultural discourse is the melting pot into which criticism, my art form, and history are thrown. If we cannot be clear about the perimeters of reasonable understanding of history, we're discouraging the same thing. The 2010s through today has been a time of unprecedented use of the phrase "Separate the art from the artist." I understand the urge to want to keep safe and sacred the works that mean something to us, that helped us define who we are at a young age, and when our heroes, these artists, let us down, the impulse people frequently have is to discard the creator for the creation. To simply enjoy the work free of the contradictions and work that must be done to keep the work alive in our estimation. I find this to be counterproductive and a little cowardly. Part of aging is putting away the proverbial rose-tinted glasses we used to look at the world, and that includes the art that so charmed and inspired us when we were younger. By trying to hold onto our perfect adolescent view of a work of art, no matter what that work may be, you're agreeing that the work should not be allowed to evolve with you and that you yourself needn't evolve at all. We cannot at once be a culture where victims of abuse and trauma are allowed to have their say and then we decide to not do the work of understanding the people who cause that harm. Obviously there's a grave difference between the physical hurt done by people to other people and, say, a children's author's conversion to hard right politics, but per the Academy Museum's warning about westerns, the one promotes violence against the other. To stand John Ford the man separately from his work does both of them a disservice. Ford's art is the kind of testament to the malleability of morality, to the frailty of Americans that we need to study more. We've tried to cover up a history of bad art with good art, but we may *need* that bad art's lessons, if nothing else to try to help make the good art worth watching in a few year's time.

Ford was a political liberal in a conservative business who retreated from his best instincts when the culture started to threaten to pierce the illusion of his own centrality in the world he made for himself. If HUAC could stop you working, it meant Ford would have to finally look himself in the mirror and wonder what else he was doing on Earth. Without his movies Ford could not be the god of Fordland, with its roving film production camps and their nightly singalongs and cookouts and regimental dances (the way McBride describes it you'd think Ford's actors stumbled through the pearly gates every night after "cut, print"). Every night on a Ford set was a party, and when the movies wrapped he'd throw lavish Holiday parties at a ranch he bought for his Naval unit after the second world war ended; indeed his social gatherings seem like the weddings and dances from Michael Cimino's *The Deer Hunter* (1978) and *Heaven's Gate* (1980). Ford used to enter the set every morning to the strains of character actor Danny Borzage, director Frank's brother, playing "Bringing in the Sheaves" on his accordion. That's not life on Earth, that was just life in Fordland; a bubble. Threats to that way of life made him compromise. He took money gigs he didn't care about, made politically dubious work (even for Ford) to stay afloat, and he talked tough one day about the need for unions to stand up to producers, and the next day wrote Cecil D. DeMille a letter saying how courageous he was to stand up to those loutish unions. Every single thing in Ford's art could change if need be, because the thing that mattered was that he got to keep making it. In high times his work reflects his socialist leanings and in low you'll find unforgivable stereotypes and the rough edged conservative family values that would be the cornerstone of the politics of Ronald Reagan, the politics that have survived to 2022 in increasingly warped and perverse ways. Ford was, of course, a confused and scared man - his history of kicking around his male stars is a classic projection of and terror at his own weaknesses and sexuality - but he was also the perfect picture of the artist who cannot live in reality. As it is in the movies, though, sometimes a bastard makes a better character than a human being. Ford was a martinet, a man who could not detect his own racism even as he fought it in others, a miserable locker room heavy, "but", as Lindsay Anderson said of him, "God made him a poet and he must make the best of that." Or, maybe more to the point, there's what Boston legend and film critic Gerald Peary said to me when I told him I was writing this book, in a note-perfect Ford impression: "He was a son of a bitch, but he's my favorite director."

PART 2

# JACK FORD'S SILENT ERA

1917-1928

Rowdy Jack Ford wasn't going to be a picture maker. His interests were in theatre and sport, both forms of public performance. When he got to Hollywood he had no money and no prospects. Mother Feeney, a woman Ford would later pay tribute to in a dozen or more of his movies, would have preferred her sons become criminals before she saw them become actors, but she got over it when Francis, Jack's older brother, started showing up in movies playing down the street from their home in Maine. Fame she could understand. The early silents Jack directed chronicle the slow dawning of a personality, a style. Many directors arrive fully formed, ready to impart their vision of cinema onto the world (Michael Mann, Terence Davies, Terrence Malick, Ken Loach, Preston Sturges, Orson Welles, Steven Spielberg) and others start off as one kind of director before veering hard into new territory, discovering themselves as they go, responding to the times and a changing audience (William Wyler, Curtis Hanson, Douglas Sirk, Robert Siodmak, Roy Ward Baker, Leo McCarey, Richard Brooks). Ford was a stupendous sequence director and a canny image maker from the word go, but he was just getting started. Making westerns with Harry Carey came with freedom and limitations because no one cared how the films turned out because their kind of movie was popular, but they weren't going to be given the kind of resources available to the D.W. Griffiths of the world. They would make do with a little and just keep creating. It was only when Ford started to feel the itch of ambition that the world started creeping into his movies. Classicism and racism and the spectacle of the creation of civilization and the attitudes that clash when you decide to make the world from nothing. 1924's *The Iron Horse* was in some ways Ford's first real film, the first one where he was able to shoot exactly what he wanted, where he was allowed to think up more than the best way to film a horse chase or a barroom brawl (though, because those are such intrinsic parts of Ford's concept of American drama and filmmaking, those both still feature prominently). The daydreaming athlete realized he had more to say, that his poetry was being wasted on cowboys. It wasn't, not exactly, but the idea of his needing to become someone would put him on the road to being the American cinema's most important poet. Ford had to leave Maine to find movies, then he had to leave Harry Carey to find himself. All the while his family history, the years of his youth spent in a sea-side hamlet, all of it begins to feed his stories of the wider world. Even when he was in Wales, Kenya, New Orleans, Kentucky, French Polynesia, Arizona, or California, he was always in Maine dreaming of the Ireland that gave birth to his parents. The melancholy of never finding home, never *feeling* at home would dog Ford his whole life (not for nothing did he let his beloved yacht, The Araner, rust into uselessness before he'd give it up) and give an edge to every one of his stories of valor and life outside of civilization, of law and order. His heroes would search in vain but never be allowed to come home. Ford could never become the boy again, though he tried. His first movies with Harry Carey are proof of the existence of a purity of life, of making movies with your friends, of having your life ahead of you and having no idea what if anything it had to be.

## Straight Shooting (1917)

John Ford (born John Martin "Seán Aloysius" Feeney) made a quarter of a hundred movies with cowboy star Harry Carey and then more with his boy when he came of age. Ford had the temperament and loyalty of an Irish barfly. The men at his left and right would stay there if he could help it ("Harry? He's in the Gin Mill."). It was easier than learning new names and anyway up against the machinery of Hollywood he needed every friend he could keep. When Universal executive Carl Laemmle found out he and Carey, a star, had gone off the reservation and started making features instead of shorts he stood up for them. Maybe they were onto something. Ford never looked back, making five reelers and above (by *The Iron Horse* in '24 he was up to two and a half hour epics) for the rest of his life, pausing only for the war effort or the occasional TV episode or war documentary. The young Ford was a more energetic fellow than he became, which means that the early work can sometimes make you look over your shoulder for the scene that flew by.

*Straight Shooting* has fleet pacing, gun fights, barroom brawls and lots of men on horseback. His heroes perform maybe the first comic stand-off, when they must, guns in each other's guts, navigate their bodies through a tiny window together. A few minutes later they're back at the bar drinking together. Ford wasn't quite so afraid of the implications of his movie's declarations here; maybe he was just young. This one's nakedly socialist. Carey plays a free-grazer whose antagonistic overlords try to steal water from him and his horses and farm land so he can't live there anymore. Because it's Ford they settle this like men, with two fists and a pistol. The story of Johnson County's dead sons drifts down river through time into Ford's view finder. If he had a hard time giving Native Americans their due (indeed he shamefully played up the comic version of Natives every chance he got in movies with only five or ten surviving minutes from this period), he can't pretend he didn't know right from wrong.

Carey is Cheyenne Harry, a character he played on and off all his working life, a good old boy who tried to live a simple life... but temptation crept up on him. It's not hard to see Ford in the character, the little kid actor brought along with his brother to the Sodom and Gomorrah of the new world with everything to prove. Older brother Francis Ford ran away to the circus and then wound up in pictures (their mother wrote him off as dead) bringing John with him when he settled down. By the end Jack would be more like the old men who tip their hats to Cheyenne in many a short, but without the pleasant demeanor and the fearlessness before their own emotions. Molly Malone, one of those perfect Ford names, is a revelation in the early Westerns, perhaps not quite the object the Gish sisters, Lilian and Dorothy, turned out to be for Griffith but stunningly modern, rather like Ford himself. Carey looks old fashioned but he's very watchable. Ford was something like Sean O'Casey on a horse back then, trading crowded family homesteads for plains and prairies, cops and turncoats for ranchers. The poor had to look out for each other. Of course, the difference was Ford's gift was not dialogue but filling a square with action and *meaning*. *Straight Shooting* takes a reel to get going but it ends with fireworks that still stupefy more than a century later.

**Bucking Broadway (1917)**

The first fully surviving Ford film comes with it a sort of hindsight anticipation. You read about *The Tornado, Soul Herders*, and the rest and the progression from drunken Jack Ford just making guys leap off their horses at each other as he learns what a camera does, how to edit in camera, what the best composition for a shot is... to John Ford the poet. By the time you reach *Bucking Broadway* the excitement drips off your face like sweat. It's earned. The first few minutes are a frenzy of emphasis. Horsemen filmed in stark geographical relation to one another in a seemingly boundless frame. Men miles away acknowledging each other, hands in close-up carving trinkets for the women just out of frame, the vastness of space used as a background alive with potential. Ford was 23 so it's obviously impressive he got it so early but there's also the idea that to the newbie enthusiast inventing his own engineering solutions to the problem of "meaning" in a movie that wasn't built to have any he inveigled some. What does the audience want to see, and how do they want it shown to them? He was making this up as much as he was learning anything and it shows. This is a marvel of visual demonstration. The story isn't so important as two shots connected by a breezy cut to make meaning. No wonder Sergei Eisenstein loved him. Young Ford was creating cinema (and the 20th century) and recreating the 19th century every time a horse rode toward the camera. He makes Griffith look sluggish.

*Bucking Broadway* is something with energy you still see today when a director seems to have cracked the formula: Federico Fellini, Leos Carax, Paul Thomas Anderson, Mathieu Amalric, Gore Verbinski, guys who make every shot its own reward. Ford by now is so confident he can make "mistakes" that look more dynamic than theory. A man is punched in the head and falls stage left. The next edit picks him up falling down a flight of stairs stage right and then runs down the z axis for 15 seconds until he's gone from sight. It's impossible *and* thrilling. Every barroom scene teems with incidental business, and every landscape has more than one plain of action. A cowboy hemming and hawing while explaining his nuptials has not one but two close-ups of his feet dancing uncomfortably as he searches for the right words. A case could be made that directors should be asked to master academy ratio before being allowed to graduate to wider frames. It means so much more when a hand extended in approval takes up the entire frame, as if Ford had pointed his camera at the sun and God nodded back.

This is a tale of men finding their emotions, of fathers leaving the room to cry about their wayward daughters, of men twitching when met with praise and encouragement, of the silent confederacy of men rent by loss and longing. About men having a drink too many and unleashing their inner beast, something to which Ford could heavily relate but not yet. It's tidy but that's more a product of film being a nascent invention; Ford was still just grabbing stories off the clothing line and seeing if they fit. It never much mattered what his cowboys got up to but there's little doubt he loved the idea of a passel of Wyoming ranch hands riding into the big city to rescue a woman from the clutches of a moneyed industrialist. It ends with a parallel donnybrook and horse chase and both are impressively huge things indeed. Ford would not now be diminished.

**Hell Bent (1918)**

Ford by now gives off the distinct impression that behind the camera he has the intoxicating bravado of a rodeo rider or a trick shot (the movie features both). Every set up is an opportunity to wow an audience into the future. Men ride horses into barrooms (the very act that won Carey fame back in his early stage days), creating Napoleonic tableaux in dusty Texas barrooms. A man considers a painting as the camera zooms into it and then it comes to life without a visible edit. True magic if e'er I seen it. The title seems equally to refer to Ford's desire to shake D.W. Griffith (who he loved and admired, calling *Birth* one of his favorite films of all time to the bitter end, but he also said Wayne's *The Alamo* was almost as good so maybe he was just being nice) out of the public's imagination as the American cinema's pet director. They want history written in lightning, do they? Here is a cinema of pictures that spring to impossible life and stare back at you. A runaway freight train of incident and faces coming right off the screen like the one that supposedly scared the first movie goers out of their seats in the Lumiere's screening room.

The eagerness to try every effect imaginable speaks to both insouciance and excitement. He tells jokes with freeze frames and uses vignettes like Arnaud Desplechin would 80 years later: for emphasis but also to remind you that this art form is as close to illusionism as the 20th century has to offer. Ford wastes not a second, shoving some stupendously entertaining sequences into each reel without abandoning the thread of the plot fully, though you can sense a growing boredom with the kind of cowboy stories he was allowed to make (he'd take a hiatus shortly after and then only fleetingly return to the genre well into the 30s until *Stagecoach* changed everything).

The story here is one Ford would tell for the rest of his career, though perhaps rarely with such a perfectly rationed sense of earnestness. Homosocial bonding grinds uneasily against romantic love as two men fall into bed with each other and then into confusion when a woman enters their life. Harry Carey is once again the lovesick cowboy, whose mustachioed chum looks on with envy as he loses himself in the eyes and arms of a dance hall girl. The best moment in the film is a few seconds of awkward navigation of a rainy street. Carey has to take a second to think about the best way to carry his gal across the muddy thoroughfare of lawless Rawhide. The romantic idyll is interrupted by an attempted heist which leads to an exciting horse chase and then finally an existential death march into a sandstorm (later a Ford specialty). Carey gives his girl his horse and has to trudge to freedom with his rival, upon whom fate does not smile. It ends with a big grin on its face, this movie, but it's a deceptively heavy thing. Ford covers a lot of emotional ground between the slapstick and horseplay, hinting at this ability to stick comedy brawls between searing investigations of the soul. The point as always is it's tough to conceal who you are out west. All that space and nowhere to hide.

**Just Pals (1920)**

Buck Jones wasn't a name I'd heard before, but his appearance in Ford's *Just Pals* brings out an ease in the director; their rapport creating a space closer to modernism and its breezier social dynamics. Harry Carey, Ford's leading man until they broke up to pursue bigger and better things, was certainly fun to watch but Jones seems to be less hemmed in by style. He'd been in a few dozen two-reelers by now and he'd go on to a hundred or so more. He's a fore-runner of the Deans and Brandos, sure, but more than that he seems to point the way toward 40s John Wayne, a guy just kind of figuring out how the world works and how his body fits into it. After the usual opening fireworks from this period Ford (a beautiful tableaux with two distinct planes of action twenty feet apart; two kids fighting in their yard, and a little boy appearing to actually board a moving train without a stage hand's help) there's a great gag where a kid is thrown off a train by one of the station hands and in the answer shot, the kid lands in a heap in a ditch. Jones walks over to give the brakeman a piece of his mind, catching the attention of a female passerby (Helen Ferguson). She looks on adoringly at his heroically standing up for the kid, just in time for the punchline - Jones is thrown in a heap in the ditch right next to the kid. They both laugh and help each other up. Ford, the poet of the barroom brawl, sharpens every tool in his kit.

Babe Ruth starred in a movie of the same name with a vaguely similar plot about ten years later, so someone remembered this. I can certainly understand that. All the Fords from this period stick in your mind like early rock songs. Maybe all you remember is a guitar lick or the reverb on someone's mic when they shout "baby!" but it lingers. This is Ford's first Charlie Chaplin picture. There's even a minor character with his mustache. Jones and his young charge bum around, getting each other to age up for whatever task is in front of them. Jones threatens to kill a chicken for their supper but everytime he brings the knife up to behead him the young fellow stops him. Would have been right at home in *The Kid*. Ford adduced a Chaplin-esque sentimentalist streak around here that he'd revisit from time to time (cannily he understood every film needed different doses of it, and some none at all - that's why I like *Arrowsmith* so much, even if it's not nearly his best work). Jones threatens to send the kid to school and he shoots back "You didn't go to school, why the hell send me?" That's what sets Ford apart from Chaplin, among a few other important things.

In one of those purely visual strokes that set Ford apart from other directors, he has Jones spy on the kid's first day of school from the classroom window. Ford took every advantage of the frames he found on every set. Observation and the way in which people fuse with their surroundings and become one with us in the audience transfixed him. There's a third act robbery, pretty standard stuff for Ford by now, but there are breaks for images that seem religious. "Nightfall across the trail to nowhere" reads an intertitle and then Jones and his ward stand on a hill, between the camera and the sun, looking like they've just descended from Olympus. Ford was still young enough to be on the look for hypocrisy. He has his evil posse praying and the subtitles use air quotes to call them out. It's very modern, like when Jeff Nichols has Joe Don Baker lead a prayer before going to kill a drifter in *Mud*. Great moment. Like Chaplin, Ford seemed aware that the more civilization modernized, the tougher it was going to be to tell genuine folk from pretenders and frauds. A simpleton like Buck Jones is a human compass, as Ford and Chaplin both imagined themselves to be. Always pointed true north toward good old-fashioned values. Of course… life has a funny way of sticking a magnet to your functions.

**Cameo Kirby (1923)**

In 1961 Breathless finally had its American debut. Bosley Crowther, writing in the New York Times, the castle walls that protected him from trends, said "As sordid as is the French film, "Breathless"...and sordid is really a mild word for its pile-up of gross indecencies—it is withal a fascinating communication of the savage ways and moods of some of the rootless young people of Europe (and America) today....it goes at its unattractive subject in an eccentric photographic style that sharply conveys the nervous tempo and the emotional erraticalness of the story it tells." Time Magazine was even more cruel: "Breathless is a cubistic thriller that has an audience because half a century of modern art and movies have rigorously educated the public eye. Filmed on the cheap ($90,000) by an obscure, 30-year-old film critic (Jean-Luc Godard) of the French New Wave, Breathless would seem to offer little to the average star-struck spectator—it features a Hollywood reject (Jean Seberg) and a yam-nosed anonymity (Jean-Paul Belmondo). What's more, it asks the moviegoer to spend 89 minutes sitting still for a jaggedly abstract piece of visual music that is often about as easy to watch as Schoenberg is to listen to."

It was the attitude that condemned a post-war Catholic authority. Godard spurned a consistent story and indeed linear time, and so when he started wasting cops and hanging out in bedrooms with shirtless lovers it was easier to condemn his cavalier inventiveness with the camera and at the editing bay. Because of course Godard was nowhere near the first man to mess about with time when he felt the atmosphere demanded it. Godard, for his part, would later exhibit fascination with Ford and John Wayne. He was horrified by his own adoring reaction to *The Searchers*, of his affection for Wayne. The moment Wayne grabs Natalie Wood in the climax, it's like someone gave all of life's beauty and horror to Godard and told him to keep them in his hand. If he dropped it he'd never see either again. All throughout the many hours of *Histoire(s) du Cinema*, Godard cannot stop running the clip of Wayne grabbing Wood. All of art, our reaction to it, our complicated love of it, in that one frantic decision, that one inexplicable gesture.

Jack Ford started going by John Ford when he made *Cameo Kirby* in 1923 and it's not hard to see why the emendation in public persona was needed. It is at once a more regal and post-modern tenor than we're used to seeing young Ford assay hitherto now. With its Booth Tarkington source material (Welles would later adapt his *Magnificent Ambersons*), its high decadence of setting (a riverboat casino, a venue for second hand La Belle Époque fashion and off kilter social grace) and Ford's sly but unyielding gaze, this is half Renoir picture and half Renoir painting. But crucial to understanding the confidence is that he keeps repeating seconds of time to drive home impressions of its subjects. Three seconds of a close-up, then an abrupt edit to show you three different seconds of the same close-up. It happens so often that it can't merely be a kind of winking version of the intertitle introduction cards, where the description of someone takes up most of the frame and in vignette in a corner the picture of the actor stands there absorbing the judgment of the screenwriter. Surely Ford didn't have the patience for that? No, if I didn't know better, I'd say he was trying to have fun. One moment twice, leaving the viewer unsure of the veracity of what they've just seen, indeed questioning what a movie really is. A series of impressions? Action (this one's got a death by gunshot in a medium about 5 minutes in)? Or time, kidnapped and tortured?

John Gilbert, dead by 38 having romanced Garbo more persuasively than any other soul, is the hero. Like Ford he'd been kicking around the film industry since 1914 waiting for his break. Here he's Don Juan dressed like Jack The Ripper. Ford loves filming his sharp sideburns and perfect features, but not so much as he likes filming people on the bow of the ship, watching space fly by. There's a shot of four steam boats passing by a small town that is so monumental it seems almost religious. He'd shot with trains before but this seemed to excite him even more. These billowed like factories and ruined unbroken surfaces like leviathan. Water becomes a conduit for all his technical ideas - a young woman (a still unformed Jean Arthur making her debut) is daydreaming while stirring a puddle with a stick and when it clears there's the reflection of her unwanted suitor looking up at her, Gilbert will later spy Gertrude Olmstead, the object of his affection, in a well - because it's the ephemeral that interests Ford. He presages the forgotten pageantry waiting (or not waiting) for Ethan and Martin when they return from their final jag in *The Searchers* here by insisting that out on the water the party must always go on. Murder and marriage and mistaken identity takes a back seat to gambling and cigars. That's John Ford's America. He'd already slant drilled Griffith's historicity and here he is inventing Godard, Renoir, Stanley Kubrick (the duels!), John Huston, and stealing a march on everyone from Clarence Brown to King Vidor, both also coming of age around now, artistically speaking. One hundred years later cinema is still in a puddle, reflecting the world Ford created.

## North of Hudson Bay (1923)

Watching early John Ford is a fascinating look at the way art travels. This or that film is from a VHS rip on YouTube and comes with English subtitles to go with the Portuguese intertitles as the film made inroads as a programmer with William Fox's money in his quest to dominate the global box office with oceans of product. I thought not infrequently of Bill Morrison's *Dawson City Frozen Time* (2016) while watching Ford's *North of Hudson Bay*, and not just because they take place in the forbiddingly frigid northern territories. Morrison's film shows the journey any given reel might take in its journey to entertain the largest possible audience, dead ending in a frozen bog near a town that sprung up around a gold claim. *North of Hudson Bay* found its way to me with Czech intertitles, and I pictured it playing their gorgeous movie houses, which would have been erected not long after the creation of the state.

It's a little shocking that Ford didn't make more movies like this, in the vein of Jack London (they were sympathetic politically and both loved tales of men at the ends of the earth proving themselves). There are close-ups and lighting set-ups that are almost Dreyer-esque among the back slapping wildling camaraderie, so maybe he just didn't think there was much to see in the snowy mountains. He and Chaplin only made so much art in these conditions - maybe they hated being cold. Tom Mix leaves his usual dusty stomping ground to go find his mother's favorite son, who's been killed. His claim partner is being held on a murder rap in a Klondike campground. It looks pretty cut and dry; they find him with the smoking rifle in his hand standing over the corpse. But Tom Mix wouldn't be sent to rescue a scoundrel, no sir! We see the crime twice, once from the perspective of the mob, once from the innocent man's perspective, an early kinship between Ford and Kurosawa here emerges. Eugene Pallete is on hand as the dead brother, charming but an incomplete man without the froggy voice. Mix takes a steamboat (Ford having developed terminal steamboat fever) and falls in love. The parade of faces here are romantically haggard, some of the best bit players Ford had yet filmed. His yen for filming pretty cowboys meant he hadn't yet found all of his people - Big Victor McLaglen, as my friend David Cairns calls him, impossibly set John Carradine, gruff Ward Bond and the rest of the boys.

The picture of the Inuits isn't exactly complimentary (simple, noble, etc. etc. etc., - collar pull) but they aren't evil like the natives would become when he entered the thirties. Ford's sympathies are queer. He does seem to recognize that there's a right and a wrong way to do this (he had little trouble with both sympathetic portraiture of black men in *Cameo Kirby* the year before, but he's got black-face and red-face all over this period and he never loses the latter). Compromises were clearly necessary working for studio money (if we're being generous) but Mix has to kick the shit out of a bunch of the natives to save his brother, even though they're just doing what the law dictates. The villain is the very white Frank Campeau, lookin' like Fritz Lang's Dr. Strangelove, who has rigged up solar powered rifle death traps like a proto-Jigsaw killer to murder folks as they sign contracts (sadism at home, wild animals and deadly nature abroad; Mix fights wolves with naught but his mitts like Liam Neeson in *The Grey*). Ford cuts right to a close -up of the ominous barrel of the rifle, conversing with Edwin S. Porter, but hinting that the scourge of the modern world is that there may soon be no man at all behind the gun and thus no ideology behind war. Mix is sentenced to die on the death trail, a walk into the white unknown from which no one returns. Men murdered by no one, others sent into nothing. No wonder Ford didn't feel at home here. Capitalism assailed him like an army of ghosts, a pack of wolves, a too-strong current.

**The Iron Horse (1924)**

D.W. Griffith was Ford's unspoken friendly rival for the length of their career overlap. Ford was an extra in *Birth of a Nation* (a moment playfully captured by Peter Bogdanovich in *Nickelodeon*). Griffith got credit for inventing a half-dozen techniques and for coining the American epic and later the melodrama. Ford's response was to just do all of that quicker and with more verve. He wouldn't be properly recognized for any of his efforts for years as much more than a quick draw until *The Iron Horse*, on which he wandered into the Sierra Nevadas with nigh 300 thousand dollars of Fox's money and refused to answer their telegrams. It could have been the first *Heaven's Gate* (they employed a small army of crew and actors and built two towns from scratch) but it was a smash, making two million and cementing Ford as someone with whom you had to reckon if you were taking stock of the American cinema. It was, however, his penultimate western for 20 years. The market was drying up but also once you've painted your biggest canvas yet how exciting can it be to go back to 5 reel horse stories. Not for nothing are his worst films the tossed off genre films he directed between his ironclad social dramas and experimental tragicomedies.

*The Iron Horse* is his *Birth of a Nation*, his *Intolerance*, his *Broken Blossoms*, and accidentally his *A Corner in Wheat*. Griffith would finally respond with his own movie about Lincoln in 1930, basically the last thing he did before going broke. In *Horse*, Lincoln is on hand to personally decree that the building of the railroad is as important to America as winning the Civil War (a reach, even for Ford), but mostly this is a note about Ford's own technological war. Making this movie was as important to him as anything he'd ever done, ergo it's as important as any conflict or civil victory. Even the notion of including Lincoln in the story (and Wild Bill Hickock and Buffalo Bill Cody in a depressing scene of bison hunting right out of *Wake in Fright* that Ford would replay for horror in *The Searchers*) was a bit of Griffithian sleight-of-hand. The story must be important if he's here. Ford had never really seen past the rubes and good sons who took up his frame because to him cinema was a man putting aside his childishness long enough to be a good husband or father. Each man here is still the Ford hero or villain, there's just hundreds of them. The film does indeed eventually give way to brawls and vengeance - a shirtless fist fight to the death is stunningly realized. The triumph here is when a man finally sees his dead father's dream come true in the form of a vast expanse of track - Ford in this case looking at his longest movie, an artform he inherited from his brother about the railroad that brought his mother and father together, Irish emigres who landed in Boston and Portland respectively. Surreally strapping George O'Brien (soon to be Murnau's lead in *Sunrise* and a precursor to Ford's favorite twink Jeffrey Hunter) placing his hands on the rails once the work has finished is, well, touching. It's little wonder Ford would keep remaking this film; the man for whom a mission is more important than his love life. That was Ford all over.

A pre-sexual romance (Ford's cinema knew no other for a *long time*) is thwarted by the young boy's father's entrepreneurial spirit. The family can't sit around watching young love blossom, he's got railroads to build! He's got to tie this great nation together, one rail at a time. The romance seems a subtle dig at Griffith - romance is kid's stuff. Their departure from the snow-covered Illinois town where the story starts confirms that Ford simply hated the stuff. He belonged unencumbered. He's still bound here but it's by *importance*. There's an undeniably stilted gait here, even if the images remain shockingly crisp and purposeful. The Ford of *Straight Shooting* would never have slowed down to drink in hopes and dreams quite so deliberately. He tries new things, of course, the sense of experimentation remains - he's finally cross cutting to introduce rogue elements unseen by the heroes, as when we see the footsteps of Native Americans sneaking up on the engineer and his son in darkness. The head of the war party is a white guy in red face, only this time that's in the script. He's working for himself and using natives as a stalking horse to steal from the railroad - Gore Verbinski would re-use this in *The Lone Ranger*. The same charitably underhanded attitude misses the treatment of the Chinese, who are introduced with the title card "There is no white labor." Shame because as a depiction of labor itself, the film is quite stunning. The real-time movement of enormous trains and the laying of track (Werner Herzog and Robert Altman are among its children) - take out the narrative and you'd really have something here. A Lumiere Brothers derivative on a nation in progress, an answer to American cinema's sentimentality through the fact of its people's work.

**Lightnin' (1925)**

*Lightnin'*, based on a now-obscure Broadway smash, opens with one of the greatest title cards of all time: "In those more-or-less good old days, the Calivada Hotel was on the border line between California and Nevada. It had become famous overnight, when unhappy ladies in search of divorce found they could camouflage their residence by having their mail - and males - find them on the "California side" of the hotel while their rooms on the "Reno side" established them as residents of Nevada." Jay Hunt is Lightnin' Bill Jones and Edythe Chapman is his wife, Mother Jones (Ford's socialist streak finds purchase where it can). They run a hotel, the site of bawdy shenanigans and drunken humor (the second or third joke has Bill's dog digging up an old bottle of whiskey he'd buried, the fourth is that one of his friends dug it up, drank it all, and reburied it first...and then Jones dutifully re-buries it and puts a cross over the spot. Whole scene a minute long). Madge Bellamy is back from *The Iron Horse* and Ford good luck charm J. Farrell MacDonald, he of the 330 + credit resume, the best man at Ford's wedding, rounds out the cast.

It's also something of its own joke that Ford would make this comedy about old codgers unhappily married after the previous year's *Hearts of Oak*, which sounds properly deranged. It's lost now, one of the latest of the extant Fords from this period, and it's apparently about a man who falls in love with his adopted daughter, who would marry him except she's in love with her adopted brother! It sounds like something Laura Gemser would have headlined. So to be making what is basically a Ma and Pa Kettle movie (admittedly with better gags) the year after is kind of alarming. The humor is all good natured and old fashioned but there's some stunning visual work in their construction. MacDonald is introduced next to a picture of himself, which would later become the Lloyd Bridges *Airplane!* joke and then the Timothy Dalton *Hot Fuzz* joke. That always works. He's smitten with Bellamy, given a crutch for no other reason than it's funny how busy her appearance is. So stricken she doesn't think to help Bill, who's carrying her comically oversized suitcase. Everything here is like a preview of the jokes that would become de rigueur on sitcoms. There is of course, an element of competition with Chaplin, as there so often was in Ford's films of the period, but the slapstick paints the way towards the likes of *Fawlty Towers* and *Three's Company* in its uncomfortable closeness and the mingling of classes and motivations.

There's some incredibly energetic business about the line down the middle of the house being a state border and the things permitted on one versus the other; there's even a foot chase where a big fellow keeps trying to nab a smaller guy but can't follow him into Nevada. There's a very funny wordless gag where our hero is about to be swindled by real estate magnates (unsurprising that the villains are the guys developing the natural world, even if literally last year his heroes were doing the same thing) and his friend has to mouth the word "No!" to stop him because his many verbal warnings haven't sunk in. There's nevertheless plenty of space for Ford's sentimentality between the jokes, as when the Jones find themselves pining for each other at the same time from a few miles away, though this is broken up with a pretty classic angry wife joke. Ford would stick to this formula rather than continue to make out-and-out comedies moving forward (*Donovan's Reef* was trashed and *Tobacco Road* is often called his worst movie, so he was probably right to keep his jokes in the margins) but he was pretty goddamned funny when he wanted to be.

**Kentucky Pride (1925)**

Something very 20s about a movie where famous horses are audience-hooking guest stars. The bipedal cast is introduced with the title card "Those creatures called humans," and true to the film's word none of them is as famous as Man O'War. Odd that we should still know a racehorse some one hundred years after his heyday but P.T. Barnum was also probably the most influential person in the development of the American character, more so than Abraham Lincoln. It would be funny to think of Ford as straddling the divide between them but he didn't have much of the huckster about him, he was too Irish and far too sincere. He'd pull a chair out from under you but he'd give you an icepack afterwards rather than sell it to you (actor Frank Baker once begged Ford for money for his wife's surgery and he nearly beat the man unconscious but he *did* pay for the surgery). *Kentucky Pride* all but proves it. It's narrated like a children's book and shot like a nature documentary but there's still room for broken hearted dreamers and scheming gold diggers and of course a sob-worthy happy ending.

This is a film about a prize racehorse (*The Shamrock Handicap* the following year picks up the thread more conventionally) told by the horse in intertitles. There is thus something of Bresson's *Au Hasard Balthazar* about the movie, with the horse's fate decided by the people around him, but rather than fully give over to plotlessness (he couldn't even if he wanted to, and he did not) he uses them as mirrors. So really it's more like the *Days of Thunder* of Kentucky Derby movies. J. Farrell MacDonald is the stable hand who announces the birth of the foal to the wealthy owner of his parents. The rich gather round to see the new horse and one of them's smoking a cigar. MacDonald tells him to put it out or he'll burn the place down so the man hands him the cigar thinking he'll dispose of it for him and MacDonald is justifiably outraged. "Do it yourself!" The solidarity between humans and animals or animals and other animals is more convincing than that between most humans. The horse and MacDonald are both heartbroken when the lady of the house (Gertrude Astor) opines that the little critter is ugly. This same horse will later roast an Irishman for becoming a cop. "What else was he gonna do? A mick like that!" is the attitude. How a horse learned enough about people to become jokingly prejudiced, who could say?

Ford is...even this early...a funny guy. He loves horses, loves photographing them, but given a chance to make a movie of nothing but horses frolicking and running, he's still working in new, overwrought human drama every few minutes. It could also simply be that he can't set up a decent shot with a horse at the center because the damned thing won't stand still. This becomes text when MacDonald thinks he has to shoot the horse but his family won't let him. The horse recognizes its own mortality "I realized I was to be killed like other useless horses." There's an idea I wish someone would run down. Does a horse know its days are numbered? Does it know when other horses are about to be killed and why? Spielberg obviously boosted quite a bit of Ford's Ireland for *War Horse* but here the two men collide like two drunk drivers. Does a horse understand original sin?

## The Shamrock Handicap (1926)

Of the 15 or so lost films that represent John Ford's early 20s period the one I'm most anxious to see, should by some miracle a vault in Buenos Aires open and out they spill along with the Peking Man's bones and *The Storm on the Sea of Galilee*, is *Little Miss Smiles*, Ford's film about a young Jewish girl who has to step into her mother's shoes as head of the family when the older woman goes blind. Ford by then had made a few films that specifically address religion - the deceptively titled *The Big Punch* has a priest going to jail on behalf of his crook brother - but I would have killed to see his dry run for *How Green is My Valley* in a milieu that would have been foreign to him. He was full of surprises during this period, branching out beyond barrooms and trains, and throughout the rest of his career he would drift in and out of the old experiments with newly concrete grammar. He would of course become a specialist in the saga of the poor family with aspirations. *The Shamrock Handicap* wasn't the first of these but it is a particularly strong example of the form and one of the first films to make hay out of Ford's Irish heritage, rather than just happy subtext.

Louis Payne is Sir Miles O'Hara, a Fordian character if ever there were one. He's benevolent with the poor O'Shea family who rent from him but tells the tax collector to go to hell. Sir Miles' only daughter Sheila (Janet Gaynor! An honest to god star! Like George O'Brien she'd star in Murnau's *Sunrise* the following year, a movie that changed Ford's life) loves a horse trainer (Neil Ross), who like Ford's father did before he was born, goes to America to make his fortune. His trade is horses, and so was Ford's after a fashion. No one shot oaters (that's horse westerns, for those of you who enjoy the feeling sunlight on your face) like he did, after all. Ford needed a shot in the arm. By running away from westerns and styling himself as a more serious-minded filmmaker he runs into a poetry problem. There are beautiful wide shots a plenty but his dialogue coverage and close-ups want for urgency. He still finds beauty staging goodbyes in sun dappled fields filled with grazing sheep but he also suspects the whole movie can't just be beautiful tear-soaked landscapes (little wonder his earnest attempt to do just that - *The Quiet Man* - was one he had to fight to finance. The reviews weren't all kind, though he did win an Oscar for directing it).

Ross makes quite a stir in America, winning the respect of his fellow jockeys by knocking the shit out of one of them and saving his life in the process - a black valet was about to cut him with a razor blade! Ford actually handles this pretty well - his humanism at last beating his leanings toward ethnic comedy, and anyway it's the Irish who have to seem like the strangers here - the black character, Ely Reynolds as Virus Cakes (!!/), is one of the jockey's butlers but if he's a figure of fun it's because Ford and Reynolds build him well in just a few short scenes; he's a gifted physical comedian and he would come back for *Upstream* the following year. His terror and unease at being in a hospital surrounded by the sick and dying has him fleeing gurneys left and right until he seeks refuge in a surgery where ether is being used by the tablespoon. Cakes is ethered but good (killer use of slow-mo, maybe the first in Ford's filmography but tough to say with so much of it missing) and when he reaches Ross' hospital room starts dancing the Charleston. Ford was never as tone deaf about black characters (it's not like he *directed* Stepin Fetchit) as he was about Native

Americans and though this is undoubtedly a peculiar cul-de-sac, it's not minstrelsy either. Small favors when you're in this decade. This one also feels very much in conversation with Chaplin (the immigration storyline, the emphasis on direct comedic beats) and a sort of dare for both men to look beyond their pet subjects. Though it's undoubtedly funny that for Ford that just meant making someone else's idea of a movie. Chaplin wouldn't branch out for another two decades, by which time he'd grown more maudlin and a great deal more *odd* than Ford could ever have dreamt.

**The Blue Eagle (1926)**

*The Blue Eagle*, one of the earliest of Ford's war pictures, opens strong, splitting his patriotic affliction in twain. We meet a priest on the bow of the ship, contemplating his place in the world. Then we duck below deck and see a bevy of diamond cut men, literally glistening with sweat, feeding the ship's furnace. Heaven above and hell a furnace room full of gorgeous meat, laboring sailors fixing for a fight, rubbing chests in the glow of damnation. They're like gamecocks or baboons, they can't help but want to tear each other apart. When they fight it's not a graceful thing, it's dumb and quick. Only an attack from an enemy ship can separate them. One of them advises the other not to die in the attack because he hasn't finished beating the hell out of him in the ring (shades of *Hot Rod*, at times a very Fordian comedy indeed). Later a den of thieves will be portrayed as a boiling hole in the middle of a rocky island, as if hell has truly opened its doors.

When the plot arrives it's like a pre-code shopping list. Rival navy men, sporting the Blue Eagle tattoo of the title, vie for the love of Janet Gaynor, and break up an opium ring with the help of a priest just in time for a climactic boxing match. There's a lot of footage missing. There's plenty of barroom dancing but a whole battle is gone. Just as well, the dancing's more interesting. Gaynor can't believe one of her suitors would give his navy cap, the swabbie equivalent of the letter jacket or class ring evidently, to a dowdier gal to get her attention. No one questions the small monkey on a leash one of the enlistees has brought with him to a party. All these long-legged antics predict Gene Kelly and Frank Sinatra strutting around New York in *On The Town*. The opium crisis hardly makes a dent in the mood. If *Wings* is William Wyler grappling with war on the one hand and life on the other, *The Blue Eagle* is Ford not really minding that the two have to meet sometimes. He'd change his tune after he "served" and saw the carnage firsthand. I don't in earnest believe that he stopped thinking that war was still a pageant of ego and honor, but I think he understood how much it meant to be people (like himself – he lobbied for years to get a Silver Star for his work filming D-Day and Midway) and he stopped being quite so flippant. After all... he was still filming all those brawls in his Cavalry pictures years after VJ day.

The attitude, and it's not an unbelievable one, is that if men are going to run into death every few feet on behalf of a nation, they deserved to kick up their heels when it was over. Big Victor McLaglen *earned* that drink in *She Wore a Yellow Ribbon*. Ford's interest in the semantic brambles one could be caught during wartime increased tenfold, that's for sure. He became a process-oriented filmmaker in a way he never used to be after the war. In *The Blue Eagle* there's no meaningful separation between the duty of the Navy and the duty of a private citizen busting up the opium racket. Some things just need doing. The dock worker's brusqueness of this film is charming. There's some stuff here that leads me to believe Simpsons writer John Swartzwelder was a fan, or at least picked up a lot of its sensibility as it repeated throughout the early 1930s. "Just a real sweet throwin' brick - not too round, not too square," says one gangster before a hate crime, sounding exactly like a citizen of Springfield ("Oh, let's say... Moe"). Even the idea of the police approaching a priest to help them stop the flow of heroin has a kind of warped TV logic to it. Someone calls into a boxing match to offer encouragement as if he was shouting ringside: "Tell him to Give 'em the old one two." Another spectator breaks in through a skylight and falls into the ring. The Wild Bills (Wellman and Wyler) got all this stuff a little more right, they dug in aesthetically earlier than Ford (Wyler's *Hell's Heroes* is the best of the early *3 Godfathers* adaptations, which Ford would himself try twice), who at this point still treated sets like cardboard. That would all change when Ford started to use the tension between indoors and out rather than merely living by it.

**3 Bad Men (1926)**

I divined the reason Stagecoach didn't do nothin' for me for the longest time: it was a sound rehash of the best ideas of *3 Bad Men* without any kinda update in its attitude. The horse chases, everyday racism, and dusty set pieces? They're all here. If anything the attitude goes back further than '26 and '26 was no time to hope for progress. '26 feels late for this based on what I've seen from Ford up 'til now. *3 Bad Men* begins, for instance, with off puttingly casual cruelty. Before the first image has been seen we're told that Ulysses Grant has stolen land from the Sioux because they found gold on their reservation. They've been displaced. And then the intertitles tell us of the hopeful emigres headed to America in the 1870s to make their fortune. I suppose the Sioux had no fortune to make. No dreams even to defer. Ships out of Turner or Homer overflow with proud Europeans spilling out into American waters and a mountainous vista becomes visible when a beautiful tree is cut down, timed perfectly with the opening of the aperture. The camera as an axe. Cinema a mass grave dug by victors. It feels downright sinister when our Irish hero is introduced singing a jaunty tune, but that is history.

The bad men of the title are grudge laden horse thieves, silhouetted desperadoes overlooking miles of terrain, ripe for the taking. Ford can't make up his mind (not a flaw) about economic expansion. It's good for the spirit to chase lucre and make yourself a man, and yet that same hunger brings men to criminality. What separates the trio of gunslingers from the naive Europeans they prey upon? They kill Olive Borden's corpulent father and Tom Santschi, the looker of the three, insists they let her keep her horses. She'd been dressed like a man and her femininity takes them off guard. Ford's women were either waifs or tomboys, but no one was ever quite the equal of a man. Olive Borden is thus one of Ford's greatest heroines, so modern in her gestures. The wheel falls off her wagon and George O'Brien, agog at the sight of her, helpfully says "Looks like the wheel fell off." She rolls her eyes and replies "You must have traveled *far* to have learned so much." When her dad is killed she unthinkingly buries her head in the chest of his killer. She's upset. Nothing else matters or makes sense. That's how it is. In *House of Gucci* Lady Gaga hugs her dead ex-husband's new wife and then demands she be escorted off the premises by security. Grief is harder than it looks. It has its own schedule, as I was told when a dear friend died in 2019.

Somewhere in this unwieldy show Ford gets a great joke about his journalist character (Otis Harlan), he's "half Scotch, half seltzer," but the movie's sort of a modern TV pilot so no surprise he makes time for the whole country. There's a little *Deadwood*, a lotta *Hell on Wheels* (which in 5 seasons couldn't muster anything as interesting as ten minutes of *The Iron Horse*, its other obvious inspiration), and in general a lotta business. The main plot looks like it's gonna be the same as Lamont Johnson's lamentably forgotten *Cattle Annie and Little Britches*, the story of some orphans adopted by an outlaw gang (Johnson's finest hour), except our heroine is in her twenties and knows a thing or two about a thing or two, per Mike Nelson. They become cohorts until civilization drives the comrades into a death march up a canyon. Ford seems to know he's making epics now (another Ridley Scott connection) so he juxtaposes kids at church in three rows with a similarly sketched barroom brawl, showing just how far civilization has come. Ford never forgets to compose for the ages, everything iconic the second it wanders into frame. Botticelli with his lines, Goya with his shadows, just shy of Melville, America in his bones.

**Upstream (1927)**

The "house full of lunatics" comedy picture is a time-honored tradition, though understandably it's not the kind of thing that gets talked about with the reverence people reserve for Screwball comedy or comedies of remarriage or any of your more sturdy styles. If one of the gang is too much for you, you're trapped with him for 90 minutes of aimless hijinks. That can be a lot to ask. Hitchcock made a few of these (*Rear Window* a stealth entry), so did Tobe Hooper, Roman Polanski, Bogdanovich, and Nora Ephron. *The Old Dark House* by James Whale, remade by William Castle in 1963, and Tod Browning's *Freaks* (whose screenwriter Willis Goldbeck would become one of Ford's best collaborators) are in this vein, fusing the theatrical and the cinematic and bending towards the horrific all the while. After all, what's more scary than being trapped with someone who hates you, or worse, doesn't seem to notice you at all? Ford's *Upstream* ranks as among his most madcap films and it gets its energy from the performers he films, all hopefuls living in a cheap rooming house with a fussy landlady, each hoping for a big break. Dwight Frye has an uncredited role. You know you're making a kooky movie when that guy just *shows up*.

Step right up, we've got dancing sisters, knife throwers, actors, jugglers, and whatever Ely Reynolds is supposed to be (that man! It's one of cinema's great tragedies that no one signed him to a three-picture deal or just filmed him eating breakfast or something). Francis Ford, John's older brother, plays the uncredited juggler. If there's a more prolific artist, with more uncredited roles in more Capital M-Masterpieces, I'd be curious to hear who that might be. Frank directed 180 movies (most of them one or two reelers, admittedly) but he acted in just shy of 500 movies and yet good luck getting people to recognize his face. Like all the Ford/Feeney men he looked like Randall "Tex" Cobb in his youth and appeared to have a head built for smashing in doors.

It's at times uproariously funny. An old lothario sinks so far down in his chair trying to rub his feet against those of a woman half his age that his head is below the table. Earle Foxe plays a dreadful thespian with a famous name. A producer comes calling because they sold out a theatre with the promise of a "Brashingham" in the lead role of *Hamlet*. "The fact that you're a terrible actor doesn't make any difference." Young sir goes to a mirror, fixes himself up, and announces to the boarding house he's off to play *Hamlet* like he's Norma Desmond in the final moments of *Sunset Boulevard*. Raymond Hitchcock plays the seasoned pro (which he was, by then a decades-long veteran of the stage) who's going to teach Foxe how to play Shakespeare convincingly. He died two years later at 64, missing out on his chance to become a member of Lubitsch's stock company. He's very good. Instructing Foxe about playing different emotions he goes to a corner and stiffens and suddenly he's Max Schreck in *Nosferatu*. Ford's staging of Hamlet is his best stab at expressionism and he excels, though you do get the sense he thinks it's too fanciful. Ford loved Murnau, he would visit him in Germany and he's one of the only directors he confessed influence. A shot of Nancy Nash crying on her bed is worthy of *Sunrise*. Grace surrounded by broad comedy, what more could you ask for?

## Hangman's House (1928)

Ford becomes something he never quite got to be in *Hangman's House*; a B picture journeyman. He begins the picture in Algiers (shades of Von Sternberg, who had to have been aware of Ford, working as he was on the Paramount Lot while Ford was at Fox, in direct competition so to speak) where he boldly sets the plot up. Big Victor Maglaglan makes only his second appearance in a Ford film playing the marvelously named Citizen Horgan (he'd already been in a couple of classics by now, having switched from boxing to acting in the late teens after a fabled bout with Jack Johnson) as our vengeful hero. He toasts his regiment, then gets an urgent cable. He's going back to Ireland, where he's a wanted man. Must be pretty important to make him risk his neck after saving it in the Algerian campaign? It is. Back in County Wicklow there's a man he's gotta kill. This is the kind of set-up a Von Sternberg or a Wellman or a Walsh would have absolutely chewed through like a prisoner eating his own arm to get quit of handcuffs. Ford was never quite those guys. He never got to bum around in the B's. Except here.

The marked man in question is Earle Foxe, back from *Upstream* not a whit less caddish, engaged to the daughter of the town's hanging judge, grown rich and grotesque in his lonely mansion. Ford introduces him (Hobart Bosworth) with a hand heavy with portent. A man outside curses his name, the mansion is crooked and is flocked by birds of prey like it's on Skull Island, and the judge himself is introduced through the flames of his fireplace. All he's missing is the tail and horns. If Big Victor can kill Foxe, maybe hang-daughter June Collyer can marry safe sweetheart Larry Kent instead. We know Foxe has to die because the subtitles tell us he was born in Ireland and left because he didn't like it there. Only the devil himself would refuse a trip back to Ireland. He also doesn't like dogs, the bastard.

Ford's still in Murnau country here, framing Collyer and Kent like the lovers in *Sunrise* whenever he can (there's even a romantic boat ride), but the Sternberg connection fascinates me. Bosworth sees the hanged faces of his many victims in the fireplace like a scene out of *The Scarlet Empress*. When he expires Ford and George Schneiderman (his regular photographer from *Just Pals* until *Steamboat Round the Bend*) close the aperture to smudge half the frame. The expressionism and impressionism are a lot more casual here than on the much more demonstrative *Four Sons*. The film appears at times like a Universal horror, the climax's flaming Xanadu presages *Frankenstein*, which confirms my suspicion that Ford was ready for sound. He was always swift with action and montage and depending on his lead actor he didn't take time to overstate things the way a lot of silent pioneers did. He needed to burn through the screen itself. He needed more.

**Riley The Cop (1928)**

The poster for *Riley the Cop* showed J. Farrell Macdonald yawning big in his uniform. It was John Ford's way of downplaying the arrival of sound, like he'd opened his yap to croon like Jolson and out came the yawn instead. There's a synchronous score written specifically for the film, there are the sounds of feet on pavement and children enjoying themselves, a bat cracks when it connects with a baseball, but no one utters a word. They *yodel* but they don't speak. This was one of JFM's last films as a Ford leading man, another go-round as the colorful leading character who watches over a community and the fortunes of two young lovers (Ford predicting the later Marx Brothers movies with his rehash of the *Upstream* romance taking stage left). Riley watches his street corner with interest and love. He helps kids (one of them played by *Cry Danger* director and future Bertrand Tavernier cohort Robert Parrish! He and Ford would fall out when Parrish pointed out that Ford could be helping the poor instead of buying vacation houses for his Navy buddies to throw parties, which was true. As for Tavernier, he'd grow up to be a filmmaker of Fordian poetic minimalism after he and Pierre Rissient babysat Ford in Paris and had to give the old codger a bath one day) frolic in the spray of a fire hydrant, lets them escape when they break a shop window, he's known some adults since they were kids. He is in other words, a complete fantasy. Ford only filmed two kinds of men: brutish and unyielding or unbelievably noble.

The story gets going when David Rollins chases Nancy Drexel to Munich and gets himself arrested trying to win her back. Riley is sent to bring him back to America ("why couldn't the lad have been arrested in Ireland?") and finds him in shadows, head hung low. Germany and Ireland still the twin pillars of Ford's heart. His beloved homeland and Murnau's (our Irish cop hero hugs his German counterpart like a brother). J. Farrell immediately falls for a German beer wench with a bow on her head as big as a dachshund ("I've been searching all my life for a girl like you… and you've got *beer*!!" is the gist of his love-at-first-sight declaration, aligning him with Homer Simpson). She tries to cheer Rollins up by sliding on the bench like she's being propelled by magnets, or perhaps like she's on a dolly track. Very cute bit of business, that. Turns out she's actually a transplant from Hoboken. Small world after all.

The central joke is that J. Farrell is a terrible jailer and Rollins is more committed to being his prisoner than the cop is to guarding him. "I'm your prisoner, Mr. Riley, and I'm going to get you to Paris on time!" It's pretty funny, as far as one joke set-ups go. He goes on a tour of Paris at the urging of the gendarmerie and forgets Rollins at the train station. There's a real Elmer Fudd quality to this fellow (heaven knows the sound effects are pure Chuck Jones), though he's nicer. He causes a stir at a restaurant when he insists his French chauffeur be allowed to join him for dinner. He pays for it when the driver orders snails for him. Ah, the French... An endless comedic well. Ford indulges in a little light psychedelia again as Macdonald watches a dance hall kick-line while drunk and it starts spinning like a Busby Berkeley number. Not sure who we have to thank for that. Neither photographer Charles G. Clarke nor editor Alex Troffey were particularly experimental technicians. Maybe Ford truly did just sort of see the future in a drunken stupor. It wouldn't have been the first time.

**Four Sons (1928)**

The line on *Four Sons* is it's the film Ford made after seeing *Sunrise* and meeting and dining with Murnau and the influence is marked, to say the least. The line *should* be that it's almost comical to imagine that anyone could watch the movie and think of anything other than Murnau. It begins with a dolly shot of a man walking through a European village waving at all and sundry looking like Emil Jannings in *The Last Laugh*; This is no mere homage: Ford is reborn in Murnau's image. Whatever Ford had been is gone, at least for the length of this film. Ford had been searching for a language more serious than his own to make epics and dramas and the like and though he undoubtedly makes a first-rate Murnau acolyte, it's fascinating to think that he looked at his own methodology and found something he thought he should bury or grow beyond. Ford's own sense of inferiority would never leave him. He'd come to talk about directing like it was a job for half-wits, scoffing at people's attempts to mythologize him and his work. Young Steven Spielberg visits and asks for advice, Ford points to a landscape on the wall "The horizon doesn't go in the middle of the frame, it goes here [not quite the top] or here [not quite the bottom]" and then shows him the door. Spielberg re-stages this in his magnificent memoir *The Fabelmans* with none other than surrealist David Lynch as Ford. Peter Bogdanovich drives Ford hundreds of miles back to Monument

Valley hoping for a sacred reunion between an artist and his muse and Ford, miserable, all but spits in his face. Ford didn't want to be an American artist, he wanted to be F.W. Murnau, who died too young to be held accountable for his early work and left behind nothing but majesty. The second line in the movie is "Books, herr postman, are friends that never deceive." Film? Film is nothing but deception.

The film is preposterously beautiful and it knows it. Ford lays on the Germanic mannerisms and appurtenances so thick it feels like a trip to Epcot but he's still in there (beer is drunk like afternoon tea). The militarism is vulgar in that Ford way (he'd direct soldiers like this the rest of his life, you can see this stuff become concrete in the Cavalry pictures), something Murnau would never so carelessly present. The march to war, no matter how great the toll it's meant to take on his characters, is nothing to be taken lightly. He fought in World War 1, after all, he'd seen what death looked like up close. Ford's decision to join up and help the war effort can also be said to be a way to follow in Murnau's footsteps (even still he carried a camera, not a gun). He'd learn to be less cavalier about his own wartime experiences as he went. He makes a handful of WW2 films but almost none with combat footage and he all but disowns *They Were Expendable* afterwards, though he was very excited to direct it. You could trace much of this country's uneasy relationship to shooting warfare for the "right reasons" back to this, Ford's true answer to Wyler's *Wings* (it even has the Z axis tracking shots). Steven Spielberg's punchline Nazis are born in a scene of a uniform inspection. The idea of an idyllic valley invaded by Germans predicts Michael Mann's *The Keep*.

Despite being quite evidently a Murnau mix-tape this is perhaps Ford's most gorgeous looking movie up to this point in his life, an unyielding experience of beauty. A man pounding iron with a hammer has an Eisensteinian or Langian quality, like we're looking at a God at toil. A shot of a young recruit having his head shaved while his mother watches teary eyed from a window and then says goodbye to him on a cramped train is eerie in the extreme, hinting at everything from the treatment of the Jews in concentration camps to the scalping that becomes an inextricable image in Westerns, Ford's genre. In its search for the naive it uncovers darkness it knows not with what to do. The film is called *Four Sons* and three of them perish. Even so it's quite difficult to imagine now so talented a filmmaker making so many odd decisions in his quest to become serious and still producing one of the greatest films of the decade. Ford wouldn't make anything as dramatically considered as Murnau for another few years but he paints canvases worthy of Michelangelo here.

PART 3

# THE COMING OF SOUND & THE DEATH OF A HERO

1929-1935

Ford learned early the sting of personal rejection tore him up inside. His brother Francis did give him a job in Hollywood, but initially he was just digging ditches. In retaliation he kept Francis employed until his death but treated him rather roughly in full view of everyone – like Francis was a totem from his childhood more than a living breathing human who needed love and respect. Everyone who stayed close to Ford got to know this awful intimacy well. Then life started taking away the people who did mean something to him. F.W. Murnau, Ford's hero, his artistic inspiration, died in 1931. Will Rogers, the actor Ford loved most of all his collaborators, the man who took the spot nearest his heart after he and Harry Carey went their separate ways in 1920, died in a plane crash in 1935. It all should have taught Ford to guard his heart more, and though he comported himself like no one meant anything to him, he never learned. People could always leave him, and he'd always give them cause to do it, but he'd never ever learn how to live with it. Ben Johnson got tired of being pushed around by the old man on the set of *Rio Grande* and walked away from him for ten years. George O'Brien abandoned Ford in the middle of a bender and was banned from his movies for almost two decades. As Ford aged into a state of permanently bent bitterness, he began to paint his greatest works about the men he could never be. The heroes of *Arrowsmith, Judge Priest, The Prisoner of Shark Island, Air Mail,* and *Doctor Bull* were projections of a hopeful man, someone who wanted to believe he could step up, and be worthy of the love he received from the people towards whom he was sometimes a dictator and tormentor. The lowly sinner in *The Informer* was a look into his soul, the man who let himself down, the man who would betray his people, turn his back on those who suffered most. It was a prophecy that came true.

## The Black Watch (1929)

On the early sound films of Fritz Lang, Tom Gunning, writing for The Criterion Collection, highlights that Lang took to sound with a staggering intuitiveness. "One cannot leave this complex film without discussing Lang's own mastery of one of cinema's newer devices in 1933: sound. Two years earlier, in his masterpiece, *M*, Lang created one of the first enduring masterworks of film sound. From its very first images and sounds, *The Testament of Dr. Mabuse* continues Lang's experiments with the role sound could play in creating suspense and terror." As *The Black Watch* opened with a battery of soldiers bounding through double doors flanked by marching bagpipers, I was hearing Lang's cacophony in my head. Some people simply understand film language. Ford was debuting in sound and would not be taking it for granted. A Scottish colonel (Lumsden Hare) stands and addresses his men at a long banquet table "Gentlemen... this is war!" Ford lets the pipers take up 45 seconds of screen time after his big speech, then each man drops his glass on the table, one after the other, followed by a singalong. It's like Ford is hearing music for the first time. *The Jazz Singer* shown up gracefully.

Victor McLaglen is being sent into the dark heart of the Middle East. Apparently there's a woman down there who's so sexy and bizarre that they worship her like a god. Can't have that, can we, Captain Willard? I am fascinated by the idea of sending men to go dethrone a queen because she's somehow so charismatic that wars are being fought on her behalf (unlike the English of course, who've never done anything so stupid). This is sort of the plot of *She*, the H. Rider Haggard story, but the men in that stumble upon the supernaturally gifted queen, they don't go down to kill her with orders from the state. I don't know, just...odd. It's *Heart of Darkness* meets *Cobra Woman*. Regardless, Big Victor has to go kill Myrna Loy (introduced magnificently, under silk slowly lifted to reveal her in close-up). Let's see how this goes.

It's fun to hear Vic's voice for the first time. It's a little reedy for such a frame. Laurence Olivier's delicate delivery emerging from a boxer's towering bulk. He bids a tearful farewell to the regiment while tenor David Percy sings him off. Indeed there's a new piece of music every few seconds; the Pakistani extras all stop for a gorgeous song announcing call to prayer. They don't call it Pakistan, of course (and the character named Mohammed Khan is played by...Mitchell Lewis, who played a lot of sheiks and beys), but that's where we are. Ford, so used to being able to just shout direction, had to dress his AD like an extra and have him mingle with the actors and whisper in everyone's ears. John Wayne's an extra here somewhere, too, pulling double detail as prop boy (Ford introduced himself to Wayne by kicking the shit out of him one day, and Wayne the simpering giant never looked back). Lupita Tovar and Randolph Scott are here, too. Oh look there's Tom London, too, maybe; an actor who managed 650 acting credits, and hey, Bob Kortman, who almost hit 300. It's a who's who of *squints* where? The drama with Loy never takes off (she enunciates like she's a balloon letting out helium and speaks in "thees" and "thous" for some reason), so someone hits upon the idea of making her go braless beneath a sheer shirt. The sets, thankfully, are drama enough. Ford lights them like they're alive, faces emerge from shadow and we're back in Murnau country again. There's a wheel of pain right out of *Conan The Barbarian* (Robert E. Howard and H. Rider Haggard together again for the very first time; H. Robert Rider E. Haggard Howard) that places him back in pre-Universal horror mode. We're in *White Zombie* by way of Murnau's *Faust*. Riveting and terrible. Orson Welles must have seen this, we know he ran *Stagecoach* once a day for a month before making *Citizen Kane*; his Shakespeare films all take place in its hideous netherworld.

**Salute (1929, John Ford & David Butler)**

I don't mean to denigrate everyone whom Ford directed alongside but well, the results do speak for themselves. Even staggering drunk he lapped everyone on *Mister Roberts*, his is the only interesting section of *How The West Was Won*, no one remembers future forced Ford collaborator Andrew Bennison, and within seconds of this collaboration with David Butler we're missing Ford's touch. This was the team director system he fought hard to abolish. There's a dull establishing shot, a dull shot of people dancing, then another dull exterior where dialogue drops from the mouths of our lead characters like a bowling ball from a broken arm. Who else could I blame? I almost quit, especially knowing the movie was about the Army and Navy football game, something about which I could not care less...or anyway I thought I couldn't until Stepin Fetchit showed up as a butler. Little but an act of god could save this from the scrapheap. Ford was many things but he wasn't god. I hear James Baldwin everytime I see Stepin Fetchit "...who, rightly or wrongly, I loathed." and see David Alan Grier briefly livening up an episode of Saturday Night Live and making it momentarily dangerous with a sketch where he plays an Uncle Tom version of Louis Armstrong ("He made history by being the first black person lynched by black people").

How to reconcile this? Just two years ago Ford was working with Ely Reynolds and while it'd be a reach and a quarter to describe those performances as progressive, they weren't this. Butler and William Fox I'm willing to blame for the sports motif, which despite his love of football was something in which Ford was usually smarter about indulging. Fox made a couple of sports and sports-adjacent films (most dull, to these eyes) like Butler's own *Pigskin Parade* and *A Connecticut Yankee* with Will Rogers, later Ford's leading man. Butler's in this one, too, so you see why he's got my mind wandering and my eyes narrowing. Bennison was also a Fox contractor and like Butler if he'd done better work we'd still be talking about him as something other than barnacle on Ford's hull (though knowing my luck, people will rediscover him like they did Mitchell Leisen [who deserved to be rediscovered, mind] and I'll look quite the fool). Looking at his enormous resume (which turns to TV after some oddball 50s work) I can't help but conclude he was like Fox's untalented Michael Curtiz, just the guy who did whatever needed doing. I cannot for the life of me think of how else to explain this movie's lousiness except to muse that Ford might have been drunk or checked out and Butler did the heavy lifting but who knows, maybe Ford truly just did bad work this time. It's unfunny, unimaginative, thoughtlessly composed, and Stepin Fetchit is in it. We won't see a worse film with Ford's name attached to it until the Korean War.

Co-lead William Janney (dragging down screen brother George O'Brien with him) is a squid-beaked scarecrow, a psychopathic virgin who coos each lazy syllable like he's reliving the second grade. I'm sure they hired him because he has the looks of a Kennedy (years before the boys became public fixtures), which used to mean something before they killed John. Helen Chandler (Mina Harker in *Dracula*!) is a little more awake but there's a reason she didn't become a storied leading lady. If the film must be watched it's for the first proper appearance of John Wayne and Ward Bond. Bond was a real gridiron bruiser, so when they asked him to play himself, he lived it up like a movie star. He blew a chunk of the movie's budgets on room service and slept with Ford's favorite extra. Ford wanted to kick his ass back to USC but Wayne stood up for him and Bond swore to stick by the kid no matter what and his Ward was his Bond. The coverage of the game recalls later TV broadcasts of Football games, haphazardly catching the action at a diagonal from the stands. There's the occasional chaotic medium insert from down below but it can't do much. Football's not the easiest sport to film (Aldrich (*The Longest Yard*) did it better than Altman (*M*A*S*H**) because he liked the idea of ugly combat, but I'm of the mind that nobody's made it truly cinematic the way George Roy Hill managed with hockey) and at least this one time Ford was content with the bare minimum.

**Men Without Women (1930)**

Curiously we're back in hybrid silent mode, though I understand there's a sound version of this film out there somewhere. Ford doesn't change his playbook though, he's still using über dynamic tracking shots (an opening example is about six feet above the heads of his navy boy heroes, presaging a ton of modern cinematography). The men of the title are submariners, out on the town when we meet them, trapped at the bottom of the ocean before too long. Maybe if they'd taken the warnings of Chinese streetwalkers seriously they'd have been spared God's wrath. One of them negotiates a few minutes of bliss for one of the younger sailors and does the hand signals from the trial scene in Michael Mann's *Thief* to notate the rising cost. A few feet away J. Farrell Macdonald is served a beer with fish in it and William Fox discovery Frank Richardson, the "Joy Boy of Song," belts "Frankie and Johnny" live. They talk in intertitles but sing out loud. It's enough to make your head spin.

The boys crash their sub into another boat and start taking on water. The lights struggle to stay on and for a minute we're in a Peter Tscherkassky movie. They need to plug some valves and clear some shafts or they'll all drown. Pretty amazing that a film with this title is all about men clamoring through yonic tubes and tunnels trying to clear passages and the like; this wasn't lost on Ford for all his "aww shucks" chivalry when it comes to the fairer sex. He was a *crude* man. The edit and photography butting up against the 30s means this not infrequently starts to resemble a Cooper, Schoedsack, and Pichel adventure picture (the hodgepodge music is pure Max Steiner, if rather less directed and catchy; three credited composers...). Ford doesn't make much use of the claustrophobia of the situation, opting for humor as often as horror. J. Farrell MacDonald breaks into the ship's booze ration instead of the Oxygen reserves, which, when deployed prompts one fellow to muse "I'd like to shake the hand of the guy who discovered oxygen." ("Curse Pierre Jules César Janssen!") One fella's freakout comes with piercing audio out of nowhere 40 minutes in. If the film is a spiritual sequel to *The Blue Eagle*, it is also, like that movie, an early Simpsons episode. It's even the bosun's first day. "Quack quack quack."

Of course it's not all hilarious jokes about alcoholism. The captain has to kill his most deranged crewman when he gets hold of explosives and starts proclaiming himself the angel of death. The one thing sorely missing from this film is a real sense of how long they're stuck down here. By my count it takes about twenty minutes for all of them to lose hope. Divers are called in with two reels left and the crew dropping like flies. This has one of the earliest instances of the *Armageddon* ending I've ever seen: one of them has to stay behind to make sure the rest of the boys get to leave the sub safely. The score plays Wagner for him (public domain Wagner, at any rate) as the sacrifice is made and his shipmates escape. Ford comes alive at last, as each man takes their turn escaping, his fealty to Murnau's German heritage (though he's also predicting Edgar G. Ulmer and his doomed men) restated as these boys say goodbye one last time.

**Born Reckless (1930, John Ford [& Andrew Bennison])**

I had no idea who Andrew Bennison was before I started seeing his name next to Ford's, so I was somewhat puzzled by his "staged by" credit at the start of *Born Reckless*. Did the studio think he couldn't handle himself? The movie opens with a would-be bravura tracking shot, so maybe? The camera starts in a parade before letting the truck with the marching band in back ride off down the road and landing on a gangster lookout coiled in waiting for a heist. The camera jerks a few inches with every foot it travels, like the tripod was in bad need of some grease. Presumably Bennison (the writer of some 40 forgotten-ish films between 1923 and 1941, who held the same "staging" job on Ford's *Men Without Women*) could worry about directing the actors while Ford slicked the dolly.

He'd have done better on his own. Bennison directed his only feature solo in 1932 and then never again. Ford would later help create the DGA to stop this from ever happening again.

The opening of the film is set on a beautiful backlot metropolis. Edmund Lowe commits crimes, then heads to his parent's apartment where his moll is waiting with a change of clothes and a bucket of paint; ma and pa think he's got an honest job. Even this is too clever by half for a gangster film. Ford doesn't have the ferocity of William Wellman or Howard Hawks, he can't pretend he doesn't like people. Lowe's sister Marguerite Churchill wants to date a man and rather than kill the guy in some twisted Zeus and Demeter rage like any self-respecting gun-toting small time hood, Lowe approves of him. He even chases away a worse guy interested in her hand. Scarface would never. The plot doesn't start for 15 long minutes. Lowe gets booked for the heist and a journalist talks the judge sentencing him into service just before WWI. Turns out the army's crawling with crooks; the guy next to Lowe at basic introduces himself by spitting out three words "I'm a BOIGLAH!" They misunderstand him and give him a bugle. Hawks would never.

Ford has no temperament for this milieu. He's too busy looking out for the little guy to enjoy killing him. He orchestrates some boffo camera movements but he can't make them tell the story. They're incidental. He's still getting his sea legs with sound. He lets Lowe walk outside a door into the fake street, dollies up to the window and watches as a cop walks up on him. In earlier times (and again later) he'd have kept the camera at the window watching the conversation. Someone (I'm looking at you, Bennison...) insisted he cut to the street so we can hear him get arrested, instead of merely seeing it. To my knowledge Ford hadn't directed a service comedy before, but they'd become the rule rather than the exception after a certain point in his career. They'd pause for death, romance, and other tragedies, but he loved it when a bunch of guys shared bunks and shot at bad guys. This one's funny about 20% of the time it means to be. The combat footage is impressive, of course, but Ford forgets we're watching a comedy while he blows up a French town, so we're not really in the mood for a massacre. The army reforms Lowe before the movie's half over. Nothing particularly interesting follows until a fog bound shoot out with stunning pace and a viciousness that suggests Edgar G. Ulmer. Then the film simply ends.

**Up The River (1930)**

"I don't see any flat tire." "No? Well buy a mirror." John Ford crashes into the 21st century. Spencer Tracy's the escaped convict who breaks out in style, pulling up in a stolen car in a new suit in the middle of an old pal's salvation army spiel. "I say to you...crime don't pay." He's back inside the next day with Humphrey Bogart, face still taut, jaw like a mule, voice pure rubber. Hollywood lore says he didn't find himself til the 40s but he's obviously a star here, though there's an argument that everyone is a star in Ford's cinema (well...except Stepin Fetchit... and that lizard eunuch William Janney). Tracy and Bogie were both dead before the 70s, having made the decade possible just by refusing to stop drinking and stepping in front of cameras. They make great bedfellows here, two denizens of the carnivalesque jail Ford occupies. Ford's 30s so far are about momentum and pizzazz; no dolly or tracking shot more show-offy than the next bon mot. He seemed to like being "anonymous" as much as he liked being present.

Tracy makes for a spectacular Bugs Bunny, asking that the warden give him a cell with southern exposure. Ford discovered Tracy on stage and gave him his film career but he was so good someone else would have gotten him in front of a camera eventually. Tracy arrives in the clink just in time for the big inmate baseball game. "One week before the big game, they had to go and pardon the pitcher." His jailhouse rock is in conversation with Vidor's offices and Wellman's barracks, predicting *Big Deal on Madonna Street* with its ants-marching prison psychology. Tracy's mean right arm might just be the salvation the farm team needs. In the meantime he's got to bone up on his knife throwing for the talent show (prison seems ok!). There's blackface comedy at the show and the black inmates seem to love it more than the whites. At this I can do little but bang my head on my coffee table. As I never tire of saying Ford knew the difference between right and wrong in this instance, he just didn't care. George Lucas would follow him down this particular cul-de-sac, and it kept neither of them from immortality, so for once it's ok to blame society as well as the artists.

Ford takes quiet glee in the perspective that the bars and infinite perspectives of the big house afford him. He frames Bogie and his girl (she's in the women's prison next door) between bars, facing away from each other - her canted to the left, him hips forward, looking right. Dynamite. Tracy breaks out again and his flat-faced sidekick ("Danny Mora from Dannemora") are next seen on a train positioned in front of a rear projected countryside like some mechanical ouroboros. Tracy talks Bogart out of murdering a guy who swindles his well-meaning, kindly old mother. The footage of Tracy getting revenge on the guy is either missing or Ford never shot it. He disappears as suddenly as he appears, heading back to the big house in time for the big game after making sure Bogart's intentions towards his jailbird sweetheart are pure. Convicts are saints in Ford's reckoning. It's bankers who are the real trouble.

**Seas Beneath (1931)**

In the opening reel George O'Brien gathers his men on deck and unveils the newest addition to their ship like he's revealing a new car on *The Price is Right*. Their prize? A shiny, phallic new cannon. Dudley Nichols the hawk writes, back for another tale of men at sea after *Men Without Women* a few years earlier and playwright William Collier helped with the dialogue and appears as...*Mugs O'Flaherty*... Sure. He'll also show up the next year as the judge who tries to send Sally O'Neil up the river in *The Brat*. Ford kept Nichols around like a good luck charm, writing 10 movies for him when he wasn't also writing for Hawks and Leo McCarey among many others. Those two shared more of Nichols' political leanings. Also on hand is Francis Ford, Warren Hymer - Dannemore Dan himself, John Loder, who got paid 1000 dollars extra to get a Nazi haircut, and Larry Kent, whose last credit is as an extra in *Viva Las Vegas*. They're running silent to outfox some U-boats, posing as a trawler. The trick is they gotta act like regular joes, not Navy men.

The navy gave Ford a half dozen serious boats and other toys to use for filming but Ford can't do much work on them. He comes alive when the boys hit the south seas port ("No fraternizin' wit wimin! Hear me Mugs!? *NO FRATERNIZIN' WIT WIMIN*!") and he breaks out the dolly track to film bustling barrooms and splits his frame in twain, showing men climbing stairs and women waving from parapets. 15 minutes in and the movie explodes, every composition is perfect and lively, like a bird spying a mate and thrusting its plume to the heavens. There's singing and dancing on bar tops, beer, and cigarettes galore. It's like the movie enters a speakeasy. O'Brien tries out the same photo scheme Robert De Niro will use in John Frankenheimer's *Ronin* on the port guard because he's trying to gather evidence of enemy seacraft. He and Marion Lessing flirt with a huge gun between them presaging...well gosh, I'm not sure. Might come to me later. Wellman makes *Safe in Hell* the same year which has a jail-bound Dorothy Mackaill fleeing to a depraved island hellhole until her beau can clear her name. Ford was in Heaven, Wellman in Hell. As usual.

Mona Maris is doing some cockamamie thing with her accent, where she's German but also Spanish? Anyway, she's one of the earliest examples of the Ford fallen woman, best exemplified by Linda Darnell in *My Darling Clementine*. Like Peckinpah, Ford had a love hate relationship with dark haired girls from south of Dover. "Here I am waiting on the Prado." "Here I am...*walking* on the Prado." The guys have to interrupt their shore leave to chase down the rather conspicuous German officers nearby, passing by the beautiful views of ocean behind them with every errand their run. Ford can't help but shoot the sea and it's stunning every time. These beautiful shadows strutting in front of the low sun, courting death, a war ahead of them and another behind. It's almost supernatural.

**The Brat (1931)**

Open on a speeding paddy wagon full of drunken partiers rounded up like cattle and a trial that's kicking defendants out one after the other like an assembly line. "This your first time?!" Asks one delinquent debutante to another awaiting judgment (Ethan Coen has his ear to a glass on the wall). Just over their shoulders bottles are being smashed by cops, driving a crooked spinster to salivate. The 20s are over. The depression is here. "Were you sober when you struck your wife?" "Yes, your honor, sober as a judge." "On second thought I'll turn you over to your wife." Ford is done with his lugubrious honeymoon with sound. He's back in action, directing thirty little comic vignettes in the first ten minutes of this one. It's a remake and it's hot to the touch. It's like *Pygmalion* meets *Ball of Fire*, or *My Man Godfrey* with no third act. Novelist Frank Albertson brings criminal floozy Sally O'Neil home to study her after she gets arrested for vagrancy; think of all he could learn from a streetwise truant like this.

She seems to be the archetype for every caricature of American urchinism with her newsboy cap and her Jackie Faux-nassis accent. ("I'm from PA, dats Pennsylvania!" she whines on the stand. Be still my heart.)

She says his idea sounds "skwewy" but she needs to eat and anyway she gets real cozy with the idea of being the subject of a book almost instantly, introducing herself as "da heroine!" to someone at the half hour mark. Albertson's family laughs at his little experiment but they all come around to her eventually. This stuff is so funny because Ford has to be the only director who's neither rich nor poor enough to get either archetype right. His stuffy butler-possessing professor is already a parody and his foundling is a cartoon character. Doesn't matter, of course, it's all funny and Ford directs like they switched his hankie for a bump. The performances are quick, the camera's light on its feet, the film trips like Cary Grant in a Hawks comedy (which Hawks hadn't invented yet).

Ford finds himself in a mood I don't think I've quite encountered, somewhere between Murnau's pastoralism, Jean Epstein's surrealism, and his usual grab-bag of ethnic comedy. There's a scene where O'Neil soars on a huge swing hung on a tree, without words as Alberton's dad, a bishop, and the butler stare at her dumbfounded. She nearly pratfalls off of it. The bishop loves her. Ford wouldn't ever repeat this particular combination again (he comes closest in *The Long Voyage Home*) but to quote O'Neil it "clicks like a nickel at an automat." Albertson does eventually get around to seducing her (the scene doesn't totally work, he's too creepy, but the construction is solid enough) but before he can passionately kiss her the phone rings. "Oh nuts," she says. "And I so felt like working..." he sighs. Ford's pre-sexual politics can't totally spoil his brio.

## Arrowsmith (1931)

Sinclair Lewis only wrote one script, *Storm in the West* in 1943 with Dore Schary, and it was never produced. It sounds fascinating (they staged the rise of European Fascism as a western) but no one bit. Not difficult to see why he wanted to try his hand at script writing, he'd been giving a pretty thorough going over by Hollywood by then (he'd be dead before Richard Brooks' stellar *Elmer Gantry* film, with Burt Lancaster as the titular firebrand and future Ford leading lady Shirley Jones as his femme fatale, became a minor hit). He had his movies turned into a number of forgotten programmers all through the '20s but he'd also been treated to classier adaptations by William Wyler, Victor Fleming, Tod Browning, and

Norman Taurog. Ford was one of the first to adapt his words in a talkie and while he does rise to the occasion eventually, it's funny to think how much he bent Lewis to his own whim.

This was, after all, not really his kind of picture. I thought at first he was taking potshots at Warner's prestige pictures, but they weren't a thing yet; Paul Muni hadn't even played Scarface, let alone started looking down microscopes. Sam Goldwyn enticed him over to... Samuel Goldwyn Productions to make the film and rumor has it he had but one condition: don't get drunk on set. Ford made the handshake deal and then sped through shooting, tossing overboard any scene he didn't think was necessary, so he could get home, or at least to the parking lot, and start drinking. There's a war going on here between awards-ready bluster and Ford's untamable spirit of adventure. There is, however, no denying that this is the first Ford film that feels like the Fords that would follow, in speed, sound, and framing. The shift to Goldwyn settled him. He was henceforth, mostly, the John Ford most people recognize. The story starts, hilariously with a little girl riding a horse outrunning the law, like Ford was showing Goldwyn he wasn't gonna fully give up his vices just because he couldn't slam back whiskey all day – later Ford would make it a point to *always* be sober on set, but he didn't always succeed. Sidney Howard adapts and he takes out all the parts where Arrowsmith acts like Ford. No womanizing or boozing. To this day people are confused about just what Ronald Colman is *doing* with Myrna Loy in her few scenes, because he doesn't appear to be sleeping with her. Colman was Ford's drinking buddy, and one of the few people he truly admired.

Arrowsmith is a Doctor in White (a type in the 30s - Charles Laughton was lampooning them in *Island of Lost Souls* as Dr. Moreau not a year later) here to make the world a better place. He delivers babies like he's fixing a sink. He gives up his career to marry Helen Hayes but you can't stimy the urge to do good. He helps the town's collection of maudlin sods with their ailments but greater things call to him. Colman's casually stupendous, Ford loved him because he never had to direct him. He's breezy (Flynn-esque, you might say) in the first act. By the end he's a drunken wreck cursing mankind (ok so he still *kinda* acts like Ford). Hilariously the film was nominated for a host of Oscars but neither Ford nor Colman were recognized at all. They don't like it when it looks like you could do this in your sleep. Ford takes every advantage of the settings and trappings (he lights beakers like they contain Dr. Jekyll's serum, more of that Universal Horror connection, and he shoots a nighttime boat ride into Voodoo country with the camera perched on the back of the skiff, careening into the unknown. It is magic). When he gets to the West Indies to fight plague he meets Dr. Oliver Marchand (Clarence Brooks), the first black character of the sound era to have a PhD. Ford's apology for Stepin Fetchit's performance in *Salute* (though not fully: the Arrowsmiths have a domestic servant in the West Indies, after all [like Mr. and Mrs. Ford did in reality] and our Doctor in White is here to save everyone, and Fetchit would be back in a few years anyway). Clarence Brooks was a fascinating figure, too infrequently talked about or cited as a man who wasn't content with what the motion picture industry would give him. He and Noble Johnson and James Thomas Smith formed Lincoln Motion Picture Company in 1916 (both D.W. Griffith and John Ford's careers outlasted the LMPC which closed in 1921) as a way to make sure they weren't playing porters and minstrels. Johnson was playing a native chief in *King Kong* for future Ford business partner Merian C. Cooper around that same time, so it wasn't a totally foolproof plan, but Brooks did ok. He and Colman make excellent foils.

Ford makes a meal out of the Caribbean setting in the third act. Some villagers burn their homes to kill the plague rats and the camera finds every expressionist angle for the job, like he's marrying Murnau to Fritz Lang. Murnau was making his own south seas adventure *Tabu* at the same time, but he would die before he could see that or *Arrowsmith* which trailed it to theatres by a few months. There's almost no chance he was still working on this when Murnau died but Colman's fury at losing Hayes in the last scene plays like an epitaph anyway. In *Air Mail* the following year he'd have one colleague risk his life to save another. Two daredevils looking out for each other, the only two guys who know what it's like to live in free-fall.

## Air Mail (1932)

*Air Mail* was the pre-cursor to Howard Hawks' *Only Angels Have Wings*, basically a perfect film, and the film that introduced Howard to that fella, what's his name? Ralph Bellamy! Pat O'Brien is Bellamy's love interest even if Gloria Stuart is supposed to be. They're cuter together but Ford didn't really think cute was enough. Their milquetoast chemistry doesn't have a patch on the punches thrown between the two carves of beef at the center. Ford was always Willy Wonka about the homosexual bonding of his heroes. "Stop... Don't... Come back..." Likely because with his lust for Wayne, Ward Bond, George O'Brien, Big Victor, and Little Harry Carey, Jr. could never be satiated (and lord knows he plowed through one mistress after another when he couldn't have his leading men). Just google George O'Brien nude and see what I'm talking about. An apocryphal story has Ford leaving his wife Mary standing on a California dock, her ticket to a cruise ship in his suitcase on the deck, as he and strapping George made their way to the Philippines for a press junket. Apparently Ford was then rather upset when George had to abandon his cohort (who would Not. Stop. DRINKING.) to attend to his career, meaning a somber Ford was left to fend for himself for 10 days. Later they'd accuse Ford of using that trip to spy for the US government, to which O'Brien could only laugh. If he was spying on anything it was the inside of a bottle. His abandonment of Ford would lead to a decade and a half's blacklisting from Ford's films. Ford's still drunk in spirit on *Air Mail*, we learn when we hear these words from a benched pilot in the opening. "So you broke your neck?" "I didn't...but I might if I start flying." You don't say...

My capsule review has been taken down from Brooklyn Magazine, a trade long ago sold to cretins, when this played Dave Kehr's restoration festival at the Museum of Modern Art in Manhattan a few years ago, but I held onto it:

*John Ford is always poised on a knife edge between hilarity and tragedy, a punch-drunk margin walker, the Irish poet gazing at his American homeland in wonder and horror. Here he struts his hour on the wings of a plane barrel-rolling towards an abyss, laughing at the greedy toll man on the other side. Howard Hawks would later turn this story of perpetually revenant airmen into Only Angels Have Wings, but Ford keeps his focus narrow: Two men, two women, and death from above. Pat O'Brien and Ralph Bellamy act off each other like Louie Bellson and Buddy Rich trading solos. They've got different styles and their attitudes about the plane as an instrument put them at each other's throats. One thinks he's invincible, the other knows he isn't. Ford puts wry, snowy silence and women between them as they break up and remarry. Better to share the sky when men crack wise one minute and beg for mercy while they burn to death the next. You see death on a screen, you hear it on the radio in the control tower, and your powerless when it falls out of the sky and hits the guy next to you. Better to laugh in its face together than play its game apart.*

I was, it turns out, being hyperbolic about O'Brien and...what's his name, but I think I was just after a metaphor that also involved percussion, what with the two flyboys punching each other. I think also I still had Hawks cavalier attitude ringing in my ears.

*Air Mail* isn't at all a movie about laughing in the face of death, which its screenwriter Frank "Spig" Wead had done flying planes and then breaking his neck, which left him without the use of his legs. It's a movie about a man newly aware of the toll of losing people. As I never tire of pointing out: F.W. Murnau had just died. "Still wanna be a flier, stupid?" Asks one old paint to a rookie as one of their rank plummets to his fiery death. The screams of the dead pilot haunt you. I had forgotten that. You can see George Roy Hill pocketing it for when he kills Edward Herrmann in *The Great Waldo Pepper*. I couldn't bear to put the sound of his death in my essay film *Beata Virgo Viscera*, if only because I myself couldn't possibly hear them again. Richard Gilmore means too much to me, I can't hear him die everytime I watch my movie. "Joe didn't suffer. He never knew what happened," lies Bellamy to the dead pilot's girl. Ford is gearing up for World War 2. Like Waldo Pepper, his German hero is dead. Now everyone's his enemy. He's even got one of Murnau's photographers, Karl Freund, by then a Universal hired gun, aiming the camera. Christmas dinners and daring rescues (*un-scored* daring rescues, to really sell how unconvinced Ford is by everyday heroism) can't sell a more optimistic America. Darker times are here to stay. It would take a more folksy kind of story to really pull Ford out of the doldrums. The vacancy of the atmosphere isn't unusual for Ford, but there's so little else to which we're meant to pay attention. There's no Arizona buttes, no busy parlors, no burning jungles. The sky should feel more different from the ground.

**Flesh (1932)**

Hang around in Hollywood long enough you'll work with Wallace Beery, says *Barton Fink*. Ford had finally been around so long that they were just throwing him workhorses. *Flesh* is best known as the movie they're making in the Coen Brothers 1991 Palme d'Or winner; William Faulkner wrote it, Ford took his name off of it. He was working for MGM and still getting used to the water in Sam Goldwyn's pool. The melodramatic tone does feel like a hastily learned second language. Karen Morley chides a warden trying to say he knows she's good at heart. "Save the sermon for Sunday, Warden! Bring the whole choir, it sounds better with music!" You can hear Daffy Duck saying it just as easily, can't you? I do love that, clearly feeling a little adrift, Ford takes refuge in German culture again, dollying down a street where lovers toast each other with full steins as accordions haunt Morley's steps. Shots of beer glasses sliding across bar tops have more conviction than anything to do with Morley leaving Germany for America (Chaplin's never far away). For a few gorgeous, gorgeous minutes we're in a great movie, Ford's *The Blue Angel* with a wrestler taking the place of a teacher...or maybe...Wallace Beery filling in for Marlene Dietrich...a little dizzying to track but it doesn't really matter.

The first image returns to the Robert E. Howard wheel of pain from *The Black Watch*. Morley is a convict whose pregnant belly is her ticket out of women's prison. The sternness doesn't last. In a few minutes we're watching big brutes wrestle while beer spills from taps as if out of a sprung fire hydrant. With his cod German accent and his massive bulk, Beery is a proto-Schwarzenegger, clumsily pining for the hardened moll in the beer hall stall. He pockets her tab when she can't pay and she's in love maybe, but maybe she's too bad for love. He does seem like Ford's kind of hero, but it's all very cute and I think maybe the issue was admitting it. Ford had been, could be, and kept being cute, but he usually hid it better and saved it for later, at least in the good movies. His camera movements still feel like the procession of a king moving through a town square, which make the cheaply programmatic nature of the plot feel even weirder. Ford would never have been asked to make *Casablanca*, but more to the point it would have been redundant, he made *Casablanca* every other time at bat between 1928 and 1938. The scripts were just no good.

"This is a Teutonic friendship..." Ford begrudgingly makes hay out of the unlikely courtship of the little dame with the tar-stained soul and the big oaf who loves her like a father. There's the requisite Sunrise boat ride and everything. Sometimes the crutch you walk around with while reviewing old Ford is knowing that he becomes JOHN FORD, CINEMATIC POET and starting to view the throat clearing as aberrant instead of normal. With his wonky, Twainian worldview and his impeccable grammar, it's little wonder he'd hit snags and corners and pockets and swamps while getting to become himself. In much the same way it shouldn't exactly surprise us that something so tin-eared lurched off William Faulkner's fingers onto a typewriter and into the mouth of Wallace Beery, playing a

German brute with the mind and heart of a child, it should stop being such a shock to see Ford make silly movies. "You want dat yo papa chould be da champion of da voilrd?" Baby, you are making a German spectacle of yourself! Moss Hart wrote some of this for the love of Mike. Maybe he, Ford, and Faulkner were out to one up each other in the game of disdain for their own work. Everyone taking a big step back, cigarette/pipe in one hand, glass of whiskey in the other, shrugging their shoulders and moving on. Maybe next time. The film does have the earliest (that I can remember having seen) version of the ending of Bresson's *Pickpocket* (to paraphrase a joke from *The Critic* "Extra! Extra! Depression over and Paul Schrader born!"), so it wasn't a total wash. Two lost souls, one a recidivist traitor, the other hopelessly in love, both on the wrong side of the bars, gripping each other's fingers while guards watch over them. All that nonsense and then, suddenly, grace. Inventing the world is like that, I suppose.

## Pilgrimage (1933)

Ford would only return to MGM fleetingly throughout the next few decades of his illustrious career. Fox would let him do what he wanted instead of the other way around. Or at least William Fox knew better than to hassle him. He paid for it, this little reunion lost the studio money, but it was worth it in the long run. Shame too, it deserves to be better known. Norman Foster loves Heather Angel (can ya blame him?) but his mother Henrietta Crosman doesn't want her only son marrying the daughter of a drunk (Charley Grapewin), but the real reason of course is that she's a demented old crone who doesn't want her son engaging in heterosexual congress with anyone but her. And since she can't do that she has him press-ganged into the military in time for WWI. Pretty fucking sadistic!

The vision of the Arkansas prairie on which this little passion play transpires is right out of *Sunrise*, but there's an uncanniness to everything. Every house looks like a matte painting until the characters walk inside. R.H. Bassett's score swoons for the lovers. When Angel tells Foster she's pregnant and he tries to defect then and there to marry her so his kid isn't born a bastard, Ford cuts from the chaos to Angel in close-up watching her man carted off on a train towards a boat to the Western front. He seems to have made peace with D.W. Griffith. Ford's brother Francis plays the mayor who tells Crosman that her son is dead. She breaks down over her needle point and has to tape together the picture of him she tore up when he threatened to marry without her permission. It's shocking how effective this is because ten minutes earlier she was the most evil character Ford had ever written. Now she has to watch the kid grow up down the street knowing she killed his father. The ending can't exactly live up to how wicked the first act is but Ford is *on*.

Ford's reliance on shots of people lost in landscapes seem to prefigure his best work to come (certainly there's a lot of Henry Fonda staring meaningfully into the middle distance in our future). He's back at his silent movie-expressionistic-painterly best. When Crosman heads to New York (would you believe she winds up in front of a boat right out of Chaplin's *The Immigrant*?), Angel and her son stand by the window of her train compartment, as she did the night Foster left her without making an honest woman out of her, with flowers. Will Crosman lay them on the dead soldier/husband/father's grave for her? Angel lifts them to the window and Crosman's arm alone, clad in a black glove, emerges from within. She takes the flowers wordlessly, and then the train starts moving. My heart stopped. Crosman takes the exact same trip her son did to go visit the graves of dead American soldiers over in Europe and her heart slowly thaws along the way. Another grieving mother asks her to put flowers on Foster's grave for her; her son was missing in action. Doesn't even have a grave to visit. She meets another lovesick young American whose circumstances are the same as her dead son's and she realizes the error of her ways. She decides to join them for one last perfect day in the country before they'll be separated. Ford's happiness defined, nothing but simple culture and music and romance.

### Doctor Bull (1933)

My complaints about the uninspired establishing shots in *Salute* are answered in the opening of *Doctor Bull*, in which every shot in the first three minutes, of things essentially unimportant to the plot, is steeped in poetry. A train pulls into a station. A mail bag hits the ground. The woman carrying it trudges up main street. The same street is seen through a window, looking slanted, just behind a woman operating the phone for the small town. The first conversation, between three women in three different shots, dialogue overlapping, has the oldest of them looking to camera (complaining that the town doctor stayed up til 3 doing god knows what the other night), one of them looking just to the side of the camera (making fun of the old woman in visual asides), and another staring into space taking both of them in. We meet the doctor (played by Will Rogers) collecting firewood. Twain's Americana and Joyce's frosty humanity side by side. A man approaches, complaining of pain in his appendix, so Rogers/Bull suggests he go to church; he doesn't recall anyone ever bursting an appendix in church. Just like that, a town is alive with poetry and gritty humanity.

Rogers was one of the first Native Americans to get red carpet treatment in America, likely helped there because he didn't look like anyone who'd come from the Cherokee nation. He was a beloved vaudevillian and before long he was starring in Goldwyn movies (he was the first man to play Ichabod Crane, if I'm not mistaken), he had a nationally syndicated newspaper column, was mayor of Beverly Hills for a minute, and was just generally everywhere. He was Andy Griffith and Lonesome Rhodes in one man. Funny to think that the Will Rogers institute is probably a name everyone in my generation knows because of the ubiquitous ad campaigns (which gave us the indelible sound of Sylvester Stallone saying "And I'll see *you* at the movies!" with the ease and charm of a hostage speaking his third language in a proof of life cassette - if anyone was ever *less* like Rogers, I'd be hard pressed to think who it might be) but it's not like we knew who he was as kids. His movies weren't taught in schools, ditto his writings, and his legendary wit was no such thing to most. He once joked he had an epitaph idea so good he couldn't wait to die so he could have it carved. Well he got his wish, he died in a plane crash right when his film career was at its apex.

Rogers liked Ford best of all his directors, not tough to see why, nevermind the talent discrepancy between him and say...David Butler, co-director of *Salute*, who also directed Rogers in *A Connecticut Yankee*. He did get Frank Borzage for his first sound film, *They Had To See Paris*, which is really funny, so it wasn't all bad news, but Borzage was an odd fit for Rogers in a way Ford wasn't. Ford and Rogers had the same idea about the function of dialogue (Ford didn't really care about the performances of his actors; that was their job, not his - wasn't it Ford who quipped that he didn't know John Wayne could act until he saw him in *Red River*, twenty years into their working relationship?) and as long as the cast could rise to Rogers' example, they'd be in tip-top shape. He was right. Everyone's good in this. Andy Devine makes the biggest impression in his first role for Ford. Like Rogers you can't imagine him in silent films, he had a voice for film. It's kind of a retread of *Arrowsmith* (typhoid hits the town pretty hard in Act 3) but without ever leaving the heartland. *Doctor Bull* might be Rogers-centric but it's really a story of a town (hence the arrival of a train opening the picture), and Ford was at his best studying communities, the way they bend and sway in the presence of this or that figure or event. It's *Groundhog Day* without the high concept. Think of a whole town quaking in fear at Lee Marvin in *Liberty Valance*, the cavalry units commanded by John Wayne, or the dance hall in *My Darling Clementine*. This, with its gingham topped beer hall tabletop singalongs (during one of which Vera Allen is found switching between coffee and beer - the woman of my dreams), the revolving doors to bedrooms and parlors, and town hall meetings, is a place straight out of Ford's poorly hidden heart. What is a film set after all, if not a little town overseen by a benevolent guiding force like Bull/Ford? Men with vices, men with virtues.

**The Lost Patrol (1934)**

While Max Steiner's locomotive of music pounds into us, a gang of soldiers crosses an Arabian desert at sundown. Who's that I spy? Why it's Big Victor McLaglen leading Reginald Denny, Boris Karloff, Wallace Ford, Alan Hale, Sr. and Douglas Walton (Percy Shelley to Karloff's Monster in next year's *Bride of Frankenstein*). *The Lost Patrol* was Ford's first movie for Merian Cooper at RKO. Don't quote me on this but I firmly believe Thin Lizzy's "The Boys are Back in Town" was written about this movie. The gang is well and truly all here. Their commanding officer is killed in the opening three minutes so Vic's in charge. This was all familiar to him, he'd fought in Iraq in WWI, and his brother had played this part in the 1929 adaptation of this same Philip MacDonald story. "Where are we going to bury him?" "Doesn't make much difference... does it?" This film influenced Zoltan Korda's *Sahara* with Bogart and Rex Ingram and it's the kind of potboiler that adolescent dreams are made of. Victor nearly splits Karloff's soul in twain when he stops him from delivering a full eulogy for their departed captain. Karloff knows just what he's doing, giving a Dwight Frye performance in a movie of stock types and anonymous faces, practically perverse with the spirit of the lord. "If you read your bible instead of hanging around in taverns, you'd know that Mesopotamia, this very spot, is the garden of Eden." He says, practically drooling, to our last recruit - blissful drunk J.M Kerrigan as Quincannon, the soldier Big Victor would play for the rest of Ford's soldiering pictures.

The winds howl and the chorus on the soundtrack hums a mournful tune as night falls on the cold desert. Karloff screams for the everloving souls of his regiment but the music keeps reminding us that the soldiering life is worth it (Ford would offer a contrary take in his next film but no matter). Every shot of the horizon is a bleak poem of wrongful dedication. Robert Aldrich basically remakes this with *Flight of the Phoenix*. Billy Wilder snaps awake to catch enough of this and direct *Five Graves to Cairo*. Ford had little use for pessimism of this sort, even as the brigade gets picked off and goes crazy, Big Victor holds the platoon together while he literally holds Karloff together by tying him up with rope when he cracks. There is an *awful* lot of speechifying between killings and the film could have handily survived without it. Funny to think Ford could direct the hell out of anti-war epics but he lost his senses when glorifying it.

Salvation rears its head when a plane flies in from *Air Mail* but just as quickly vanishes from the horizon. In a perfect re-statement of Ford's sense of humor, the pilot is shot mid-swagger. "I say you chaps...!" thud. Groundskeeper Willie would be envious. Wallace Ford and Big Victor are the last men standing. They light the plane on fire to signal an oncoming patrol while Karloff frees himself from bondage and goes AWOL. He strides into the desert with a cross like some cracked messiah (an image answered by the crosses bookending Ford's later *The World Moves On*). Big Victor buries his whole regiment as Max Steiner's score cries for him. He puts on his dress uniform and picks up his saber and the whole last twenty years of military drama flashes before my eyes. He winds up blasting away at the six arabs (played by white guys, Francis Ford among them) and laughing as he knocks 'em down. Not quite the stirring tribute to the soldier it seems at first. Almost like war is bad for us.

**The World Moves On (1934)**

A close-up of a cross morphs into a wide of a will reading. There's talk of keeping business in the family and then a perplexing exchange takes place. A man approaches Madeleine Carroll and starts flirting with her, but she cuts him off. "Is this a joke!?" The ferocity is startling. A duel is fought over the insult and the offending lech is killed. Believe it or not this was the first film passed for screening by the Motion Picture Producers and Distributors of America under their new, more strictly enforced production code (when people talk about pre-code what they mean was "after it was written and before anyone read it."). The man's murder happens in about one minute thirty of screen time and they don't even alert Carroll's husband, Reginald Denny, to the matter. Franchot Tone doesn't want to bother him. Hey, it's just a duel to the death, it's not like his horse ran away or anything. Tone killed the man not over the insult, per se, but because he's in love with Carroll himself. Their families are prosperous merchants, English expats in New Orleans (which looks like how backlot Mexico used to look in all those bullfighting and Zorro pictures). They part ways but the families are brought back together just in time for World War I.

Their descendants are played by the same actors and when they meet it's déjà vu all over again. "Haven't we met before?" There's a wedding with lots of talk about England and Germany never ever arguing for any reason ever, so naturally the war breaks out the next scene. Tone joins up, much to the chagrin of his father. There's a hilarious edit where two elders are speaking "I think Europe is insane! Six months ago you were all at a wedding in Germany!" then HARD CUT to a picture of the wedding and some soft focus double exposure footage of it. Doesn't really mean anything, we were also just at that wedding, it was about 10 minutes back, but it is very funny. David Lean and Noel Coward would attempt this same kind of thing a few years later, but about World War 2 and with less frankness and panache. Of course Lean wouldn't have cast Stepin Fetchit as a bewildered soldier (actually one of his less embarrassing performances) in Tone's platoon so six 'a one, I guess. Though it's not like Lean didn't have some *other* bad ideas about casting.

The grab bag of techniques (stolen battle footage from Raymond Bernard [which was practically a tradition in WW1 films at that point], miniatures, sharp edits, double exposures, big center frame subtitles) and the speed of events make this feel almost postmodern. Carroll doesn't want to hand her family's factory over to the production of shells and bombs to kill people. Tone is kind of an asshole about it but he softens when she asks him to see her off the next day - a swell scene followed by the marching of soldiers in the rain reflected on a window through which Carroll watches mournfully. Ford seems to know it's a great shot because he cuts to it twice between a shot of the camera creeping up behind her to see what she sees. It's matched with a shot of a slow push-in from across the room when they reunite a few weeks later. There's murder in his eyes. He's been changed by what he's seen on the western front. When he grabs her we aren't sure he's not about to kill her, but no, he wants an emergency wedding. It's like he's editing Hemingway. "I never told you...I think you were dead right not to make munitions." This one gets borderline erotic when Tone finally gets Carroll into their marriage bed, once again making me wonder just what the censors cared about after all. I guess the music is romantic and not mischievous and they're married so what's the harm, but.... I got shivers. Tone loses it all in the depression (lotta plot for 90 minutes, which is *very* pre-code) but it makes him a better husband and saves his soul. We should all be so lucky. The shareholders say the only thing that can save them is another war and Carroll loses it. "Why? So that the guns don't go hungry?" Smash cut to footage of Hitler. That's not a joke. Ford's last "early" work is one of his best.

**Judge Priest (1934)**

Will Rogers starts this one by staring right to camera and banging his gavel, once more predicting Godard. Then begins another Grampa Simpson-style old man argument as three witnesses and a judge try to recall which battle was fought over what and when. There, square in the middle of all of that is Stepin Fetchit, braying, squeaking, bowing, and scraping, becoming rich doing this deathless shtick. Rogers frees him so they can go fishing. I guess that's liberalism of a kind (frankly we're still very much living in this world). Everyone in town remembers the good old days; there's even double exposure ghosts dressed for an antebellum ball. Ford fully gives into the cornpone values that Rogers and Mark Twain peddled most of their lives. Jonathan Rosenbaum calls this the purest expression of Twain perhaps ever committed to film and so in that vein we just have to accept the garish nostalgia, the Dixie Alzheimer's that so characterizes the worst of America's vision. Looking back and only seeing the good. Twain is one touchstone. Walt Disney's *Song of the South* is another.

Ford's disdain for bureaucracy shines through, with Rogers gleefully reading comics during a trial while a racist lawyer goes on and on (once more, tough not to think of *The Simpsons*, and Spielberg's *Lincoln*). Men just want to be left with their memories. Rogers' son wants to date the girl next door (introduced with the same gaggle of tricks used on Sally O'Neil in *The Brat*) and Rogers wants to pass the time drinking and playing croquet with his fellow confederates (and Fetchit, who loves the Judge; they're both the right kind of adversaries, the sort that don't let politics get in the way of legal slavery). Hattie McDaniel shows up Fetchit as Rogers' maid and preps her *Gone with the Wind* performance. Rosenbaum and McBride have no trouble with Fetchit's performance and in this instance we heartily diverge. I found it tough to focus on the compositions and atmosphere with all the Civil War decorations still up everywhere. Rogers, McDaniel and a choir of black back-up singers belt "My Old Kentucky Home," and it's like we're watching America's *Alexander Nevsky*. Or...if you like... *Triumph of the Will*. That's Henry Walthal, the hero of Griffith's *Birth of a Nation*, as Reverend Brand. Mae Marsh, who played a woman who dies rather than let a black man touch her in *Birth*, becomes a Ford regular, too.

Rogers recuses himself from sitting in on the climactic trial, not wanting to seem biased (he and the district attorney don't get along). Justice remains important to Ford (and he sees no inherent contradiction in valorizing the confederacy in the pursuit of "justice" and fairness). It's tough to muster much interest in the case; who's being railroaded and why. Rogers and McDaniel singing picture-breaking duets is much more interesting and one of the only things this film can offer that doesn't rankle in hindsight. I suppose I ought to be able to see through these things, to be impartial, as Rogers attempts to be, but I just don't know how. There's something sickening about all the sentimentality festooned in stars and bars. Looking back from your rocking chair is one thing, looking back *there* is quite another. I felt like I was drowning. Tomorrow belongs to them.

**The Whole Town's Talking (1935)**

A good number of early Fords have been painstakingly restored but as I do not have access to every vault I occasionally had to settle for subpar copies of some of the early Fords. It matters little, the care with which Ford composes is the same as that of Beethoven. Even a shoddy recording can't disguise the practiced hand, the feverish machinations of the mind, the ample beauty. Still it was quite something to turn on *The Whole Town's Talking*, based not on Fannie Flagg's story of the same name but by a lesser known tale by W.R. Burnett (and it would have to be lesser known, the guy wrote *The Great Escape, The Asphalt Jungle, High Sierra, The Westerner* and *Little Caesar*), and it looked just like a Preston Sturges comedy (whose best work is all in tiptop shape...except *The French They are a Funny Race*, which looks as bad as it feels). Burnett's *Little Caesar* catapulted *The Whole Town's Talking*'s star Edward G. Robinson to fame. Both Ford and Robinson must have been in the mood to play around a little with their images because *The Whole Town's Talking* is the most urbane thing I've seen Ford do and the earliest comedy I've yet seen Robinson headline. This was Ford's first film at Harry Cohn's Columbia, and they dolled him up real good.

Robinson's a mild-mannered advertising clerk by day, failed novelist by night. He happens to look exactly like an escaped killer (the shot of him examining himself in the mirror is both gorgeous and priceless - Robinson makes staring at himself, for the thousandth time, seem like an act of shaken faith in the universe; the guy was such a star. Bonus points: he has a magnificent drunk scene which Ford shoots like a death scene). He draws the short straw at his job and is set to be fired except the bosses need him, he's the only one who ever does any actual work around the place, so they fire Jean Arthur instead, who responds by walking to her desk and cracking the newspaper. Arthur hadn't yet been in the Capra films that would announce her immortality but she's fully formed here. She'd worked for Ford twice before but without sound she wasn't the whole genius yet (she also stood opposite Buster Keaton in *Seven Chances*, and worked very hard to become something like his antithesis; brash and loud and openly contemptuous; there was rarely anything sly about Arthur, she could put you in your place and you'd just stand there and take it). Anyway Robinson-as-Jones takes his lunch break and newly fired Arthur sits down to commiserate, making his day. He says he's got a stamp from Shanghai to impress her, and she does, too, after a fashion: she'd already been in two unspeakable Fu Manchu movies.

The cops move in on Robinson. The guy who dimed him out

wants credit, so the press grab him to take his picture ("Shoot this man!" they say, and his face goes whiter than...it was a few seconds ago). The jokes aren't particularly sophisticated but the delivery is impeccable. Arthur responds to interrogation with incendiary looks of confusion and then sarcastic satisfaction. Ford could tap the untapped when directing actresses. Tag Gallagher suggests it was because he just let everyone be. Which makes sense. If you're not getting micromanaged, your mind might start to wander, and you might find something there you weren't expecting. Arthur gets the best stuff, or anyway she makes it the best stuff. The form here is pure Americana in the way of a lot of Ford, but the shape is different. These comedies are what we associate with Hawks, Capra, Sturges, and Mitchell Leisen (there's even a kind of art deco double exposure hysteria montage - Columbia's in-house editor supreme Viola Lawrence is unbelievably good at her job as you might expect). Ford has zero trouble finding his feet in the imposing offices and pre-modern decor. Every shot of Robinson in the office predicts Jacques Tati. This, the performers, the pacing, the best of the dialogue ("Mannion just robbed a bank!" "You're drunk!" "I know that, but it's true!"), all of that makes up for the second act plot, which makes no sense.

Robinson eventually winds up acting opposite himself so the "Nyaaah Seees?" start flying (handled pretty well considering this technology was in its infancy - Only Boris Karloff in *The Black Room* does better work with this gag) but he also acts opposite a softball team's worth of minor legends. Francis Ford and J. Farrell MacDonald are both back, so is boy wonder Robert Parrish, who'd hang with Ford for the rest of the 30s. The film also supposedly stars (deep breath) Arthur Rankin Sr., Clarence Wilson, John Wray, Jay Eaton, Edward Hearn, Al Hill, John Ince, Arthur Stuart Hull, Edward Keane, Cornelius Keefe, Charles King, W.E. Lawrence, Frank Marlowe, Charles Marsh, Charles McMurphy, Ferdinand Munier, Robert Emmett O'Connor, Pat O'Malley, Steve Pendleton, Joe Sawyer, Reginald Simpson, Charles Sullivan, Harry Tenbrook, Billy West, Lloyd Whitlock, Ivan Christy, Jules Cowles, Arthur Hohl, Donald Meek, Etienne Girardot, Edward Brophy, Paul Harvey, Ernie Adams, Eddie Baker, and Kernan Cripps. Between them they have (quick math) 1 billion screen credits. Charles Sullivan alone had almost 600. The whole town indeed.

**The Informer (1935)**

Ford wasn't the world's most demanding director when it came to actors he knew he could trust to get the job done. Victor McLaglen was a fine presence but to Ford he wasn't a great actor yet. *The Informer*, based on a book written by Ford's cousin Liam O'Flaherty, was too important to leave to his usual method. He started tormenting Big Vic. He'd get him drunk on set, lie to him about call times, bring him in hungover, berate him in front of everyone in a pattern that would become all too familiar for Ford leading men. He looks very drunk indeed during the scene where the head of the organization grills him. It was inhuman. Vic said he was going to quit acting and kill Ford but it *did* work. He won an Oscar. So did Ford. His first and well deserved. Graham Greene called it Victor's best performance. Walter Matthau is born in its reflection; it was understandably his favourite movie. Sam Fuller, who was a friend of Ford's, once claimed the same thing; certainly his own work bears out the affection. There's no denying this is stirring, uncommon work from McLaglen. He looks like he's driving a truck going 150 miles an hour while it leaks fuel, hitting guard rails and narrowly avoiding pedestrians. Maybe he *is* the truck.

He's a drunk and a washout, bounced from the IRA. His best girl is a streetwalker now. That boat to America to start over is only ten pounds. The wanted posters with Wallace Ford's face on them promise twenty. Freedom and love for half the price of betrayal. Surely it can't mean that much now? Surely the cosmic scales won't tip for this one man? Ford had to cut out of a lot of the references to the Black and Tans, the turncoat police forces patrolling Irish streets for troublemakers, and the IRA (Ford had little trouble chastising them as indeed he frequently browbeat *all* traitors, but he would, let's say, forget this position for a period in the 50s). They become more elemental forces, which eerily helps the picture. It's already such an expressionistic alienating work. You see as much of Victor's silhouette as you do his face, like he wandered in from Fritz Lang's *M* (there's even a trial) or G.W. Pabst's *Pandora's Box*. This also makes the emotions run higher. When you don't have as firm a grip on the whys and hows, the sudden intrusions of violence are more frightening. Take Wallace Ford's execution by the police, Una O'Connor playing his mother screaming and wailing at such a pitch you can hear it over the machine gun fire. It's awful.

Ford manipulates the images in a way I haven't seen since his first silent westerns; fittingly there isn't a spoken word for the first five minutes.

The wanted poster keeps appearing in inconvenient places torturing McLaglen, just like Ford, everywhere he goes in double exposures and superimpositions. Light and wind are pushed up and down as if on faders, like Vic's being interrogated by the city itself. McLaglen is hounded by a blind witness; the film is about what we can't see but know anyway. Victor's at first sure the man knows he turned in Ford, then he pays him for his silence even though he still doesn't know anything. Every drop of change outs him as a judas (twenty pounds, thirty coins) and he helps himself not a bit by threatening to throttle everyone who looks at him wrong. You can tell he made this for RKO, the sound is pure RKO, peaking whenever Max Steiner's Oscar winning score tells us our hero can't handle another moment of scrutiny. RKO films seemed almost like they were alive, like they had blood and guts. Certainly when Val Lewton took the gig producing horror at RKO (*Cat People*, *I Walked with a Zombie*, et al) he learned the lessons of this movie; what we can't see but are desperate to prove? That, too, has claws.

**Steamboat Round the Bend (1935)**

I was as excited to find Ford back on a boat as I was absolutely furious that this was another Stepin Fetchit movie. Star Will Rogers was dead before it was released. Ford's last aquatic frolic was a decade in the rearview by now, however when this opened with a shot of a boat on the river and then a passion play with a bearded Moses (Berton Churchill) before the cross on the deck of the boat, I knew I was in for as good a time as possible given the circumstances. Further cementing Ford and Rogers' twin affinity for Mark Twain, this is set on the Mississippi River in the lead up to a riverboat race. Our Moses is conducting a temperance sermon, demanding everyone throw away whatever booze is on their person. Next cut: disgraced former steamboat captain Rogers hawking booze on another deck. He gets into a bet with the captain (Irvin S. Cobb), seeing who could get their boat from one port to another faster for pink slips like in the early *Fast and Furious* movies. Convenient on two counts: one of the drunks present for the sermon on the mount was once an engineer ("You just drunk yourself into a job!") and Rogers' nephew Duke (John McGuire) just killed a guy over his new girlfriend Anne Shirley ("She a swamp woman in she?"

asks a trepidatious Rogers) and he needs to track down the only witness along the river. The race is on!

Turns out Moses saw the crime so Rogers suggests McGuire turn himself in. Truly gorgeous vignette follows when they wake the sheriff (Eugene Pallette!) and he just tosses them down the keys to the jail, too sleepy and lazy to walk down and arrest him himself (Garrison Keillor was taking this all in, you can be sure). They can't afford him a lawyer so Shirley and Rogers get to know each other while they hatch a scheme to save him. Pallette runs a wax museum in his downtime (there isn't all that much crime to stop around these parts). They use it when the relatives of the man McGuire killed come around looking for blood. First to scare them by using the Jesse James figure as backup and then to dumbfound them with the whale that swallowed Jonah. There's a bizarre burlesque of Ford and Roger's previous film *Judge Priest* when they make the Robert E. Lee figure salute and the swamp dwellers all mechanically salute the dead man. Little less funny when you know Ford, Rogers, and Fetchit were mechanically saluting him themselves the year before.

A lot happens while McGuire's behind bars. He learns to play the saw, reducing all and sundry to tears. He marries Shirley with Pallette performing the honors. It's all enough to make you forget this movie's supposed to be about a steamboat race. The shots of the mighty crafts in the river is a stupendous spectacle. Ford just sending behemoths into the sunset for our enjoyment. So much modern filmmaking makes too large a deal of the sight of a big *thing*, Ford seems to enjoy being lost in the crowd watching them sail by. The clip of the men feeding the furnace while the rear projection world passes by has a bewitching falseness. Shirley looks very cute in her captain's uniform. Rogers lassos Moses and drags him aboard the boat to get him to testify on McGuire's behalf when they get back to port. Will Rogers fishing a bearded prophet from the drink is exactly what I go to pre-WW2 Ford to see. This film has some impossible and cockeyed sight or sound every few minutes. The thing that gets our heroes over the finish line? All that rum Rogers had been hawking. They throw it into the furnace and win handily and McGuire goes free, saved from the noose with eight seconds to spare.

## The Prisoner of Shark Island (1936)

When you adjust for inflation the 20 pounds Victor McGlaglen gets to rat out Wallace Ford in *The Informer* comes out to about 1500 bucks today. Makes sense when he's giving out free food to everyone at a bar or giving a society lady boat fare back to England. Samuel Mudd gets fifty dollars to fix up John Wilkes Booth's leg in *Prisoner of Shark Island*, which is about 800 dollars today. Not bad for a few minute's work. But a heavy toll when you consider how much hard time he did and what happened to his name in the wake of the act of benevolence towards a stranger. Warner Baxter plays the scene of discovering the money as if he's the star of a one-act play on the subject of benevolence. He makes a banquet out of it, letting no second go empty of gesture and feeling. Gloria Stuart kisses the money goodbye when they think the weird stranger who gave it to them has come to reclaim it. Turns out it's just that a neighbor is finally going into labor and a doctor is needed down the street. A perfect short film. Then the plot starts.

Ford keeps trying to have a reasonable debate about the actions taken here, all of them based in fact. His Boothe (Francis McDonald) is joyless, made-up and lit like a villain. Claude Gillingwater plays Mudd's confederate father-in-law who seems like a blowhard when crowing about states rights but he's also a loving family man. Mudd is a slave owner and his slaves throw the local carpetbagger off his property because they'd rather stay and work for him. Indeed one of them willfully puts his life in danger by getting a job at a prison to make sure Mudd's doing ok in stir. Ford shoots the aggrieved mourners who wanted justice for Lincoln as a rabid mob hungry for blood above all. The judge in the trial tells the jurors not to be bogged down in that "legal nonsense...reasonable doubt!" Mudd's attorney is a kindly union soldier who wants to help, but he does lose so it's not all good news. It's an extremely antiquated and dispiriting early version of "fair and balanced". In his final performance for Ford, Harry Carey plays the warden of the prison Mudd is sent to.

Bert Glennon had already photographed a dozen great films by now, several by Josef Von Sternberg, and this shows the everyday brilliance of a man at the height of his craft. Nunnally Johnson scripts and between lionizing Jesse James and later writing the marvelously entertaining, crypto-fascist *The Dirty Dozen*, he and Ford appear to be meeting in the middle. Amazing to think that they go way out of their way to talk about what an inhuman place the prison at Dry Tortugas is (John Carradine gives his first iconic villain performance as the head of operations, which ought to tell you how it's depicted) but neither man stopped for a minute to think if it was such a horrific place for a wrongly accused man, perhaps it was just as bad for the guilty? Frankenheimer sort of remakes this in *Birdman of Alcatraz* and anytime there are innocent men in prison Paul Schrader's ears prick up. Robert Redford makes the inverse with *The Conspirator* in which the life of the lawyer and union soldier Frederick Aiken is ruined for defending Mary Surrat, the only other conspirator who wasn't immediately hanged after Lincoln's murder. People can't stop reading this chapter of history, but they won't ever finish it either.

Watching this movie I kept hearing David Strathairn as Secretary of State Seward in *Lincoln* addressing a confederate delegation: "You'll not be conquered people, Mr. Hunter. You will be citizens, returned to the laws and the guarantees of rights of the Constitution." The means at the disposal of confederate apologists was vast and unyielding. No one ever told confederates to tamp down their hatred. It's all well and good for Ford and Johnson to make this (incredibly beautiful) work of romantic nostalgia that paints union soldiers as bloodthirsty yokels but where were the classic Hollywood films about the fear that gripped free men upon hearing that the man who passed the 13th amendment had been killed? If they could kill the most powerful man in America, surely that meant anyone was fair game? Where was the other side of the equation? Ford had just two years ago made a movie that predicted the rise of Hitler and knew that was a bad thing, why could he not afford the same suspicion to the supporters of Robert E. Lee? There is, after all, a reason there wasn't an influx of Nazi tract movies in America, right? Hollywood may have eventually made room for black actors, directors, and screenwriters and likeminded collaborators genuinely interested in their experiences but not before decades of confederate art had been put brick by brick in front of the idea of American cinema (and America itself) as a place of inclusivity. This may be Ford's most stunning work of revisionist horror, even if it does make sure that Mudd's black servant gets his happy ending, too. The union forever, hurrah boys hurrah.

## Mary of Scotland (1936)

It didn't happen but I could see Joseph Mankiewicz watching this get made while working for his uncle at RKO (grossly oversimplifying things here but this is a hypothetical not a history lesson) because when they introduce Katherine Hepburn's Mary Stuart, queen of Scots, there's a sort of galloping fanfare and entourage to go with it. All I could think about was the ten minute parade that precedes Elizabeth Taylor's arrival in Rome in *Cleopatra*. Hepburn wasn't quite Hepburn as we know her yet but she was a holy terror. Ginger Rogers came to audition for the part of Queen Elizabeth and Hepburn kicked her in the shins. She asked to *also* play Elizabeth in this movie at which John Carradine scoffed "How will you know who to upstage?" Ford was gung ho on the film (and on Hepburn, with whom he's meant to have had an affair - now there's an image) until they started filming. He suddenly realized he was making a costume drama based on a stage play. You can't do much with that.

He gets a lot of mileage out of dozens of crowd scenes and parades (all of Scotland turns up to serenade their new queen and Ford and Joseph H. August light them with typical expressive zeal) and certainly no one could hold a close-up like Hepburn. She seems to suck the camera in like a blackhole, too pretty for words. Ford tries his best to make this interesting (there are great shots of people raging at the sky, lit in dazzling chiaroscuro) but it's mostly talking. Ford never went this far back in the past ever again. Moroni Olsen and John Carradine are the only actors up to the task of holding their own against Hepburn. Fredric March knows he's licked so mostly leans back and lets the charm waft off of him. He is wearing a kilt the whole film, which does a lot of work for him. They did eventually settle on Florence Eldridge to play Queen Elizabeth, her rival, and she gets off one of the best notes in the movie, when they present her a drawing of Mary. She looks at it with wry disgust, then grabs a mirror and compares the two images. This takes twenty silent seconds while Eldridge's face is a picture of misery. Hepburn directed her own love scenes and though the camera doesn't really do anything, there is a tenderness in them missing from the rest of the film.

Fans of Coleman Francis' anti-masterpiece *Night Train To Mundo Fine* aka *Red Zone Cuba* will be pleased to know that Carradine has a musical number in this and it's actually quite lovely. He strums a lute and sings mournfully before Mary gives him the sack. He sounds almost like

Paul Robeson. He should have quit while he was ahead; the troops break into the palace and kill him a few seconds later for treason. There's a coup and a sword fight and stuff but it's mostly just shots of guys pulling their horses to the ground. Not hard to tell Ford was yawning between takes. His energy is infectious. Even when they blow up the king the film's pulse doesn't rise above resting. Ford would have hated to hear it but Orson Welles would have nailed this.

**The Plough and The Stars (1936)**

Playwright Sean O'Casey was very popular in European and American writers' circles when he was writing his hits and he was briefly in vogue among directors looking to show their solidarity with the oppressed. Hitchcock directed a dreadful adaptation of *Juno and The Paycock* in the 30s, which explains *Rope*, in which he tried once more to make the theatrical cinematic and succeeded on his own newfound terms. John Ford also fell into the same trap, trying to wrest the play's political life into something more poetic but the trouble started before they'd even begun rolling. RKO wanted stars (and perhaps more to the point they wanted stars who weren't Irish in this story about The Troubles) and they wanted him to tone down the politics. Do that to an O'Casey play and you don't have much left. Arthur Shields, Eddie Donahoe, and George Nichols Jr. directed as much of the film as Ford, who walked off the set when it was announced they wanted reshoots. Ford was so pissed at the RKO bosses he wouldn't work with them ever again. Well...that's not entirely true. He'd form Argosy pictures with Merian Cooper a decade later, which meant he was using RKO money but he was calling the shots.

Sure starts alright, though. Barbara Stanwyck enters her house and finds husband Preston Foster brooding over a cigarette as he stares out the window. Little gathering of courage from her, then "A penny for them, Jack." Without looking up. "They'd be of no interest to you." I don't think anyone's ever looked less Irish than Stanwyck (she was English and Scottish, but there's no "almost" in horseshoes and Irishness). Also funny to think of arch conservative Stanwyck playing a woman who married into the Irish Citizen Army but she really was that good, even if her accent comes and goes. Foster can't help but seem wooden next to her. "A man must fight." He says with the conviction of a substitute youth pastor. They seem to be back on *The Informer* sets for another tale of a conflicted man at the mercy of time and tide and the woman he wants to impress but can't. Again I can't say for sure who shot what here but the domestic scenes are a hundred percent more dynamically appointed and lit than Hitchcock's attempts at the same. If nothing else he's on surer footing in cramped parlors than he was in the castles of *Mary of Scotland*.

This doesn't have much of a reputation but I think it's basically good. The trouble is Ford does better work with the camera than with dialogue, which never mattered much to him except as a direct and blunt extension of characterization. The best parts of Ford could be silent. Having him direct reams of O'Casey dialogue is not the best use of his talent, though he obviously disagreed because he thought this would be his major statement (which explains why he was so mad when the studio started tampering with it). Some artists just don't know why they're good. I was taken aback by the scenes of the English openly machine gunning the Irish in the streets. I knew RKO wanted to tamp down some of the political content but it doesn't get much more cut and dry than that. Massacres. Irish history is pockmarked with them. Stanwyck goes out into the streets to look for Foster after he's been drafted and the film becomes like the last act of *Les Misérables* by way of Terence Davies' *Sunset Song*. She screams that the violence is all pointless and for once the ideological contradictions are more interesting than sickening in Ford's 30s pictures. She isn't wrong, but also, if the Irish hadn't fought back would there still be an Ireland? Thornier stuff than I expected after so much Confederate poetry.

**Wee Willie Winkie (1937)**

John Ford, freak that he was, loved Shirley Temple. Not initially, of course, she had to earn his trust and respect (no quicker way to Ford's heart than to not need a second take) but he was so enamored of her that he loudly berated her husband on the set of *Fort Apache*, out of the usual Freudian impotence. Though he was John Agar, so Ford was probably right to give him shit. Ford was even godfather to one of her kids (imagine that woman's children being raised by a perpetually drunk and grouchy John Ford in his last decade...). If this one seemed an odd fit for Ford (most serious people loathed Temple's schtick. Frank Nugent of the New York Times said he yearned to see her become a "has-been by the time she's 15 years old." Ford gave him a job.) it was only because he wasn't a maker of children's entertainments. He was no stranger to the kind of sentimentality Temple's movies trafficked in. Add to that this is only fleetingly a Temple film and there's no leap required to make it fit snugly in his body of work. Graham Greene called it "horrifyingly competent" in a review that got him and his publisher at Night and Day magazine sued for 3500 pounds (in today's money...best not to think about it). That's roughly a hundred pounds a word. Understandably Temple and Fox took issue with him discussing her in a grimly sexual way.

"The owners of a child star are like leaseholders — their property diminishes in value every year. Time's chariot is at their backs: before them acres of anonymity." it begins. By the time it's over he's talked about her ass in slacks and lays this number on her audience. "Her admirers — middle aged men and clergymen — respond to her dubious coquetry, to the sight of her well-shaped and desirable little body, packed with enormous vitality, only because the safety curtain of story and dialogue drops between their intelligence and their desire." I mean, yeah, I guess I might have sued, too. But as crass as he's being, he wasn't wrong about the weird response to Temple from the adoring public. It's always fucking bizarre when someone who can't drive becomes so famous they can't walk down the street without being assailed by screaming fans. When shooting on WWW wrapped, someone drove by her house and shot at her. The gunman was never caught.

Based on Kipling (kind of a shock it took Ford this long to adapt him) this one has Temple palling around with a Scottish regiment in India. Perfectly this allows Ford to have June Lang set the record straight about the difference between Indians and Native Americans. Ford made *Stagecoach* two years later so he evidently wasn't listening, but then, this is the man who gave us the phrase "print the legend," so we oughtn't be surprised. Temple is in kilts with a toy gun marching with Victor McLaglen before long, much to grandpa C. Aubrey Smith's consternation. She also converts an extremist (Caesar Romero, devilishly handsome and dignified...which is more than can be said for Willie Fung as "Mohammet Dihn." Hollywood can truly make your fucking head spin) to the cause of imperialism through kindness and singing. Ford gets off a couple of splendid compositions; maybe because he knew if he was going to be heard over Temple's cadence and bagpipes, he had to really nail the assignment. There's the usual bravado and manly crying and boxing and marching and so on and the camera's never in the wrong place, there just isn't much you can do to make something like this interesting. Temple sat on the board of directors of Disney and Del Monte and later became ambassador to Czechoslovakia, and one suspects it was to prove to the likes of Greene that there was more to her than curls and dresses. Shame that no one ever thinks of a non-evil way to prove their worth, but in America I guess there aren't any. In the end she was every bit the little colonizer she plays here.

**The Hurricane (1937)**

It's almost as if, recognizing that the world was robbed of Murnau films, Ford took it upon himself to give us more of them. *Four Sons, Flesh, Pilgrimage,* and especially *The Hurricane* are all right out of the F.W. Murnau playbook. Hurricane is a tribute to *Tabu: A Story of the South Seas*, and about a woman who comes to French Polynesia to be with her tyrannical despot husband and instead finds her heart aligned with a native dissident. Her husband loathes and persecutes the strapping native with abandon, representing everything wrong with the world that isn't Europe. Ford couldn't be happier to be back in Murnau's old house, shooting boats and seascapes with Winslow Homerian grace and exuberance. He also lets something slip that explains some of the colonialist attitudes he has; an advanced form of repressed self-loathing. When Mary Astor and Thomas Mitchell pass an empty stretch of beach on their boat, he blows it a kiss. It had the "misfortune" to exist in the worst of the Hurricane waters and it was obliterated. Paradise, he calls it. Ford believes him. Which means he believes there are some places man shouldn't go, some beautiful places withheld from us. Then Astor is showered with leis as she departs the boat and the cast of actual pacific islanders greets her with cheers and embraces. "He's the governor of a flock of birds. Birds don't belong in a cage," says Mitchell of Raymond Massey's ice cold villain.

My friend Ben Sachs, once lead critic for the Chicago Reader, said wisely that Ford's vision of the political attitude of this time was supported by the climate; there was no contradiction between something like *The Hurricane* and *Prisoner of Shark Island* for him, or frankly, for most other white people. I'm routinely flummoxed by the appearance of apparently good faith incarnations of both socialism and the confederacy throughout his body of work. It's not that I don't imagine anyone capable of both (Michael Bay and Steven Spielberg routinely rocket from one end of the spectrum to the other), it's that Ford is so earnest in both idioms. Watch something like *Judge Priest* and yes, you can tell he's laying it on thick for the sake of his audience, but he still does it with all his might. And then *The Hurricane*, his most beatific study of a community yet, free of condescension, and anti-colonialist with a vengeance. It's like reconnecting with Murnau's ghost re-introduced him to the better angels of his nature. The winged German libertine on Ford's shoulder.

Jon Hall gets six months hard labor for punching a racist, he breaks out, they catch him. Massey could save him but hates every native with a passion. Astor tries to plead with him but he says that if he just listened to his wife every time she had the right idea he couldn't very well be a maniacal governor, could he?! Astor starts looking after Hall's pregnant wife Dorothy Lamour as Hall keeps trying to escape and keeps getting more and more time added to his sentence. Ford's montage is downright Sternbergian during this section, the trials and torments whipping by like fistfuls of sand. It's nearly the equal of the escape sequence in *Shark Island* for sheer brio. Hall returns to the island in time for Massey's bloodlust to reach a fever pitch, a baby to start crowning, and a historic hurricane to hit. It morphs from a sensuous survey of paradise into a relentless spectacular a la Cecil B. Demille, complete with dozens hiding in a church bound for the next life. Hysterically, Dino De Laurentiis financed an epic remake of this in 1979 with Jan Troell directing and Mia Farrow in the lead part. Every step of the way towards the final cut a disaster, but my favorite is that apparently Italian director Franco Rossi was shooting second unit on a beach, and he and his crew got drunk and left all their footage to get swept away by the tide. Like god himself was trying to tell them you can't remake John Ford, and certainly not by throwing millions and millions of dollars at the problem. How could you ever hope to recreate this wind-swept appassionato, a lament for the sin of innocence? Paradise lost. On some days my favourite film of Ford's not named *Wagon Master*.

**The Adventures of Marco Polo (1938, Archie Mayo, John Cromwell, & John Ford)**

Sam Goldwyn really thought he had something here. He spent 2 million on it and even when the world and the heavens and the rest of creation told him it was a terrible idea, he just kept throwing money and directors at the problem. Douglas Fairbanks had written a treatment for the film, but Paramount sued them mid-deal when they found out they were trying to get their prize possession, Gary Cooper, to be the lead. They finally did get Cooper, but he felt rightly that he was dreadfully miscast. John Carradine and Verree Teasdale both dropped out before shooting started, she over illness. Sigrid Gurie's career, which had started ten seconds before they started rolling, was destroyed by the film. Lana Turner shaved her eyebrows off for her minor role and they never grew back. John Cromwell walked off set after a few days shooting. Cromwell doesn't get much ink these days, but he wasn't all bad. He'd just remade Duvivier's *Pépé Le Moko* as *Algiers*, which is perfectly respectable (if memory serves, anyway; it's been a decade and obviously the Duvivier looms larger in my memory, being, you know, an obviously great film by Julien Duvivier), which is probably why Goldwyn thought he could make this, with the backdrop locales and whatnot. But even Cromwell couldn't find his footing here. So Goldwyn went to William Wyler (and apparently offered him Errol Flynn to replace Cooper if that pleased him more, which is the usual professionalism you expect from moguls), but was rejected. John Ford babysat the production, shooting action scenes for a montage that didn't rely on much established mise-en-scène before Archie Mayo took over and finished the thing. Mayo had been around since time began and retired 8 years later and then died in Mexico twenty years after that. He did direct the last Marx Bros movie, *A Night in Casablanca* (which is nobody's favourite, but that's not really his fault), though. You can feel his touch in a scene where Marco Polo discovers spaghetti, and when his valet goes up and down the Venice canals calling out his name while singing. Even weirder, maybe, than all that, is that Ralph Ceder, a Hal Roach comedy short director from the 20s, was 2nd unit director...one of the first times he'd taken the gig in his 20 some odd year career. A few years later he was back working for W.C. Fields on *The Bank Dick*, one of the best comedies ever made.

"You will observe that it is very large!" This is all very little cinema, all things considered. The sets are minimal, the actors are white, it's like

*The Shanghai Gesture* on dialysis. Cooper is so strapping it doesn't matter he knows he shouldn't be playing this part. Mayo had directed some of *Moontide*, which stars the even more strapping Jean Gabin (and shirtless Jean Gabin, to boot) so he did know a thing or two. Of course Fritz Lang directed the rest of *Moontide* so uhhh... Anyway, Gurie is quite despicable as Polo's love interest. She seems to have decided that "Asian" means "sound like you're defrosting after a hundred years in deep freeze," so her every syllable escapes like a fat baby bird hopping out of a nest and sinking to the ground with a dramatic chirp. She looks like Kazuo Hasegawa in *An Actor's Revenge* and suitably sounds like she's been overdubbed by an actor doing a comedy drag performance in a 70s kaiju film. Just what in the living world Goldwyn saw in her is beyond me. I hung in for the Ford directed action scenes but man, rough sailing. Cooper's mountainous face was all the relief I got. There's a scene that's practically Mel Brooksian where Cooper sees his hosts feed a dissident to a tiger through a hole in the floor. He carries Ernest Truex (the abysmal comic relief, reminding me most of the overdubbed singing voices in the hysterically wretched musical re-edit of Bert I. Gordon's *The Magic Sword*, which has been all but lost to time and must be seen) around like a baby for some of the film. That's alright. Cooper seems at home there. More so than when he has to explain to Gurie what kissing is. A grim, grim display, leavened only somewhat by the two guards who have to show the emperor what they were doing later and re-enact it. There's very little meat in these gym mats.

An hour into this movie and the "adventures" of Marco Polo include "going to China," and "kissing a woman," so when some horseback combat stuff started I almost wept (though I'm not even sure Ford directed it). This kind of assignment, I suspect, is what made him want to go back to Westerns. He missed horses or anyway doing this tepid non-event was the wrong vehicle for his obsessions. The blissful few seconds of Dutch tilts while horses gallop into frame are like a visit to the paradise of *The Hurricane*. Alas, they're a mirage. The movie has another 40 minutes to go.

## Four Men & A Prayer (1938)

When the film begins with the big superimposed "INDIA" over a map of the region, one does think they're in for a trip to the dentist, but George Sanders is in it so I settled in just fine. David Niven, too, his voice about six octaves higher than I'd ever heard it before. For being practically still in the caul, his face already betrays about six decades of drinking. He and Sanders and Richard Greene and William Henry ("what a crop!" as Sam Richardson might say) are all called in to get their dad, C. Aubrey Smith, acquitted of a dishonorable discharge. It's like a gayer riff on *The Sons of Katie Elder*, later remade by John Singleton as *Four Brothers*, which doesn't matter at all but it's funny to think of Mark Wahlberg watching *Four Men & A Prayer*. Loretta Young does say the phrase "negro orchestra" as a feature of an evening of 'slumming' she had planned for Greene before his urgent cable took him away, so maybe he would have enjoyed it. The boys get together to resume their playful bickering while dad gins up and prepares to kill himself in his office. The game is afoot. There's a crime for these sprightly tuxedo-clad little fellows to solve.

Ford frames them perfectly, of course, moving the boys like chess pieces (there are routinely stunning close-ups throughout), but the attitude is entirely too polite. The boys are all sexless (Sanders in particular looks like a little freak with his glasses and pith helmet), despite Young flouncing around, bound in furs to protect Greene and Niven from the sight of her skin. The boys have to part company and trot the globe looking for clues to their father's death. It's Noel Coward meets Graham Greene. Witnesses keep turning up dead. The best scene is, naturally, a bar fight. Henry and Sanders head to India to inquire about an incident in a barroom and quickly the locals start attacking the regiment. A chair hits a light, a man hits the player piano, which starts chirping out a march, and in the darkness bodies fumble and punch and tackle each other like a thicket of crocodiles. It's a warm-up for Andre De Toth's lights out gunfight in *Man in the Saddle* (a better movie), Chuck Jones, Tsui Hark, and Sammo Hung (while neither of those fellows is a Fordian, per se, they do get a lot of mileage out of brawling). Also in that vein a scene where the boys are on a riverboat (being a Ford fetishist is like being a fan of some sport no one's heard of - seeing a riverboat made me shout affirmatively at my television). An uncredited Chinese Bartender appears and offers Henry and Niven a scotch speaking like Donald Duck. Niven answers him in the same voice, to Henry's consternation. "My good friend Donald...Mouse....good type." Scene over. *What?* This comes up one more time at the end when the fellow appears out of nowhere from around a corner during the climax and once more offers them a scotch in the same voice, and Niven answers him in kind. Never explained. *I...*

Young is a valuable asset on the mission, but she flirts with the suspects to get information and Greene is livid. They argue magnificently. "As far as I'm concerned Geoffrey Leigh, you can jump in the lake...(looks again at her surroundings)...river!" John Carradine and Alan Hale, Sr. are among the interviewed witnesses, JC especially subtle as a foreign general. Young witnesses a massacre and suddenly the film isn't quite the sparkling caper it was a minute ago, but it recovers instantly as Niven and Greene start arguing over who gets to romance Young. Ford treats death like a comma in this film and elsewhere. Very odd stuff, but it kind of works? Certainly the movie never breaks a sweat even while racing towards the finish line. William Faulkner apparently wrote some of this, which doesn't help unravel any of its mysteries at all. Young finds out her dad is arming the world's worst people as head of an arms dealership and Greene doesn't believe that she didn't know. At this point there are 10 minutes left in the movie. Ford still takes time out of the climax for the boys to wrestle each other on the ground at a boat dock, crowds bustling around them. They finally find their man while soaking wet from an aquatic raid on his residence. Four strapping, glistening weirdos marching on evil, then walking backwards from their audience with the king.

**Submarine Patrol (1938)**

It apparently took 10 people to write this movie and one of them was the author of *As I Lay Dying*. It took ten adults to write a movie called **SUBMARINE PATROL**, which frankly didn't have to be about anything because the title pretty much tells you the score. Indeed the first ten seconds will make you feel like you put your finger in an electric socket. The camera speeds into a navy yard before a honking coupe drives up, smashing a sailor who does a flip in the impact. This goes unpunished. Richard Greene is back from *Four Men and a Prayer*, once more playing a rich kid. He asks for a better station than the rest of the crew on the boat he's boarding like Spencer Tracy asking for a south facing cell in *Up The River*. He gets his wish: chief engineer. It makes headlines, "Millionaire playboy enlists!" like he's Bruce Wayne. On the boat with him are old Ford favourites Ward Bond, J. Farrell MacDonald (who looks fully like Elmer Fudd by now), Warren Hymer, and John Carradine, as well as Lon Chaney, Jr (!), Dick Hogan from *Rope*, Charles Trowbridge, a practically *infantile* Elisha

Cook, Jr. (!!!!), and Slim Summerville and Preston Foster who were just in a remake of Ford's *Up The River*. Nancy Kelly is Greene's love interest and her dad is played by George Bancroft, who played the titular *Wolf of Wall Street* in the 1929 film to which Scorsese was paying homage, and who was about to be Marshal Curley Wilcox in *Stagecoach*, which is starting to feel like the SATs after all these energetic but forgotten Ford programmers.

With his straw boater and his entitled attitude, Greene and the mates get on like oil and water. He does teach them all how to have a good time, at least, and they need it. These boys are highly strung. Greene's petulance is mostly winning, and the shot of him running off of Bancroft's boat after GB kicks his ass and tells him to stay away from Kelly is quite something. That boy could move! Foster is the disgraced captain of the SC-599, Greene's boat. He and Greene are both gonna have to swallow their pride. MacDonald served with Foster's dad, so he'll crack skulls if necessary to maintain order on the young Foster's behalf. The shot of the crew navigating the Hudson river, a rear projection New York skyline behind them, a lovelorn Kelly looking on as they pass, is grace itself. Murnau's aching solemnity tempering Ford's patriotic sturm und drang.

Greene's ship docks in Italy same as Kelly's, so he takes her to dinner where a comedy waiter (Henry Armetta) weeps all over them. Bancroft punches Greene's lights out when he catches them planning to elope, but they're obviously in their 30s. He comes to apologize after Kelly dresses him down and Greene returns the favor, leaving him out cold on the deck as the boat leaves the harbor. Now he's stuck with them on maneuvers, so he gets shanghaied into the engine room in time for them to do battle with the submarine that's been giving them so much trouble. "GET BUSY! YOU'RE IN THE NAVY NOW!" screams Greene when Bancroft finally gets around to apologizing. *The Long Voyage Home* strikes me as an attempt to really get right all the stuff Ford had to squeeze into his Navy movies without much figuring out how best they all work. The gorgeous work that pops up here and sporadically in *Men Without Women, The Blue Eagle,* and *Seas Beneath*, gets the "A" treatment at long last. Which isn't to say it's without humour or chummy antics, but just that by the time Ford revisited it, he'd become scientific about his poetry. Greene's presence explains Ford's later love for Jeffrey Hunter, who did all this a little more believably in the 50s. When orders change and he has to flee their wedding, Kelly and Bancroft sail after him. There's a really charming call and response bit where they pledge their love to each other from a few hundred feet away on the bow. "See you in Gibraltar!"

PART 4

# FACTS AND LEGENDS
1939-1941

It shouldn't be so unusual that a director made his best and worst films in such close proximity, sometimes out of the same milieus or even possibly the same shooting days. Ford, by now, we can say is done developing. With *Stagecoach* he is the poet. The poet may write bad poems, but he is ever the poet. With the war films we'll see his best and worst impulses dueling each other on the broad decks of battleships. One day a horrifying battle cry, the next a haunting portrait of still-living ghosts, or a plea for sanity, against all odds. There is perhaps no indication from the last decade of wildly uneven work from Ford that he was about to step up and produce a dozen of the best American movies of all time, but that's the exciting thing about Ford. At the end of 1938 he was a director; all too human, all too given to whims and unquestioning devotion to the pages of whatever script was in his hand. Then, like that, in 1939, he was John Ford, the greatest American director of all time. The rest was still true, but it was true in the context of work of such undeniable greatness that it becomes a much thornier and much more exciting and compelling exercise to work out all those contradictions, and all those many ideological missteps. A man with such love and such hate in the same heartbeat, in the same blood.

## Stagecoach (1939)

Watching Ford films in order has its rewards beyond the simple discovery of the poetry with which he used his camera. It can also make every shot seem like the answer to the riddle of the sphinx. When *Stagecoach*, his first western in more than a decade, opens with silhouetted riders against the Arizona sun, Monument Valley like the anvil of God just beyond the reach, it feels not simply like a choice, a return. It feels like a man finding himself. The world was a different place. The depression had come and gone, Murnau was dead, the war was on the horizon (something he'd commented on directly in *The World Moves On*), and Ford found clear skies again. The "directed by John Ford" credit comes with trumpet fanfare and then the film begins, horses riding toward the camera from the low hills, the sky a full 2/3 of the frame.

The political contradictions of the film are intentionally molasses thick, even if the stuff with the Apaches is too thorny to be intentional and he'd timidly admit as much later. The men in town (introduced in a dolly shot, the camera like the stage of the title meant to be moving men from place to place, from uncertainty to destiny) don't know which natives to trust, but we're told the Cheyenne hate the Apaches worse than any white man could. But it isn't the Cheyenne who fall under their horses to the thunder of rifle fire while white heroes pray for the cavalry. Ford will later make the Cheyenne the noble, mute heroes of his most lugubrious epic, proving that empathy isn't a language easily mastered when you speak American first, Irish second, and Hollywood third. "We suffer from a disease called social prejudice, my dear..." says the drunk to the floozy. Ben Hecht's uncredited punch-up of Dudley Nichols' script is finally the match Ford's been searching for. Nichols had been writing for Ford for most of the 30s but it isn't until this that he writes him a classic and even then with help; Ford kept him around until his bigotry started clouding his judgment, which coincided with Nichols getting insulted by Ford hiring Phil Dunne to rewrite *Pinky*. Nichols did write *Bringing up Baby* for Hawks the year before, probably his best work full stop. Everyone found themselves not a moment too soon.

The idea of the stage is also a stand-in for Ford's cinema; a shelter for his favourite actors from the dregs of what Hollywood was giving them whenever they weren't working for him. John Wayne becomes a star with the flip of a rifle, Andy Devine, Thomas Mitchell, and John Carradine lean back into themselves like Henry Fonda in his chair in *My Darling Clementine* a few years later. Mitchell is once again a drunken reprobate doctor ("half scotch, half soda"), getting as loaded as he can before throwing himself on the chariot out of town and away from judgment. Claire Trevor and Louisa Platt re-enact the old testament with their eye contact. Devine seems to invent Paul Henning's television empire with his unabashed yodeling. George Bancroft knows he won't upstage anyone so just enjoys himself. The dialogue has the criss-crossing intricacy of all twenty four hooves pulling the stage.

Wayne is a big kid, sweating and earnest, even with his reedier tenor, the voice unmistakably star material. His gallantry so moves one, oblivious to the world having grown more callous than even a gunhand could comprehend. He does seem to have truly walked out of the desert like a Sam Shepard hero. Carradine's parodying the confederates he's essayed for Ford throughout the thirties, which makes the south the villain, even if they don't lose near so many as the Apache, who don't even get names. Ford likes Mitchell and Wayne better, at all rates, even if Carradine's the most fun to watch. You can practically see Sam Peckinpah sitting on the floor like Ringo, watching and taking notes with Spielbergian wonder. Welles was. Ran the picture almost every night of the *Kane* shoot.

Ford's camera has perhaps never been so sharp, his montage so clean. The film flies by. Every western henceforth will be made in this film's reflection, straight or broken, the Franklin Roosevelt of genre. Speaking of: Berton Churchill's crooked entrepreneur predicts Donald Trump and the grifter neo-conversative establishment of "today" with his second act opening monologue. "What this country needs is a businessman for president!" Ford knows he's full of hot air and the only thing he hates worse than a hypocrite is a producer. "You're drunk, sir." Churchill admonishes Mitchell. "I'm happy, Gatewood!" Ford does admit that it takes at least this make-up of bastards and children to make the world, even if the world itself doesn't seem all that interesting. What's waiting for them when the ride stops? Family life. Intransigence is more romantic. When the film shoot is over, life has to begin again and Ford wanted no part of that. Out here you had to have the back of the man next to you, no matter what, even if, like Ford, you were a sadist with a drinking problem. Donald Meeks' lowly little coward even finds room in his heart to start worrying about Mitchell. "Good or bad, handsome or ugly, rich or poor, they are all equal now."

Mitchell doesn't have to quit drinking to prove himself worthy. Indeed he takes a gentle draught to celebrate delivering Platt's baby. He cautions Trevor against falling for Wayne (she's sent to do the housework in the makeshift camp - the film's strongest stretch with all those figures moving down hallways, in and out of darkness - a funny fate for the woman they won't sit near; Ford's sympathy is for the skilled laborer) but then gives in. Who more deserves happiness? Wayne himself is about to skip out on the judgement and the cage waiting for him in Lordsburg, but stops running the second he sees the Apache war fires. Ford doesn't blame him for trying to flee, either. The film is about the question of finding a moral bedrock in the desert. Something Ford himself struggled with all his life. Is there a universal morality? Should there be? Everyone but the capitalist has their moment to prove themselves, to join what Robin Wood called the Hawksian Self-Esteem Club, in reference to *Rio Bravo* in his BFI book on the film. Maybe because Nichols had been working with Hawks so much, a little of Hawks' elastic morality found its way into this, one of the few films I've seen where characters have to prove themselves against the attitudes of the rest of the cast, each given equal prominence in the narrative. The film's moral pendulum swings roughly every scene.

Ford's characters are usually innately good, they just need everyone else to realize it. Not so, here, where his ideal heroes (Wayne, Trevor, and Mitchell) are viewed through the lens of the 'civilized' likes of Carradine, Churchill, Bancroft, and Platt. But who's mettle is proven when they're beset by the Apaches and there's no cover for miles? That is Ford's point. Ideals are fine, but what do they mean in theory? Even the othering of the natives serves a sort of a point; look at Carradine's glee when he's finally allowed to start killing innocent people. Look at the hideous solution he has for the idea of Platt's potentially lost virtue. Ford has the natives kill him before he can kill her, sparing her the "fate worse than death" that crops up so often in these films (Robert Aldrich will make good on this dreaded promise in *Ulzana's Raid*, and Ford will prove it's not so big a deal in *7 Women*. In *The Searchers* Ethan Edwards thinks miscegenation is about the worst thing under heaven but even he gets over it. Ford was breaking bread with Apaches and Navajo every other week back then, he didn't believe the things Carradine's character does, which *is* a relief when you remember it). Salvation comes not just in the form of the murderous cavalry, but in the natives dispatching the prejudiced dandy. Ford here demonstrates his famous editing-in-camera. He offers no shot of Carradine dying, but rather just the pistol going limp. He's a symbol, nothing more. Throughout his career the higher-ups would beg for coverage of events in case something didn't work or they had to change it at the last minute. He refused, famously putting his hand over the lens the second he got the take he wanted. It's not simply knowing which shots work; it's knowing the camera can speak in complete sentences and not putting periods and commas where they don't belong. Carradine's death is both misdirection and a semicolon to the *Pieta*-like image of Platt realizing her prayers have been answered. The optics of the final set-piece are still fraught, but there's no denying Ford's talent in obtaining them. This one film seems to have every last ounce of America in its frames.

## Young Mr. Lincoln (1939)

Here we have the battle of perception, of trying to find the man in the legend, but having a little trouble keeping the legendary out of mannerisms. Lincoln is introduced sitting side saddle on an old chair, his dirty shirt in comparison to the Whig party bigw(h)ig and his fancy suit running against him in a legislature debate. "I'm just plain Abraham Lincoln," he tells the disinterested crowd. He's more interested in a copy of Blackstone's Commentaries on the Laws of England that a moving family gives him (this is answered decades later when Spielberg has his Lincoln quote Shakespeare and Euclid ("it is a self-evident truth that things which are equal to the same thing are equal to each other. We begin with equality. That's the origin, isn't it? That balance, that's fairness, that's justice.") - the split in the soul between rationality and art; Ford defined. When Gore Verbinski's Lone Ranger John Reid holds up Two Treatises on Government by John Locke as his "bible" we feel Ford's influence. Fonda's face is the perfect foil for Ford's camera (and his body cuts the frame like a human diopter; he's just so interesting. Daniel Day-Lewis clearly studied the way he slaps his knees), open and bright and curious and soft, like we're seeing a brain line with information in real time (there's even footage of a ripple in a pond forcefully replaced with ice floes in the harsh winter to further cement the idea that the gathering of experience is gradual and unromantic, just before we see that he's buried his beloved Anne Rutledge - information isn't all easy or nice or safely acquired while reading upside down). Ford himself is now in his poetic prime, every single shot is perfect. No other word for it. Ford has never had much time for close-ups because he likes to frame people in doorways and in landscapes. Fonda speaking to the departed Rutledge while the ice gently passes him by in the background is perfect, maybe more than perfect, maybe immortal, and Ford knows it.

Ford was a master of the Z axis from the jump - all those cowboys in his silent pictures wandering up streets or calling to each other from high cliffs into lower glades a mile away - but *Young Mr. Lincoln* takes to the Z with a vengeance. He's got parades bisecting town streets diagonally, making every piece of the frame active. Lincoln sees the veterans of the Revolution and doffs his cap, a reminder how close at hand war always is. Albert Henry Woolson, the last Civil War veteran, died at 106 in 1956. The rioters about to lynch Eddie Quillan and Richard Cromwell, they're running at the camera and only Lincoln breaking through them to get to "us" saves him from dying. Ford's point is clear enough: safety from prejudice is as much an illusion as anything on a movie screen. Without the better angels of our nature, per his famous inaugural address, what chance do we have as a civilization. Like Ridley Scott, Ford was interested in the creation of meaning from chaos, the making of civilization. Lincoln is always going to be the best subject for this because his story truly does beggar belief. Just a guy, raised in the woods with death all around him like any other settler's kid, who rose from the dirt to become the most enormous figure in American politics. Choosing to set the story in his past frees Ford from having to reckon with the fullness of his legacy. AJ Edwards rewinds even further back in time in his unjustly forgotten 2014 film The Better Angels, which fuses Malickian graceful pointillism with Ford's earthy earnestness. Lincoln had already appeared in two other Ford films (*Prisoner of Shark Island* and *The Iron Horse*) but here he's a full on living saint, introduced to "The Union Forever," a counterpart to the use of "Dixie" in *Judge Priest*, which, to cap it off, Lincoln accidentally writes on his Jaw Harp. In keeping with the changing of things, its other nickname, the Jew's Harp, has understandably fallen out of favor.

William Wellman, and not for the first time, makes a darker vision of this with Fonda in *The Ox-Bow Incident* in 1943 where justice doesn't prevail. Ford always foxtrots up to the line of the darker version of events but can't bring himself to do it. The liberal humanist, the socialist, and the historian always battle it out inside of him, which is probably why he so related to Lincoln. Imperfect actions in imperfect time, but he did eventually do the right thing and paid the ultimate price in so doing. Ford's version of Lincoln is a man unafraid to punch a guy to stop a miscarriage of justice (Aaron Sorkin learns the wrong lesson from this, as usual) but his gift is talking circles around the prejudiced. George A. Romero tips his hat to this in *Day of the Dead*. Being smarter than a bully can buy you a minute to think. The central trial feels almost like a stand-up set, with Lincoln getting laugh after laugh from the amused jury. Lincoln's words, Ford's images. They're just too persuasive. My own biases being what they care, I'm suckered by the moist lens keenness of this version of Ford's cinema while I recoil from it in *Priest*. The thing about images, good images, is that they can overwhelm us a hundred years later. It's like watching footage of a seraphim. Its goodness is blinding. "We are not enemies, but friends. We must not be enemies. Though passion may have strained it must not break our bonds of affection. The mystic chords of memory, stretching from every battlefield and patriot grave to every living heart and hearthstone all over this broad land, will yet swell the chorus of the Union, when again touched, as surely they will be, by the better angels of our nature."

**Drums Along the Mohawk (1939)**

Here she is, the first Ford film in color. And what better occasion than to drink in Claudette Colbert? Linda Darnell was supposed to be in this, but Colbert's probably the greatest consolation prize anyone could have asked for. When she's caught in a storm and her little blue hat gets ruined in the rain, she looks right through the lens and winds up six inches from your face. The colors are Turnererian from the word "go," the blocking right out of a Rembrandt. She and Henry Fonda are excitable newlyweds out to make their lives when right in a row just about everyone in creation attacks their homestead. There's a rich, ripe Disney-esque quality to the images, shot by both Bert Glennon and Ray Rennahan, the colors are so wet Colbert's dress looks like it might start dripping. Within minutes an eyepatch-clad John Carradine approaches them, so their union couldn't possibly be a happy one. He looks sharp with his tri-corner hat and his cape. What a marvel of a man. He's untrustworthy, sure, but Colbert loses her goddamned mind when Chief John Big Tree walks in unbidden.

Big Tree plays Blue Back, Fonda's old friend, and he's one of the close indigenous friends Ford kept for most of his life. Fonda forgot to mention to Colbert that he's friends with an Oneida, though John was a Seneca, born Isaac Johnny John. Fonda has to teach Colbert about empathy real fast in between her bouts of hysteria. This is what I've been waiting for from Ford this whole project, some sense that he isn't merely paying lip service to the idea of the humanity of the movie villains. Blue Back does, rather disconcertingly, give Fonda a big stick and instructs him to beat Colbert with it if she gets out of line, but I mean...he's trying. *Ford*, I mean. He deliberately made the British seem less villainous than they were during this campaign in reality because the Nazis were beating the hell out of them at the time and Ford didn't want to steer his audience towards enmity on the eve of battle. This was his preparation for the war (he joined up not long after this, making films for the war effort), though he also prepares for Michael Mann. A scene of a militia roll-call gets redone in *Last of the*

*Mohicans* (somehow more beautiful than this and just a better bit of drama, too), as do the scenes of carnage across the verdant New York wilderness. The movies have, let's say, basically the same message: what might be frightening to you is just life to someone else.

Ford gets many, many miles of mileage out of the sun drifting in through gaps in the canopy, looking as luscious as can be in newfound color. Ford films bonfires like Prometheus lit them himself. There's an unbelievable shot, predicting a similarly famous one in *How Green Was My Valley*, of the militia heading to battle, coming down right side of the Z axis, while on the left is a cattle pen. The world moves on. Edna May Oliver wins her Oscar by making her dialogue seem like it, too, is in technicolor. "I'm a *Widow*! Lemme see your hands, lemme see your hands..." She seems like the first real Fordian woman since Olive Borden in *3 Bad Men*. She has a Marx Brothers stateroom scene with two drunk Mohawks who come to steal her bed while she's still on it. Steven Spielberg and Cy Endfield studied this one, with its muddy streets after battle, the horror on everyone's faces after skirmishes. Fonda earns Ford's love forever by getting through a shell shock monologue in one 3 minute take while Colbert and Ward Bond run in and out of frame attending to him. Fonda looks like Jesus from some old painting, wretched and beautiful, lost eyes seeing into forever, when Colbert finds him abandoned by a fence post after a battle. Francis Ford gets crucified when he tries to get reinforcements. This was Ford's first film about the revolution and he went back to monochrome for his next few films about the labor crisis, seeing no beauty in poverty that needed exaggeration. The period is so vivid in our art, Ford wasn't going to deny people the sight of our founding fighters in full rich pastels, nor the eerie glow of jack-o-lanterns or flaming arrows piercing the militiamen. Colbert has a symbolic baby just as the young nation is born into independence.

### The Grapes of Wrath (1940)

The first shot in this film about the birth of a labor movement is answered numerous times throughout film history. It's an image of a man walking down a road towards an intersection, something of a nod to Murnau's *City Girl*, with its figures occupying odd corners of the frame. Here

Tom Joad walks down the Z axis, but he's in the first third of the frame, not the center. Carol Reed takes the bait when he has Alida Valli walk dead center past Joseph Cotten, whose only crime was caring that millions of kids were going to die. Jim Jarmusch will have Tom Waits and John Lurie split the frame as they walk separate ways in his best impression of a 40s film, *Down By Law*. Henry Fonda will later perform this same walk again in *The Fugitive*, Ford's best impression of a European film. Alfred Hitchcock will send Cary Grant's callous ad man to this very crossroads in *North By Northwest*, and a road just like this, bereft of symmetry once more is how Jerry Schatzberg opens *Scarecrow*, also about men with nothing moving through the country looking for a parcel of land to call their own, if only for the night.

This is the first film Ford made where he's unafraid of how loud he's talking about what matters to him. Fonda's Tom Joad starts the film with nothing, knowing how little the world wants to help a fellow man. He can't even hitch a ride honest. He's gotta hop on the sideboard so no one knows a truck driver gave him a lift. Conservative (at least by Hollywood standards) Fonda playing a labor hero is one of the many miracles of this film. Ford once again treats him like the risen Christ. Every landscape Joad has to traverse on foot is rendered mythic by the light and the arrangement of the horizon. No surprise that an ex-preacher gets his mojo back after one look at Joad. He is salvation. John Carradine plays Casy the preacher. Ford liked Carradine, there was no one who'd dig into a part like he did. He's got the holy spirit, for sure. They survey the old Joad house like they're exploring a haunted house, complete with tattered rags as if a killing had claimed the tenants. It has, after a fashion. They run into another man living a ghost's life, squatting on the property. He squints at the sight of Tom and Jim Casy. "You remember the preacher..." "I ain't a preacher no more." "Well you remember the *man*!" The essence of man, his soul, his dignified spirit, is what's at stake. Take away his home and his right to provide for his family, what is he? Ma Joad (Jane Darwell) asks first thing if they beat Tom's humanity out of him, made nothing but the worst of his emotions. After answering the question of whether he broke out of the joint enough times, you can see just how that might happen. Daryl Zanuck was nervous that people would call the film Communist propaganda (Steinbeck wasn't a card carrying member of the party yet, but all he was missing was the card) which is one of those self-fulfilling prophecies no one ever heeds (Ford found out after the War that he was labeled a subversive for making it, which hastened his turn away from the cause). If it's communism to want to not get beaten to death by cops, aren't we all communists when push comes to shove, and maim, and murder? Paul Thomas Anderson tries this from the other end in *There Will Be Blood*. Come to think of it, *The Master*'s Freddie Quell's just Jim Casy or Tom Joad with no conscience, no need for a soul. Ford would later help edit the 30 minute documentary *Mission to Yenan*, which showed off the lives and rituals of Chinese Communists. They dared not release it.

Ford never took this time getting so right what he does here. This is the first Ford film that feels as heavy to comprehend, to simply stare at. He'd never been this careful, not even on *Stagecoach*. The first film to stand tall next to the best of Murnau. Nothing by Ford is totally innocent of sentimentality, but this gets as close as he got. "Is grandma bad?" "Grandma's dead." Fonda's final speech, so often parodied, brings the film in touch with Hollywood's order of myths. "Wherever there's a cop...beatin on a guy...I'll be there." Not every day you present something and off peak Bruce Springsteen grabs it for his own. The movie's theme is "Red River Valley," which Woody Guthrie'd recorded already. There would be no *Bound for Glory*, Hal Ashby's Woody Guthrie movie, without the visual example set by Ford here. The sound of trucks idling and the sights of kids starving takes up as much time as any of the dialogue or the story. Robert Capa followed Steinbeck to Russia and his pictures ran in the resulting tome *A Russian Journal*. Capa's spirit lives in the faces of this movie, maybe Ford's finest photographic study of the human face. They aren't traditional close-ups, it's like he caught them by accident and couldn't look away. The fences they press their face against is what turns them into objects, not the camera. Ford saves the real close-ups for flash-lit faces, desperate and angry and tired. Persecuted. That's what the camera does better than anyone and Ford uses them sparingly. It's the landscape that brings freedom. The close-up takes it away. Ken Loach agreed. Ford likes to turn men into momentum. Carradine gets the best shot in the film, and the best line, too, different scenes. When he's explaining union logic to Fonda, he's a jutting art deco phantom, struck out of darkness into soft light. "That's why I can't go back to bein' a preacher again..." says Carradine, coming dangerously close to admitting there's no god. "Preacher's gotta know. I don't know." Nobody knows. Nobody ever will.

**The Long Voyage Home (1940)**

Ford had worked with Faulkner more times than nearly anybody by now, so hopping over to loose Eugene O'Neill adaptations is unsurprising. This finds Ford back in his late 20s hang-out vibe. He's got the band back together. John Wayne is here doing a...well, I hesitate to use an active verb with regards to his Swedish accent, but that is the idea. Regulars Ward Bond, Arthur Shields, Barry Fitzgerald, John Qualen, J.M. Kerrigan, crazy eyed Jack Pennick, and Thomas Mitchell join first time-Forders Wilfrid Lawson and Ian Hunter. A movie like this doesn't have a protagonist so much as a throng. But Mitchell's the guy we spend the most time with. After looking so desperate in the last few Fords, he looks strapping and vivacious here. A hero right after Ford and O'Neill's heart; a drunk with a heart of gold. Wayne, comically huge, looks at him like he's his mother.

Gregg Toland, the iron eye of Hollywood, was about the only technician Ford ever let win an argument. He'd repay him for shooting this so perfectly with his only directorial credit during World War 2. Everyone liked Gregg Toland. He invented modernism, how could you not? People (including, in a disappointing turn, David Fincher) like to claim he and Herman Mankiewicz are the real authors of *Citizen Kane*. This assumption requires never watching another movie Welles ever shot. Good luck with that. Ford and Toland paint Rembrandts along the Z Axis. At the risk of Kubrick erasure, this might be the Z Axis movie. Everyone running in and out of shadow all the time, up and down the long docks. A working class eulogy in straight lines and fog. Marcel Carné had already painted its companion piece with *Port of Shadows*, but Ford would never kill the hero of his film...or would he?

Heads know that Ford's most Fordian films aren't his westerns, but his boat pictures. "When a man goes to sea, he oughta give up thinking about thinking about things on shore. Land don't want him no more!" says Shields to Mitchell, who's running away from everything all the time. O'Neill's fatalism is a better fit for Ford than Faulkner's drunkenness, shockingly enough. Mitchell framed against backdrop skies, drunk and sad, that's why people watch movies. It's funny to think Ford will, during this decade and after he'd seen combat firsthand, make what people consider his "art film," but in truth any movie where the heroes get drunk and fight is Ford's idea of art. This, *The Fugitive, The Quiet Man, The Sun Shines Bright,* those are what Ford thought was art. He just heard tell that "art" was supposed to be about suffering and dying for the right cause in silent, stark compositions. William Wellman heard the same thing and made my beloved oddity *Track of the Cat*, which is 70% perfect and 25% ridiculously outdated and let's say 5% wild card. I love *Track of the Cat* more than I like *The Fugitive*, but they're essentially the same thing: self-loathing road trip martyrdoms. So is *The Long Voyage Home*, but it's got something the other two lack: fun. Fincher knicks this movie's version of life at sea for *The Curious Case of Benjamin Button* and if the whole film was Jared Harris on a boat shooting at Nazis it would have been a classic instead of an impression of one.

It is fun watching this crew grind against each other like coiling anchor chains. Ford frames this as a Marxist issue: everyone on the boat, per the Captain, is just an interchangeable set of hands getting cargo from one port to the next. The personalities that escape are a byproduct of Ford's socialism. He believed workers were human beings. The world largely disagreed.

Steinbeck, O'Neill; Ford seems to be making up to me for adapting Kipling and whistlin' Dixie. The film is about going home and throughout it's like Ford is realizing what he'd been doing in Hollywood and just wanted to be a kid again whipped by Maine winds. Salt water in his hair, boats ever on the horizon. Mitchell is sacrificed (Like Fonda's Fugitive afterwards) like Ford himself. He'd never get his youth back and the land may judge you but the sea will swallow you whole. O'Neill's circuitous language finds purchase with Ford's rep company. This is a mighty film animated by mighty ideas and a bunch of lowly gorgeous mugs just a step ahead of the hangman. The death of Mitchell is the saddest thing in any Ford movie. It's the only time Ford loses something he believes in. Mitchell reads a condemned man's letters, and once more William Wyler pays attention, he does the same letter reading scene in *The Ox-Bow Incident*. "You'll never be dead to me...because...I love him...Oh Tom, Tom...you must come back to us...Elizabeth." Only Béla Tarr seems to be on its wavelength with his heavy paws.

**Tobacco Road (1941)**

The arrival of Gene Tierney is like the arrival of modernity itself.

The Hellion from *Leave Her to Heaven* can only mean one thing: Ford's about to cling to the present minute like a barnacle. The film certainly starts like the clappers, as my friend Neil Young (the critic) would say. A car shoots through wrought iron gates "Brighten the corner wherever you are!" This movie is in all caps. Cars explode, dogs are as sleepy as their masters, it's like a worse remake of his own *Lightnin'*. Ford throws a rock at modernism. It's almost unbelievable. This film is scored to perpetual banjo. It put me in mind of an Appalachian joke book I bought for a friend from Boston's oldest book store. The set up and punchline for every joke was "A man had sex with his sister...then she revealed she'd also had sex with their dad." *Tobacco Road* is slightly less gross, but just slightly. It's a parade of cackling hillbilly stereotypes. Ford likes them, basically, but there are weddings with huge age gaps, everyone's always praying, singing, stealing, and crashing their cars. Everyone's poor, so it's still of a piece with *Grapes of Wrath*, and believe it or not Nunnaly Johnson wrote this. It was adapted from a shocking broadway success. Stay with me now but it seemed that New York liked laughing at the south.

*Tobacco Road* is like the hillbilly joke book rendered like a Lotte Reiniger animation, Joel and Ethan Coen make *O Brother, Where Art Thou?* and *Burn After Reading* in the same mold (you can argue Hawks' *A Song is Born* follows the same impulses but that's sort of a stretch seeing how that movie is good), which is to say: here's what Ford laughs at. If he don't he does a good job pretending he does. This is Ford's riposte to his friend Frank Borgage's *Moonrise* some 8 years before it was made. Every close-up is intimate and byzantine and baroque. Every joke is absolutely fucking terrible. Ghastly. Unspeakable. A dearth of laughs for 1 hour and 20 minutes. Charley Grapewin runs around hollering most of the movie, and everyone else just tries to match his volume. Only William Tracy gets close. Tierney hardly whispers. She's in another movie, a sentry, silky pre-make of *Gator Bait*. I'd have like to have watched that one. Dana Andrews shows up, like a breath of fresh air, hiding his good looks under a hat and mustache. Ward Bond and Slim Summerville are back, too.

When Ford can calm down, it becomes an extremely poignant study of poverty. Leaves falling beside mute witnesses to the end of an era. These are hardly the entitled confederates of *Judge Priest*. They're gonna get thrown off their land. "Shall We Gather At The River" mocks them as they prepare to get lost, maybe forever. For five gorgeous minutes this is as heartbreaking as anything Ford ever made, but it has to resume its manic hootenanny and the spell is broken.

Beauty and sorrow even here, even under the screaming and dancing and the humor about domestic abuse. This one will wear you out.

### How Green Was My Valley (1941)

There's a beautiful empathy to this period in Ford's career, and not simply in his finally making movies with a defensible value system from a historical long view. He had taken to opening his movies with the name of the author of the source text above the title. "Richard Llewellyn's How Green Was My Valley" is the opening title card. Like Ford was merely a conduit, a narrator passing on the memories found in Llewellyn's book. The author was clear enough and Ford himself made no great claims for his own memories in his work beyond the types he appreciated (men and women, one might presume, that reminded him of the better parts of his childhood - hence his keeping his brother Francis around for as long as he could). *How Green Was My Valley* is a rapturous accounting of the highs and lows of a young man's understanding, as much Proust as any other author, a lot of it is the childhood Ford wished he had had and a little of the one he did. Ford was always talking around his own experience, very rarely addressing it directly, as if he was afraid of what he'd find if he stared straight on. The name above the title absolved Ford, in some ways, of whatever followed. This film beat *Citizen Kane* for best picture, which is just as well. Orson Welles' reputation as the least appreciated man in Hollywood starts there. He was an art punk. Ford was Hollywood's brusque, distant, alcoholic father figure.

Master Roddy McDowell, as he's credited, plays the youngest observer in the valley, the one who witnesses the births and deaths and loves and marriages and betrayals. The film is one of the near-musicals of which Ford was so fond. Song was one of the few languages that can communicate like the moving image, and he knew it could say things a spoken sentence couldn't. Two people harmonizing at a wedding reception marks them as kindred spirits when class seems to separate them. This collection of parties, buttressed by funerals, is what Michael Cimino was invoking when he made *The Deer Hunter* (with a little *Liberty Valance* for good measure). It's got the hazy stream-of-consciousness of Virginia Woolf, even if the compositions (especially of the mine where the men of this little hamlet toil) are pure Eisenstein. Sara Algood delivers a rousing speech in defense of husband Donald Crisp in a raging fake snowstorm and it's like we're in *Potemkin*, watching the working class rail at the dying of the light. Clarity and dreaminess hand in hand, like the best of cinema. Terence Davies has greater affection for the technicolor musicals and iron jawed melodramas, but he's born here, with the wash of montage and the martinets at the head of every table. The narration, voiced by Ford's one-time RKO stablemate Irving Pichel, keeps the film from touching the ground.

The miners union is the great battle at the heart of the story. Socialism is a four letter word to some of the old timers. You can still hear Zanuck sweating over the front-facing labor content in *Grapes of Wrath*. "Unions are the work of the devil!" cries the local hunchback zealot. Zanuck wanted this to be his next *Gone With The Wind*, hired William Wyler to direct it and all (whom we can't seem to escape as a point of comparison; he was a few years away from *The Best Years of Our Lives*, which would do for Goldwyn what Ford did for Zanuck here - give him so much awards gold he'd lose a day polishing it all). Wyler ducked out at the last second leaving Ford a cast that included his newest good luck charm Maureen O'Hara. Ford was better suited to the material - he also called Philip Dunne's script "perfect." Dunne hated the book on which it was based, which may explain why this came out like a half-remembered fantasia and not a story of a minor miner's sexual awakening. Roddy McDowell's sexlessness here would haunt him forever; he'd never ever play a credible threat to anyone's virtue on screen, a sort of British Anthony Perkins. He'd later direct *Tam-Lin*, one of the greatest of the English folk horror films, which you might call *How Grey Was My Valley*. Ian McShane's the McDowell stand-in in that, and in lieu of beautiful Welsh countryside, he's got Ava Gardner to marvel at. A lateral move, at the very least.

The film is about the difference between theoretical positions and the reality between us and them. The four grown Gwilym boys leave home when their father won't support the miner's strike but return home when it's settled. O'Hara is less lucky. She loves Walter Pidgeon the preacher but has to settle for the mine owner's son, Marten Lamont. The whole town knows there's no love there and don't sing for her nuptials until the rich father (Lionel Pape) demands it. Everyone talks tall about leaving town but the only way anyone seems to is in a pine box. The howl of the whistle always promises more and more loss, more harrowing sights for every would-be widow in town. The Gwylims lose more than their fair share down the mine. The soundless delivery of the news to Anna Lee is one of

Ford's most striking sequences. The sea of depressed coal-stained workers drifting by as on the right of the frame is the desolate sight of loss. Lee stumbles back to the clean house and collapses in the doorway. The world cares not.

PART 5

# IT IS HERE THAT WORLD WAR 2 BEGINS

1941-1945

John Ford was commissioned as a lieutenant commander in the United States Navy Reserve as early as 1934 (around the time of *The World Moves On*, his film with Hitler as the implicit villain in stock footage) so by the outbreak of the Second World War he was ready to be put to use. One or two of the films he made during the war (most for the OSS, office of strategic services, the predecessor to the CIA) are missing and some of them have dubious claims to Ford's authorship. I have to presume this is because the US Government knew that any information expressed here would be inadequate by the time of the next conflict (which happened to be Korea, for which Ford returned, camera in hand). Warfare, techniques, technology, all of it was ever changing. So why bother preserving the films when the next time someone tried to kill you, it'd be with a much bigger gun? When World War 2 started the Allies best friend was the M1 Garand, a rifle that could fire eight shots in a magazine, instead of the bolt action rifles used by the Japanese and Germans. By the time we invaded Vietnam everyone was using M16s and AK-47s. Attitudes changed as the amount of people you could kill in a few seconds went up.

Ford's war films aren't particularly well-regarded (no one's wartime movies are, but I will say I have a soft spot for Wyler's film with Jimmy Stewart kind of politely coughing over the idea of getting the clap from good-time girls while stationed overseas) but something odd happened in the years after. Ford's usual ideology and dramatic tenor was then flooded into our images of the second world war. When Americans wanted to make war films, they'd all take Ford's approach for his westerns. Men doing a job, holding it together, being the best and most honorable men they could, risking everything for the man next to him. The artists who fought, like Sam Fuller, Lenny Bruce, Blake Edwards, Lee Marvin, Rod Serling, Mel Brooks (and earlier Murnau and William Wellman) were less sentimental than Ford. Ford wasn't in the bush with a knife in his teeth, but he did see a hell of a lot of things blow up. He was at Omaha Beach on D. Day and at Midway during the attack there and was wounded while capturing it on film. His films during this period are his most functional, his least poetic. There would be a time to think on the experience later. But for now...he had a job to do.

**Women in Defense (1941)**

Written by Eleanor Roosevelt, narrated by Ford's favorite old girlfriend Katherine Hepburn, this strikes me more as an editors' gig than a director's. I don't think Ford was filming women looking down microscopes, but if he did that's nothing to be ashamed of; functional, yes, but interesting to look at. Hepburn's mid-Atlantic drawl is tuned up to 11. Rats are given experimental drugs…errr...*vitamins*. For who knows what purpose. There's a very moody shot of a woman in a munitions factory, her face a chiaroscuro mask of import. Naturally there's some clothiers making outfits for factory workers (Missus Roosevelt *if you please*!). All these trousers on factory workers reminds of me of the best Hepburn story. Barbara Walters, having only seen her in pant suits, asked Kate if she owned a dress. "Yes and I'll wear it to your funeral." The footage of the women at lathes and presses is pretty slick. Ford inventing steam punk fetishes by accident. Footage of ball bearing placement with tweezers makes me itchy with stress. The footage of the woman woozily giving blood has a strange sexual edge to it. This was a queer way to start the war, and better for it.

**Sex Hygiene (1942, John Ford & Otto Brower)**

"This Film, previously classified as Restricted, is now unclassified" proudly boasts the opening title while a spritely horn march chirps away underneath. William Beaudine and John Ford now officially have at least two things in common: John Carradine and hygiene pictures. At a soldier-filled pool hall one of the more impatient and anti-social recruits makes a big show of going out to go have some real fun. Ford dollies in on the disapproving but silent faces of his peers, and then cuts to the white cue ball rolling right up to an 8 ball. Pretty suggestive. The footage of the soldiers in formation has a little organizational excitement missing from, say, *Salute* or *Men Without Women*. Ford repeats, for the first time since, the fourth wall subsuming trick of the painting on the wall in *Hell Bent*. Ford can't make the sex film itself (diagrams, close-ups of slides, pointers tracing urethras, however sensually) interesting but he tries like hell to make the marginalia worth looking at. "Most men know less about their own bodies than they do their automobiles." The image of a military official with a rear projector painting him with the image of a naked penis is worthy of Kenneth Anger. As is the guy with sores on his face wearing a party store Zorro mask to conceal his identity. Did Ford shoot any of the close-ups of genitals? No way, right? Right? (Of course not, that fell to Otto Brower, director of *The Gay Caballero*, the marvelous Bela Lugosi musical *Postal Inspector*, and at least a few minutes of *Duel in the Sun*, along with a few hundred other people. Editing the film was Gene Fowler, Jr., the director of *I Married A Monster from Outer Space* and *I Was A Teenage Werewolf*, the unofficial sequels to *Sex Hygiene*).

### The Battle of Midway (1942)

Roland Emmerich's excellent *Midway* features a few second cutaway of a giddy John Ford filming the battle of Midway, one of the best moments in a film filled with boyish spectacle. Ford's footage from Midway is supposed to be in technicolor but it looks not dissimilar to his home movies aboard his yacht with Henry Fonda and John Wayne. It's true on-the-fly reportage. Ford seems as taken with the local fauna as the marching soldiers. "The birds seem nervous," says Donald Crisp, the narrator. Sure they do, Don. "Red River Valley" returns from *Grapes of Wrath* over the beautiful sun-dappled footage of the soldiers at nightfall. He has Jane Darwell and Fonda (both of them also from *Grapes of Wrath*) have conversations humanizing the anonymous soldiers on screen. The footage Ford and his cameramen captured is very thrilling and the post-production sound is marvelous.

## Torpedo Squadron 8 (1942)

A B-side to *Battle of Midway* about the men who flew in a now wiped-out regiment of fighters. He captured footage of them standing by their planes just a few hours before they died. Ford is adequately haunted by the idea that he was standing with these poor guys just a short while before they were obliterated by enemy fire or drowned. Drawing on their planes, fidgeting next to each other, smiling nervously, aware, I suppose that this could be the last image ever taken of them, the last things they see, but not knowing. No one knew, really. Their humanity is uncomfortable. The war machine runs on their blood. We know it now. What did these men know?

## At the Front in North Africa with the U.S. Army (1943)

Mostly a travelogue but Ford manages some great images, largely by waiting until magic hour and catching things in auburn colors and silhouettes. There are the occasional flurries of activity - the Nazis bomb the unit at one point - but it's tough to prepare for combat, so it comes out like people staring at something you can't see. Mostly I was reminded of Attenborough's *A Bridge Too Far*, which is 50% people dealing with accidents, misinformation, and disappointment. A lot of the war to a lot of people was driving, waiting, driving, waiting, getting shot at, shooting back, driving, and waiting. Ford was in harm's way a lot. Here he films the casualties of bombing raids and strafing runs, survivors draping blankets gently over their corpses on the road. Francis Ford Coppola must have seen this, a lot of it ends up in *Apocalypse Now*, from the perpetual fire blazing away behind people casually going about their business, to the serene orange skyline mocking the brutality and banality of warfare. The final scene of battle ends with a long shot of prisoners walking under the enormity of cloud coverage shifting overhead, and then, against all odds, a rainbow. It's otherworldly.

## We Sail at Midnight (1943)

A little number about getting ships from New York harbor to England that its best recalls the beautiful naval longueurs of *Submarine Patrol*. There are meetings with officials before a cut to the earthier scenes of the ships being loaded with supplies, right out of *Long Voyage Home*. The footage from the bow predicts Peter Hutton's voyages in the 80s and 90s. The moody backlit sunset b-roll holds its own against a paucity of purpose.

## OSS Training Group (1943)

A truck full of recruits is bussed to a camp in Maryland to learn how to be better spies. Everyone here needs to conceal their identity so it's more of those Halloween costume masks for everybody and no, it doesn't stop being funny. "They burn with a desire for vengeance!" We're told, but they all look like they're headed to the mansion in *Eyes Wide Shut*, burning with something else. The live pistol display, gun positioned directly in front of the instructor's groin, is similarly charged. Watching these guys swing on ropes and shoot guns and perform calisthenics in their uniforms and blacked out eyes it's like a Jerry Warren-bought superhero caper. The recruits point their guns directly at the screen, and once more Edwin Porter ducks. "The student is taught the gentle art of murder!" we're told before two guys start picking each other up and fondling one another. There's so much talk of testicles and how to properly grip them when attacking someone, you'd think the war was won by Johnny Knoxville. The final sequence coaches you on nighttime killing missions. The men whispering and creeping, the lights flashing, it's like a panty raid reimagined as Laura Palmer's last night in *Twin Peaks: Fire Walk With Me*. This movie is hot under the collar.

**December 7th (1943, Gregg Toland & John Ford)**

Ford loved Gregg Toland. He'd shot some of his best work for him on *The Long Voyage Home* and *Grapes of Wrath* and Ford was in the mood to return the favor. They were both at work on Ford's propaganda unit when Ford decided he could do just that: why not give Toland the chance to make his first feature? He sent Toland to Hawaii to make a film about the place, to show what had happened after Pearl Harbor, to make people understand the 50th state. "Grandsons, uncles, in-laws!" Why they're just like you and me, down there. The film Toland turned in was a truly bizarre melding of fact and fiction, and the official narrative has been heavily vetted. The producers weren't so sure about it. Ford chopped it up and gave them a 34 minute version, with a heavier focus on the attack on Pearl Harbor. It should perhaps not surprise you to learn that Toland and Ford never worked together again, although that's not entirely fair. Toland was dead by 1948.

George O'Brien, the heaving beauty from Murnau's *Sunrise*, has a brief voiceover part, his first Ford part in years. He'd once more take larger parts in the Cavalry pictures and *Cheyenne Autumn*. By then he was really only working for Ford, and only because he and Ford liked each other so much. In the last years of his career he was only in an hour of TV directed by Phil Karlson, a Three Stooges western, and in a film by Ford's co-director on *Salute*, David Butler. Odd stuff. Walter Huston is in the longer version of this movie, playing a pontificating old goat named Uncle Sam. He's meant to be narrating bits of the story of Hawaii's place in America and whatnot, but all I can think about is that he'd just played the Devil and with the fake beard he looks like Colonel Sanders. Huston was also born in Toronto, no matter how American he sounded. In amongst the parade of the dead Toland pays tribute to there's an Antonio S. Tafoya from Albuquerque, son of Jesus A. Tafoya. Funny coincidence but there are thousands of Tafoyas from that part of the world and my grandfather was from Colorado and joined the Coast Guard.

Toland's images of Hawaii are stunning, of course. The patchwork combat sequences have real bite. The longer film's more pedestrian approach to delivering facts about Hawaii (and the attitude toward the Japanese) aren't exactly transcendent. There's some really odd staged stuff where a Japanese official is accused of burning documents while the attack is still happening. He's very visibly looking at his cue cards. There's some appalling Japanese voice as a white actor pretends to be Tōjō Hideki, who, like Toland was dead by '48. Though he was publicly executed. That bit of playground racism is rather hard to ignore. If they'd just left out the plot and the patriotism, they could have had another *Que Viva Mexico* on their hands. The odd mix of ethnography and footage of random mechanical tasks being performed, the mid-film dream sequence where America imagines volcanos and dancing girls, slumming stars rounding out the cast; it's kind of like an Edgar Ulmer film, not for the first time in Ford's infrequently imagined netherworld. *Isle of Forgotten Sins*, starring John Carradine, comes close to achieving this very odd mix of the real and the so-fake-it-becomes-real.

**Undercover (1943)**

Another film within-a-film here (Ford clearly trying desperately to make these things more interesting), *Undercover* was meant as a training manual for spies. It cribs footage from Hitchcock's *Secret Agent* (Hitch was also making films for the war effort around this time) and finds time to put down Peter Lorre's performance, and implicitly Hitch himself ("This is the ideal agent...for the enemy!"). This town ain't big enough for the both of them. Crane Whitley and...I believe that's Eddie Foster, but I genuinely have no idea, are the two agents who start things off, both wooden as a summer camp bunkhouse. Ford's camera does some dancing around them to enliven the proceedings. Without that, you could mistake this for an Ed Wood programmer. The guys are pretty blase about the idea of espionage. "I'll let you know when I'm ready." It's like they're planning a lunch.

Ford himself shows up in this as a recruiter and he might be the best actor in the bunch. He's certainly got something about him, flicking his pipe dramatically, sunk and folded into his chair, eyes fixed on the scene partner like his life depended on it. "How could I miss?" "Very easily...by going on like you've been going, by knowing the answers before you've been asked the questions!" Ford snaps. One suspects he's holding back. Andy Devine probably got worse than this from Ford on the set of *Stagecoach*. There's a close-up of Ford writing a recommendation that for some reason had me thinking about early Buñuel. Something so supple about the sight of Ford's hands, while the score teases us. The guy Ford dresses down pushes some paperwork away (scored to a harp glissando like he's Mickey

Mouse) to pick up Movie Star magazine. Not a very serious agent after all.

There's plenty of stuff in here about GM and the bosom of capitalism, but they also fail to say "we're spying on or for the United States," so the film has a kind of Sam Newfield anonymousness. In *Radar Secret Service* you literally lose track of who the bad guys are and what they want. The uniforms here are obviously meant to be German, but the narrator just keeps saying "enemy area." It's purposeful here, unlike in the Newfield, but there's a science fiction quality to all this vagueness. They inspect Foster's Student Al like he's just stepped off an assembly line. Stuff like this makes you realize that built into state-craft and spying is an inescapable element of class. "It's a good cut, but it's too expensive for a mechanic." Blending in means pretending you're richer or poorer than you are. Our agent uses the wrong kind of Canadian dollar at a bar and gets found out. The term "life insurance" is a double entendre. "Professionals who charge you exorbitant prices are loyal to only one cause! Money!" "The Merchant Marines a breeding ground of political resistance!" Ford never makes it easy on you. Making anti-red spy films for the CIA isn't exactly the thing you expect from the man who made *The Grapes of Wrath*, but that's Ford all over. Just when you think he might zig, he zags. Too much of the third act is rendered in whispered voice over and the framing's basically functional throughout, but someone does call someone else a "goddamned idiot," which is really funny to hear in a film of this vintage. "If this were a Hollywood movie, this would be the beginning, but in reality it's far more likely the end!"

**They Were Expendable (1945, John Ford & Robert Montgomery)**

Lindsay Anderson, among others, noted that the war changed Ford. He became obsessed with military pageantry and procedure, of things done the right way, the way he'd seen them done firsthand. Anderson admitted that he was not the fascist he sometimes presented, that socially he was basically a liberal, but like many a provocateur, it was easier to pretend to be a bastard when you didn't want to admit you weren't one. Anderson calls *They Were Expendable* Ford's finest film but Ford never gave him the satisfaction of telling him he understood why. He described a production plagued by problems; he broke his leg on set so Robert Montgomery, a real

PT Boat captain during the war, stepped up to film some things. He didn't have final say on the score, the Miami crew couldn't get him some of the lighting he wanted, he would frequently send second units into the wild to film things that interested him more than the story, which he was wary of directing because he'd met so many Navy men in the war. He didn't want to offend anyone. It didn't work. Lt. Robert Kelly and U.S. Army Nurse "Peggy Smith," on whom author William L. White had based some of the characters, sued the studio and actors John Wayne and Donna Reed personally, for their portrayals. You can see why Ford had second thoughts. Anderson persisted, told him he thought the film was good. Really good, in fact. So Ford finally watched it, and agreed.

The film has a particular kind of atmosphere I love, the kind of tipsy Tropicalia of great films like Edgar Ulmer's *Club Havana*, John Huston's *Key Largo*, Howard Hawks' *To Have and Have Not* and its remake, Michael Curtiz's *The Breaking Point*. Of course Ford isn't a fatalist like those fellas, so his film's on the straight and narrow. He'd rather film biblically accurate navy battles than sweat it out in dance halls by the dock. Ford was hard on everybody on sets but he really gave it to Wayne and Montgomery on this. Wayne got an earful because he'd dodged the draft thanks in part to a family deferment and his money hungry bosses at Republic, who were cranking out Wayne westerns all through the war years. Wayne kept writing to Ford to go be part of his unit, but it never happened and Wayne also clearly didn't care that much, he could have just joined as a private like everybody else. Get your ass shot off in Bataan or fall off a horse a few times a week? The pay was better at home. Montgomery was Ford's favourite on the film (he'd seen him land on Omaha beach) until they had directing disagreements. Ford watched Montgomery frame up a shot he didn't like, let him shoot it, and then threw the finished film at him, ruining it before it could be developed. "Well if you like it so much take it home with ya." Montgomery would later make the striking and ambitious noirs *Ride The Pink Horse* and *Lady in the Lake*. His beauty had dimmed slightly and he was correct in thinking that if he wanted to keep playing interesting parts he might have to create them himself.

Ford says goodbye to his shipboard milieu here, or anyway, it's the last of his films to be fully set among a crew of sailors. He directed a bit of *Mister Roberts*, but nobody would call that "A John Ford picture." It isn't, as Anderson called this, a heroic poem. Donna Reed is another of the true Fordian women, performing surgery in dim light with a grave expression, but anxious to dance when she's finished her job. The close-ups of Wayne and Reed are uncharacteristic of Ford and some of his best work. Wayne's being kept in a hospital wing while his unit goes to battle feels a little like Ford punishing him for cowardice. Wayne suffers a shrapnel wound and Reed tells him he might have lost the limb to blood poisoning if he waited any longer. This, I can't help but feel, is a comment on Ward Bond, another heroic draft dodger who was kept out of WW2 thanks to a secretly fought battle with epilepsy which he got from drinking so much. He was struck by a car after a premiere one night and almost lost his leg. He was still recovering while they were filming this. Bond, Montgomery, to say nothing of the other Ford players chosen for the job (Charles Trowbridge, Murray Alper, Jack Pennick, Robert Barrat, and newcomers Donald Curtis, Paul Langton, Leon Ames and Cameron Mitchell) all blend right in. Maybe even more so than in *Men Without Women* or *Seas Beneath* this strikes me as the work of a director being awfully careful. The point is the mission, not the men. Only Wayne stands out because, well, he's John Wayne. Ford keeps an awed hush alive for most of the movie (a highlight: a dinner party scored by an unseen trio of harmonizing sailors) allowing the imperative dread just on the surface. It suggests with a gentility and reverence, that everything these men do could be the last thing they ever do. Anderson wisely points out that there is no humiliating othering of the Japanese here. They're a complete void. It keeps the film from the racism of *December 7th* or some of the westerns. The closest the movie comes to feeling bad for someone is when Montgomery and Wayne blackmail Jon Gilbreath, a hotshot and very uncredited submarine captain, into giving them half his torpedoes. "Who played Tess of the D'Uerbervilles at the academy in the year 19 hundred and 32?" Asks Montgomery. The man folds. It's meant as a lighthearted gag but Ford watches him walk away for 10 long seconds. Is the guy about to go kill himself?

I've seen *They Were Expendable* three or four times now and each time it grows in my estimation. He's learned what he needed to from Gregg Toland about shadow. Joseph H. August, his preferred cinematographer and fellow WW2 vet, would shoot *Portrait of Jennie* for Selznick after this and then die. Pretty incredible obituary. He shoots a scene of the crew humoring one of their fallen comrades as he languishes in a sick bay like it's *The Creation of Adam* by way of Edward Hopper. It's a great "war film" because it does seem to be mostly interested in "the war" rather than the reasons. This is one of Ford's most casual exercises in dynamics; there are running gags and cute performances, and the score is cartoony (not in a bad way), but every few acts hell-fire rains down from above. Some people won't come back. Ford knew enough by then to know that's how it was. He claimed he didn't have any kind of a say in the edit, but that wasn't true. As always, Ford was afraid people would know that he cared.

**It's Your America (1946)**

Arthur Kennedy is waiting for us as the camera dollies across the deck of a ship, spotting the twinkly ocean over his shoulder. People weren't sure for years if Ford directed this. It took me about eight seconds to commit to the idea that he had. Kennedy addresses us directly. "I feel like...a bigger guy..." he whispers sexually at us. Whoever wrote this really thought they were doing something. "I never used to shoot my mouth off. That's what this damn penny's for." Cut to a penny in his hand. What?! The cast is stacked. Walter Sande, J. Carrol Naish, and Ernest Cossart hadn't worked with Ford before (Naish would be back in a few years for *Rio Grande*) but Preston Foster obviously had. The sentiment is unbearable. Ford and Kennedy together paint an all-too realistic portrait of a soldier in need of a heaping dose of American values. "When you know America you'll know what your fighting for." This one was for G.I.'s returning from the war and it's nicely shot and the performances are all exceedingly earnest. All the talk about pennies and Abe Lincoln mostly reminded me of the educational short "Money Talks" where the shadow of Ben Franklin appears to a young boy to teach him about budgeting.

PART 6

# THE SUNLESS, REMEMBERED

1946-1952

One of my favourite pieces of writing is Manny Farber's pan of *The Quiet Man* for *The Nation*; he didn't like the movie and found an awful lot to criticize but in so doing he unearthed the great strength of Ford's films from this period. The simplicity, the stately enormity of their images, the fugue of silent, unspoken feeling; it becomes a nest for his viewer's own longings and observations. Ford's movies create room for us. Farber produces such stunning and curt turns of phrase in trying to divine what he sees as missing from or too pronounced in *The Quiet Man*.

*The noble close-mouthed hero developed his tungsten muscles in Pittsburgh's mills, learned about Ireland's beauties at his mother's knee, and lost his urge to fight when he killed a ring opponent. All this is revealed by way of dialogue, so that there is nothing for John Wayne to impersonate except John Wayne. Maureen O'Hara plays the windlike heroine out of Wuthering Heights, and the Ford stock company (Arthur Shields, Ward Bond, McLaglen, Natwick, Fitzgerald) goes through the dated mimicry of such stereotypes as the tippling village cabby, the thick-headed, bellicose squire, and the jovial village priest who curses, jokes, and fishes from start to finish of the film.*

*Some of the technicolor photography is pretty original—a dense, gray atmosphere takes most of the hue and intensity out of the scene and makes for a curious picture that takes place in daylight yet has some of the sunless, remembered look of a surrealist painting. Ford's ability to lyricize a movie with scenic effects is manifest wherever the camera moves...*

I named a vampire movie after his description of the movie's visuals. *The Sunless Remembered*. Good writing makes you want to create in its reflection and though Farber was denigrating the picture, it drew from him some of his best words and phrases. This second great period in Ford's career saw the birth of one colossal work after another, movies of high classical quality and nagging moral equivocations that tether the work to the earth. This must rank as among the most full and rich periods in an American artist's life. The great and the terrible, cavalier and undressed, entwined like lovers.

**My Darling Clementine (1946)**

John Ford had one film left on his contract at Fox in 1946, his home since the 20s. Ford had been loaning himself out to other studios since the '30s but he wanted freedom above all else. The way he shot *The Iron Horse*, with no producer in sight. He was once quoted as saying that the most important thing to do on a set is stand around until someone gets nervous and calls a studio boss, then when he shows up to ask how things are going, whip around with your viewfinder and hit 'em in the head so hard he bleeds and make it look like an accident. Then they'll leave you alone. He didn't want to make this film, but he needed an out and he had a personal connection to the story; he actually knew Wyatt Earp. He'd met him when working as a prop boy in his youth when Earp, like many a cowboy, was closing out his career as a consultant on movie sets and would say he got his understanding of the way the gunfight played out first hand but mostly everyone agrees that was bullshit. Dennis Hopper's *The Last Movie*, Joel & Ethan Coen's *True Grit* and Howard Zieff's *Hearts of the West* are tributes to stories like this, or at least comment on the tragedy of dying so far away from your horse. It's fitting then that Ford's last hit before striking out on his own with Argosy pictures is one of his most melancholy westerns, a farewell and an overture. He built Tombstone, AZ in Monument Valley, AZ because he liked it better there. Brought Bond, his brother Francis, J. Farrell MacDonald, Jane Darwell, Earle Foxe, Jack Pennick, Russell Simpson, and Charles Stevens with him, so it felt even more like home.

*My Darling Clementine* is about form, or rather about creating something succinct from chaos. Earp rides into Tombstone ("What kinda town is this!?") and finds drunks, floozies, and the men who killed his brother running free in the streets. The marshal is only too happy to pin his own star on Fonda's shirt. He gets the job and a would-be wife to go with it, Doc

Holiday's old flame. Doc himself has taken up with Linda Darnell (as would I). He wills Tombstone into a new shape, stepping into the place like the good shadow of Doc. The way that Ford chooses angles to film the town so too does Earp place himself in just the right place to ensure that people feel strong armed into doing the right thing instead of the easy thing. A few words of direction here, a strong shove there, and the set is re-designed in his image. He even changes himself, haircut and a shave, looking at himself in the mirror over and over to make sure he can process the sight of himself. Him, Doc and his brothers will become the mirror image of the Clantons, heading into battle to destroy their egos.

Fonda's body language is a little Shakespearian display all its own. For every perfectly lit corridor and rain-soaked street, every poetic scrap evidence of life lost and lived, every extinguished campfire and soaked rain coat, there's the kinda sight you can't plan on. Like Fonda kicked back in his chair doing isometric exercises ("Aurora borealis?!"). Sometimes he forgets that he's the auteur in this town. When Cathy Downs, the Clementine in question, asks Fonda if he's going to church he forgets that he can do and say anything he wants. Off they go, arm in arm. His dancing is the prettiest spectacle, absurd limbs going this way and that. His best close-up is in total darkness, watching Clementine rush in to assist Doc Holliday as he repairs his no-good girlfriend's gunshot wound. Every pack of silhouettes in barrooms feels ancient and immortal. The final gunfight is a web of misdirection and obstruction. Horses kick up dirt, and from the dirt a fatal gunshot. Doc Holliday hanging from a fence absurdly with his handkerchief in his hand like he's surrendering. Some movies are made timeless.

**The Fugitive (1947, John Ford with Emilio Fernández)**

I wonder who the first director was to use Brechtian alienation in their stage direction? Other than Brecht, himself, of course. G.W. Pabst, maybe? This film opens with starkly stunning images of Henry Fonda doing a bit of his Fugitive thing (running and looking around all nervous), credits including Pedro Armendariz and Gabriel Figueroa (indeed the transportation of Ford, Fonda and co. to Mexico is sort of its own alienation device: kind of a "The John Ford Stock Company Hits Spring Break" thing that relies on the audience knowing about the director and his baggage; i.e. Michael Sicinski's description of *The Death of Louis XIV* as "The Albert Serra Gang Meets the Sun King"), and then an elemental character list. A fugitive, an Indian Woman, El Gringo (that's Ward Bond, if you couldn't have guessed), an Organ Grinder, A Hostage, etc. It's based on a novel, not a play, which took me by surprise. Even more surprising: the novel was by Graham Greene, who had been sued after writing a negative review of a Ford's own *Wee Willie Winkie* back in '38. You can call that burying the hatchet, I guess, but it's not like the film did anything for Greene's career (Joe McBride hates this film and called it revenge for the review). It made zero dollars and zero cents at the box office, and its only defender for years was Ford himself. Now it's him and me.

Going to Mexico to make a movie was placing himself in the tradition of Sergei Eisenstein, who'd gone down there to make his own failed experiment in the early 30s. These were the thick of the anti-clerical wars rocking Mexico, which provides the backdrop for Ford's film. We don't really talk about the Cristero wars these days, do we? Years of corrupt and violent regimes wound up leaving the keys to the Mexican war machine in the ignition during the roaring 20s; roaring for a different reason. One government would promise one thing, another would step in and kind of half-heartedly enforce the promises of the last guys, then a third government would step in, vehemently opposed to what the last several guys have been up to. That kind of explains how President Venustiano Carranza and his successor, General Alvaro Obregón left the country in a shambling state with enough violent tension that after both men were killed (Carranza by later president Lázaro Cárdenas) Plutarco Elías Calles let a war ravage the country. Obregón and Carranza and indeed Adolfo de la Huerta, their successor, none of them were staunchly anti-catholic, they were mostly busy trying to keep six or seven pots from boiling over in their own administrations (and failed, mostly. Hence all the assassinations…). Obregón, however, was killed by a catholic dissident, after Calles started a campaign of repression against the Catholic clergy, and this morphed without much provocation into the military killing thousands of people. Calles' legacy will always be complicated by the war, though his aims were otherwise less bloodthirsty (he succeeded in redistributing a lot of land to the poor, though he, like so many others, was publicly anti-communist) against the Cristeros, a derogatory term for the Catholic fighters. They were feeling pushed out by the clamp down by traditionalists against the Catholics (a process that had begun decades earlier), fought a brutal war against the constitutionalists, and all in all 250,000 people are thought to have died in the conflict. One of the interim presidents who inherited the war was Emilio Portes Gil who worked hard to get it sorted out, offering amnesty to everyone he could and trying to get people to stop killing each other (he'd later give amnesty to Augusto Sandino to try and save him from assassination by the US, which didn't work). Anyway for those three years Mexico saw more bloodshed than at almost any other time in its history. Greene's research trip to Tabasco in Mexico made him a lifelong catholic, but a problematic one. The church didn't love that his faith found expression in stories of drunk priests. It is against this backdrop that many classic novels have been written, including Greene's *The Power and the Glory*, B. Traven's *The Treasure of the Sierra Madre*, Juan Rulfo's *Pedro Páramo*, and Malcolm Lowery's *Under The Volcano*.

Ford, unsurprisingly, was so taken with the Mexican landscape and his friend Emilio Fernández's crew and rep company, that he threw out most of the script and just kind of vibed for the whole shoot. He'd later describe the experience like it was an awakening. Fernández and Figueroa rubbed off on Ford in the best way. The two had been making unbelievably beautiful work together for the last several years, including the classic *Maria Candelaria* and their own John Steinbeck adaptation, *The Pearl*, that same year. Fernández was part of the international cadre of directors Ford loved, along with Akira Kurosawa. This was Ford's first film with Argosy, the production company he mounted with Merian Cooper using RKO as distributor (hence *King Kong*'s Robert Armstrong in the cast, a magnificent turn as a loutish cop). The platonic ideal of the independent production. Fonda plays one of the last catholic priests on the run from Calles' soldiers. He travels from place to place, a step ahead of the law, bringing himself as low as he can stand to continue on his way. A harrowing Welles-esque chapter finds him degrading himself for wine; I like the scene better if it's unclear whether he's going to consecrate it, but I doubt Ford intended the breathing room. J. Carroll Naish appears to Fonda like Yōsuke Kubozuka to Andrew Garfield in Martin Scorsese's Silence, testing him, leading him to his downfall, but every religious hero has to have one. The ultimate humbling.

Greene intended the priest to be one of his conflicted martyrs at the crux of historical derangement like Holly Martins but Ford turns him into the Risen Jesus in two shots. The film's imagistic ponderousness turned everyone off but this is how movies are now. Less good of course, but Nicolas Refn's every movie is like *The Neon Fugitive*, so everyone who imitates him (David Lowery, Robert Eggers, Denis Villeneuve, Trey Edward Shults) is doing the same bit. That's a lot of undeserving little orphans running around. We've already established that Paul Schrader and Robert Bresson have stripped a lot of Ford for parts, but this is like their user manual. Ford being Ford he makes this a matter of the Calles stripping Cristeros of their crosses and throwing them in jail. Sandino didn't quite come to that same conclusion while he was in Mexico, and though he may not have been able to shoot a picture like Ford I am inclined to take his word about this. Ford tries to reframe it as an issue of social cooperation, but he renders it treaclier than usual. Ford's vision of Mexico is roughly equal to Walt Disney's (indeed this and *The Three Caballeros* are all but aesthetic twins, so richly designed and easy to fall into, so very blinkered in their perspective) and something like the inverse of Eisenstein, though there's little denying that few who ever set out to capture Mexico's essence did more than write postcards. This at least is striking. Overpowering, even. Light has never looked so much like god's own cigarette.

**Fort Apache (1948)**

Back from Mexico and humbled, Ford opens on the site of his last true runaway success: A stagecoach in Monument Valley. "What a country! Mule creek! Dead Man's Squaw! Schmitz's Wells! Hangman's Flats! Hassayampa! End of the Rainbow: Fort Apache," crows Henry Fonda, shunted to the edge of civilization after a botched performance elsewhere. He'd rather be in Europe, but his daughter Shirley Temple doesn't mind being out in the desert. With her hat from Boston and her California smile she's out of her element, but once again playing the willing exile as she did in *Wee Willie Winkie*. She stumbles on "and introducing John Agar" taking a shower. This is probably his best work, and it's probably because Ford hated his guts (he wasn't the only one who got that treatment and did their best work, if that hasn't yet been made abundantly clear). Agar had gotten Temple pregnant so it's about two minutes of screentime before Victor McLaglen is spanking him in front of the rest of the squad. Some introduction.

The film is one of those great Ford triumphs about ceremony and circumstance, about the proper addresses and salutes to give this or that officer. Ford made these to get himself back in the black (he was, by all accounts, a miserable bastard on the set of these films, only bright eyed when Danny Borzage was serenading him on the accordion or when he was making fun of Agar and Ward Bond), but he's better at them anybody, and he makes discussions of rank fascinating and cinematic. Cronenberg's clinician speak seems to be born in its mirror image. Hawks movies were about friends, brothers-in-arms. Ford's movies are about colleagues. It's a harder challenge; don't we all love to see people getting along, laying bricks of conversance atop one another? Ford's heroes have to earn each other's trust and respect, which does make for a more satisfying conclusion when they finally earn them. Agar surprising Bond and Irene Rich is a good example. The distance between them melts, and the most beautiful sight in the world flashes across us: a father, overcome with pride, hugs his only son. Then he and Victor and the rest of the boys go drinking. Ford could by now do this in his sleep. It helped that he had a cast who knew not to screw up, Monument Valley in the background and a new ally in first-time screenwriter Frank S. Nugent, a Ford foundling.

Nugent would write nearly a third of Ford's remaining films, among them *The Searchers*. He could turn a terse phrase worthy of Ford's tight frames. "You could follow their line of retreat by the bones of their dead," says Wayne of the last people who went up against the Apaches. There are borderline Hawksianisms throughout. "Sergeant Beauford." "Private Beauford." "Private Beauford." Wayne is like a Myna bird here. Ford was about to learn he could act when asked to when Hawks used him in *Red River* the next year. Wayne was about to get asked to do more heavy lifting than he ever had in his life. Here he's just on hand to be the ignored angel on Fonda's shoulder. He and Pedro Armendáriz are great together on their mission to appeal to Cochise to stop torturing and killing their men. It gets mighty dark indeed between the drunken carousing and scenes of Shirley Temple capering around in a bonnet and petticoat. She crosses the Z axis with odd posture and an unearthly glow, like some Dreyer villainess headed to damnation. George O'Brien, the strapping sinner from *Sunrise*, is back and beautiful as ever as Fonda's displaced rival. Ben Johnson joins Ford's company for the next few years; here as Fonda's stunt double. Even then Fonda was prettier than Johnson. Prettier than Shirley Temple. Hank Worden, who had a small part in *Stagecoach* is back, too, years before he'd play Mose the holy fool in *The Searchers*. No mistaking that head; an otter grown to manhood.

Nugent cannily makes the heart of the movie the difference between what's right and what's proper. Fonda barks orders and refuses to allow Temple and Agar to wed, but then has to dance with Agar's mother at a regiment dance. When push comes to shove he'll slaughter Apaches and make a liar out of Wayne, even with the latter watching helplessly from the sidelines, having implicitly begged him to forget propriety when lives are at stake. Ford shoots the dances like the gun fights, diagonally down the Z to overwhelm his audience with pomp rather than turn them into abstractions. Wayne has Ford's proxy here. Allegiances, states, borders, nations, none of it matters more than a man's word. Peckinpah rehashes this discussion in *The Wild Bunch*. Women watch wearily and warily as their men ride off to certain death singing loudly and proudly. To Ford no scene is more important than any other, so there's no contradiction to placing musical comedy beats nearby. Nugent helps Ford put his past on trial, maybe the whole western genre. You could get away with a lot between singing and dancing. People always say that they don't know what *The Searchers* is about. It's about living with hatred. It's about hating what you love. It's looking back on your life and realizing you could have said more and better, you could have *been* something. Realizing everything you gave up in the name of your prejudice. *Fort Apache* said it first, *The Searchers* just said it after Ford had made *The Sun Shines Bright*. Nugent knew what he was doing, and I suspect Ford did, too. Agar watches through binoculars as the man who said he wasn't fit to marry his daughter is overrun by the enemy in his hubris. The point is some of us don't even get beaten this bad. Some people just have to live with the hate, with no proof you did everything wrong. "And marry that girl!" cries Wayne as he dismisses Agar from the massacre. My heart caught in my throat. He'll lie with pain stamped on his face when they ask him if Fonda died "gallantly." A great movie.

### 3 Godfathers (1948)

Peter B. Kynes' *The Three Godfathers* was adapted a half-dozen times across a half century. It was the last Kynes story to be adapted and it stands as his Hollywood epitaph despite his work being turned into one hundred movies and TV episodes. Ford must have seen his first leading man Harry Carey in the first adaptation of the story in 1916, or at least heard about it from the old cowboy, and it clearly struck a chord with him because the two men made it again in 1919 as *Marked Men*, lost, as with so many early Fords. Indeed, Ford adapted it three times until he felt he'd done it every way he could. The second, starring Hoot Gibson, was lost. The third was one of Ford's most sentimental westerns and is wholly a product of Ford's shift into full bore violent romance. It also stars Carey's son. It's one of my grandfather's favourite films. He identified with Pedro Armendáriz's Pedro Fuerte, though he was as much Jeffrey Hunter's Martin Pawley in *The Searchers*. Maybe we all are. I always found it so pure and frustrating that the reason my grandfather never spoke about his Native ancestry (which my grandmother had to cobble together from context clues without his help – we're either Sioux or Navajo, she reasoned, but more honestly we're neither – we have no tribe and you're nothing without a tribe) was thanks to the way that whites treated him as a child. And where might these whites get the idea that a little boy with an indigenous mother and a Spanish father and later step-fathers deserved to be treated so violently? Could it possibly be from movies where John Wayne denigrates both races? That's not the whole story, of course it's not, but it's always been there in the back of my mind. He so loved these movies…movies that would never love him back, starring a man who turned his back on every native who once welcomed him into their community.

John Wayne, Pedro Armendáriz, and Harry Carey Jr. ride into town and make friends with a nice man (Ward Bond) and his wife (Mae Marsh) but nearly blow their cover when he puts his tin star on. They're in town not to make friends but to rob the local bank. They're awfully conspicuous for bank robbers, all but introducing themselves to the whole town square by first name. Neither of the three leads was quite cut out to play villains yet. At least not for Ford. Bond lets them go after a high-speed chase ("they ain't payin' me to kill folks...") knowing there isn't water where they're going. He organizes a posse and swindles the bank manager out of a hundred bucks in the doing. The crooks are honest and the cops are thieves. But everyone's basically ok in Ford's book. Nugent does a great job with the moral murkiness, knowing better than to try and add too much to Ford's love letter to Harry Carey with his son standing around.

Everything conspires against them. Carey Jr. gets beat up good on his way out of town, Bond cuts off their water supply, a dust storm blows 'em off course, and their horses get loose. Wayne is more like a big brother to his cohorts but he's got to grow up fast when he discovers a dying woman (Mildred Natwick, which...I mean Ford had to have been messing with her. She even says "It's getting dark" right before she expires) in labor in an abandoned stage, a full 40 minutes in. Frank Nugent gives Wayne one of his finest scenes when he has to describe why he went over a hill to get water and came back empty handed. The best part of the speech is all Kynes ("We can have cloudbursts in this country from now until I get religion, but them tanks'll never hold another drop o' water.") but Ford frames Wayne in a single medium close-up as he dispatches a week's worth of action in 3 minutes of screentime. Excellent stuff, you can see everything you need to in his words, but it is rather unlike Ford to leave it to the imagination. He *trusted* Wayne to do it. Armendariz mans up first and goes to help the dying woman deliver her cub, while Wayne sits in the dirt like a kid, angry with himself because he can't help. Everybody's going nuts and it's great, neurotic stuff. They promise Natwick they'll take her baby out of the desert and they forget their lives of crime. Armendariz makes you want to cry, he's so locked in. Carey, Jr. sings at her graveside, the wind howling and whipping their sallow faces in the pale glow of moonlight. Together they all make one Harry Carey.

The second hour is half adorable proto-sitcom antics and bickering, and the odd shape of death coming to rest over each of these characters. It is unsurprising that this became a comedy in the 80s ("The title makes me laugh!" goes Patton Oswalt's local film critic bit) and a heartbreaking anime in the 00s. "Hand over the pot, we'll slick 'eem up a mite." The bulk of what follows is repetitive action (more kinship to Bresson, and David Lean yanks the salt flats run and Wayne's canyon chorus for *Lawrence of Arabia*) which is new for Ford, and he'd never do it again. Carey, Jr.'s death scene, with Wayne holding his hat up to keep the sun out of his eyes, is one of his best scenes. For a film with a comic streak, it might be even more biblically minded than *The Fugitive*, his other great silent film of his talkie years. Three wise men wandering the desert on Christmas carrying a child with no father. Suffering becomes tantamount to godliness, here, and the sins of these lost boys are washed away in the blazing heat. Wayne drips water on the child's face as the wind howls at his back. He hears ghosts, then sees them, as he traipses the final miles to civilization, which just might have him now. Ford thinks they'd be lucky to have anyone who'd die for the poorest among us. "Loose them and bring them unto me."

**She Wore a Yellow Ribbon (1949)**

If *Red River* was Wayne's first great role, Ford wasn't going to be beaten by much. He let him play Nathan Brittles, the 60-some-odd-year-old cavalry captain who sees his usefulness setting with the sun, when someone like Ward Bond or even Victor McLaglen would have been a more appropriate choice. By now Ford was adept at color photography; this one's so pretty you want to dive into it and have a soak. Wayne himself was almost never so dignified in appearance, with the gray hair and mustache. Big Victor is quite obviously older than Wayne, but they make a fine pair of lovers. Seen more sunsets themselves than lay before them. Ben Johnson, Ford and Merian Cooper's big find in the 40s looks like he could be Wayne's kid. He's got the dusty voice and drink lined face to match even Wayne's gruff exterior. Handsome George O'Brien's back, too, thank heaven, and so is John Agar, and Harry Carey Jr. The heavies are played by Chief John Big Tree, George Sky Eagle and Noble Johnson, who was friends with *Arrowsmith* star and cowboy Clarence Brooks, and who had played the chief villager in Cooper's *King Kong*. Wagner the blacksmith (Mickey Simpson) looks like he fell out of the 21st century. This is a good group of guys. Wayne, concerned with McLaglen's Sgt. Quincannon making it to retirement, arranges for him to star in a drunken brawl so he'll be confined to quarters for his final weeks and out of harm's way. True early "Dudes Rock" canon.

Ford was aware he was chasing his tale/tail with this one and had fun with it; kept his brother Francis on hand for the whole shoot to make sure he was collecting wages. In the movie *The Informer* Victor McLaglen and Wallace Ford talk about the "Tan that killed Quincannon," a character name from The Lost Patrol and later J. Farrell MacDonald plays a sailor called "Sails Quincannon" in *Submarine Patrol*. In *Fort Apache* McLaglen shows up as Sgt. Festus Mulcahy, but by *She Wore A Yellow Ribbon*, he's playing Top Sgt. Quincannon. The answer is simple. This man has been lying his way across the map with a stolen identity since the end of the civil war. Or not, but it's a little fun to think about. Anytime David Niven had to improvise in scripts, he'd always mention his friend "Trubshawe," apparently a real guy he knew.

Cinematographer Winton C. Hoch should have been canonized or knighted or something for this. *She Wore a Yellow Ribbon* has some m*sterpiece^ of composition and lighting every few seconds, it's almost ludicrous, but the tone mostly stays breezy except when Wayne's remembering the wife and daughter he buried. Even reading the names from Custer's massacre doesn't seem to bring him down so much as fill him with a kind of awe that that many guys let their guard down (Ford having just dramatized the massacre in *Fort Apache*, it's fresh in our heads). The red mist over the graveyard where the Brittles family rests seems to invent 80s horror, but he mostly seems happy for the company. Sylvester Stallone would try to recapture this performance every time at bat and managed it once in *Cop Land*.

Maybe it was the clarity of the color, the red clay under those ocean blue uniforms, that made the absurdity of life on the prairie come alive for Ford. Hence Victor chastising a sleeping dog and hard drinking Mildred Natwick dressed in his old duds. She and Handsome George do some passionate necking and Joanne Dru riding side saddle in her cavalry coat is quite fetching. Everyone's got something court martial-able on the brain. Victor gets locked in the brig for drinking on the base, in one of Ford's best brawls. The blocking is superb throughout, Preston Sturges-esque in some cases, which is fitting for a film that's a battle-of-the-sexes comedy for much of its runtime. Ford doesn't extend much psychology to his natives this time around. He's got two competing ideologies here, both uttered by Brittles. "Only the man in command is to blame. Mission failure." and "Never apologize, Mister, it's a sign of weakness." Lindsay Anderson liked that so much it became the title of his collected writings. Ford doesn't blame the Cheyenne for killing white people, and after all it's Wayne who watches with glee as they descend on a ne'er-do-well arms dealer and burn him alive. "I think we're ok, too," as Steve Zissou says.

^Village Voice editor Danny King once told me he wouldn't allow any variation of the word "Master" into any film review. I try to stand by this.

**Pinky (1949, John Ford & Elia Kazan)**

Before he died Harry Carey was directed by Elia Kazan in the movie *Sea of Grass* and was later quoted as saying "That's the best director I've had since Jack..." As much as you can tell why Zanuck didn't think Ford was up to this, it's difficult to watch this and not see every way in which Kazan was stealing from Ford. The shot-reserve-shot stuff doesn't have Ford's poetry, he never would have allowed an editor to insert 15 cuts into a two minute dialogue scene. He would have had it in three. I think that's probably Ford directing the first shot of Jeanne Crain walking home, and frankly it might still be him when Ethel Waters hugs her and brings her inside (plenty of Z axis blocking), but we know he would have resisted Zanuck's house style elsewhere. The close-ups on Crain are all wrong, Ford would have bucked them but, well, Zanuck wanted an Oscar film (why else greenlight a script with a social message and risky racial politics in this decade). You don't win Oscars without close-ups. Kazan still has that studio-bound muscularity, but he's also like one of those neo-folk singers who always opened up indie shows in the 00s who likes everyone to forget they own a cell phone and a laptop. "Well I just blew in to sing ya some tunes, ma'am, now lemme check ma iPhone for da setliyist." Kazan wanted to make movies with the bare-chested rawness of both the forgotten parts of America and the breast-beating, shirt ripping hugeness of the new method actors (man, thoughts of Brando in *Streetcar* bring out thoughts of chests, don't they?) Of course the earthiness of the one sort of puts the lie to the other. You don't believe Brando and Dean are their characters, they're movie stars, no matter how much they scream and cry and rend their garments. That's why *Wild River* is his best: Montgomery Clift wears a huge coat the whole film and doesn't scream when they beat the hell out of him. I mean there are other reasons but that's one of them.

Kazan lets Crain get away with a very stage bound style of performance. Ethel Waters mops the floor with her. Part of why Ford left was he couldn't torment Waters the way he could Ward Bond or John Wayne. Richard Brody called bullshit on the movie *Whiplash* (a perfectly stupid modern Kazan impression) because its villain lets homophobic slurs fly but won't use *racial* slurs. Ford had the same realization and called in sick with shingles. All three of the main actresses got nominations, which is typical. Crain's best work is when she doesn't say anything (voice over fills us in so she doesn't just look blank), Waters is great all the time and Barrymore is Kazan's platonic ideal of an actor; good and intuitive but like a giant bird, cackling and cawing. Cruelty is its own end in Kazan's cinema; he gives birth to the Lars Von Triers and Michael Hanekes of the world. At times the film looks just like *Tobacco Road*, but even in its fine-tuned edginess it can't approximate that film's bizarre form of realism. Ford getting the old heave ho a week into production is a nifty little metaphor for the arrival of modernism, though for my money Kazan was only a quarter modernist. The only true work of modernism in his catalogue is Barbara Loden's *Wanda*, for which he claimed more credit than he'd earned and which he produced after he'd been ostracized for diming out his Actor's Studio friends to HUAC. Even in defeat he couldn't help but be an utter bastard to everyone who'd ever trusted him. Kazan already had a best picture Oscar for *Gentlemen's Agreement*, one of those movies I wish we didn't make anymore but we always do. He was thus only too well-fitted for *Pinky* even if, of course, he wasn't. Ford would have made a Ford film. Kazan made an Oscar movie just like Zanuck wanted (he even pitched this as *Gentlemen's Agreement* with Blackness for Jewishness). Would have been odd to hear the slurs intact in a Ford film. That part of modernity escaped him.

Here's my friend, poet/critic Fernando Croce on the film: "The film's own internal struggle rests between a tidy Zanuck social tract and a raw Kazan exploration—Frederick O'Neal's rascally magnetism and a ferocious flash of Nina Mae McKinney attest to the latter's touch, much like the knotted tribunal bespeaks John Ford's groundwork. Reactionary hicks maintain the divide yet liberalism is a squeamish Boston doctor (William Lundigan), the lass must go at it by herself. "Let's try to face it like rational people." "What's rational about prejudice?" The close of Kazan's novice period, seen with embarrassment by subsequent reviewers though thankfully not by Altman, who recalls it pointedly in *Cookie's Fortune*." Someone ought to pay Fern a million dollars for these pieces.

Kazan's sophistication keeps him at a remove from the text, from the soul of the piece. A shot of Crain walking up a flight of stairs is excellent, if a hair clinical; she's ascending (very deliberately) to the world of the wealthy white elite, who's dying in her bed - it's De Palma before De Palma. So are later tracking shots of Crain and William Lundigan walking through town talking over their problems. With Ford you never get a sense of straining for meaning, which is all Pinky does. Would have loved to have seen how he handled all the weird rationality race-as-science discussions between doctors Crain and Lundigan. It's not new to say that the problem with *Pinky, Gentlemen's Agreement, Guess Who's Coming To Dinner, In The Heat of the Night,* pick your civil rights victory in 12 reels, is that the ideal audience member for such a film is as much a fabrication as the characters changed by their encounters with characters unlike themselves. If there still exists a man out there whose belief in bigotry is hanging by a thread so flimsy as *Pinky*, his conversion to liberalism can't mean all that much.

Scott Ashlin, aka El Santo, in his review of Jordan Peele's *Get*

*Out*, prefaces his thoughts with an anecdote that will probably ring true for a lot of people; I know it did for me: "A friend of mine who was born in Bristol, Virginia, spent most of his adult life in and around Washington DC, and retired to the South Carolina coast once said to me that the difference between Southern racism and Northern racism was that Southern racists hate black people in the abstract, but like the ones they know personally, while Northern racists like black people in the abstract, but can't stand the ones they have to deal with face to face."

People like to believe that they're progressive enough to mutter under their breath and not be held to the same standards they set to the fictitious racists most of them won't ever meet. When I was a kid a guy approached my father in a restaurant line (we were, if you can believe it, in a Trump casino - the year was 1994 or thereabouts) and gave him a coupon he couldn't use because he was leaving town that day. He then leaned in and whispered to my horrified father "I wanted it to go to a white family." That man probably would chafe at the idea that he was racist, but then so would people idly scrolling dating apps and implicitly swiping through people who don't look like them. The people who would fess up to their own racism are beyond help so trying to give people waffling in the middle positive role models in film or negative reflections isn't going to change anyone's outlook, because a more powerful impulse in America than "I vow to do better" is "Well I'm not like that." In *Pinky* a white-passing black woman's self-loathing is rewarded with a free house and a fortune from a woman who for some reason has no friends and is not the monster her bigoted friends and relations are. She leaves her white fiancé, which, despite her intention to heal her community reinforces that there's only one place for Pinky and it's not where white people live and that's the happy ending. If I don't think this film is up to whatever task it set itself, well... I don't think any movie is. This work is done in reality, in your own heart. Movies can do a lot for our spirits, but this is America. They can't do everything.

**When Willie Comes Marching Home (1950)**

The writer Richard Sale is known to a certain breed of film fan as the guy who wrote the novel *The White Buffalo*, adapted by Dino De Laurentiis, so seeing his name under the screenplay credit got me more excited about this trifle than I had been. His turns of phrase aren't quite as ornate as in the western but they'll keep you awake. Sale was in the middle of a 15 year screenwriting and directing binge (with, as on *Willie*, his wife Mary Loos helping him out), keeping the lights on while he wrote books like Buffalo and The Oscar, which was disastrously adapted by Harlan Ellison in the 60s. The only other Sale film I've seen is Frank Borzage's fantastically weird *Strange Cargo*, which was kind of Borzage's *The Fugitive*.

Heading up a cast that includes Alan Hale, Jr., Charles Trowbridge, Vera Miles, Whit Bissell, J. Farrell MacDonald (in his last role for Ford, uncredited; the end of an era), and William Demarest, Dan Dailey is the titular Willie, and he's montaged from his comfy home in nowheresville playing trumpet with a jazz combination to air force training when World War 2 breaks out. Ford films the base like a modernist jigsaw puzzle, predicting Zhang Yimou, and then relives *Air Mail* as Dailey crashes his plane, snapping the wings off (Spielberg, as ever, scribbles this down in his legal pad for later). When they find Dailey can shoot as well as he can sing they send him back home so he can train other recruits. So much for being a big hero. Dailey was kind of an oddball good luck charm. He worked for Borzage, Douglas Sirk, Busby Berkeley, Michael Curtiz, Stanley Donen, and finally Larry Cohen. Ford used him twice more after this. This was the favorite for best picture that year (though it lost to his *Pinky* replacement Elia Kazan's film *Panic in the Streets*) and did win the Golden Leopard at Locarno (beating Hitchcock, John Huston, Jean Negulesco, and...one-time Nazi collaborator Wolfgang Liebeneiner), which is both perplexing and not. It's a goofy service comedy, sure, but Ford sneaks in some of his weirdest compositions; it's a hybrid musical and despite the voiceover and editing hassling you from one scene to the next, it has terrific rhythm; in short it's always interesting on the terms of a given scene and as radical in its way as *Wagon Master*.

Ford repeats shot set-ups from reverse angles to show the monotony of Dailey's experience on the base. There's a ridiculous shot of a plane crashing while in the foreground the extras climb a fire truck to help out - I can't imagine how they did that so carefully, but Ford just kind of throws it away. Then he blows the plane up. Dailey's rank keeps rising and his decorations keep growing but the war's going to end before he gets to see a second of active combat. The people in town, including daddy Demarest, start to hate his guts for hanging around on the army's orders. It's not exactly Kafka or Joseph Heller but that's the idea; it's at least funny and weird. Becoming a hero and a hated pariah at the same time and for the same reasons. Locarno had a sidebar of social realist cinema the year *Willie* won top honors, and yet there's perverse integrity to a musical about the failures of the American propaganda machine doing so while former Nazis compete and *Berlin: Symphony of A Great City* plays in retrospective. The defining image of the movie might be Dailey trying to sleep on an airplane that's going down, drowning out the noise of the sputtering juggernaut. They abandon ship without their hero, who nearly dies in the crash. He gets picked up by the French resistance and things get even more interesting.

The French immediately include him in their operation and when he sees an experimental rocket going off, the French entrust him with pictures of it and a map to the site and have to smuggle him out of the country. His ability to sing is his disguise - music is the universal language, which is why Ford always includes singing in his films - as they throw him into a phony wedding ceremony to elude the Nazis. Then he, drunkenly, rides with a torpedo boat back to England. He becomes a hero by the same faulty logic and accident prone game plan that made him so hated back in Illinois. Ford would never publicly say that this is how the world works, but he said it plenty of times in his work. Dailey stays drunk through most of his adventure in Europe and then gets put in a psych ward by accident for his troubles. He has to literally escape to get back home, the one place in the world he was trying to flee. Ford had no trouble saying that.

## Rio Grande (1950)

John Ford wanted badly enough to make *The Quiet Man* that he relented when Republic, the king of the B studios, asked him for a cavalry picture as collateral. Those were making bank, so if Ford wanted his way he could make them one of the confounded things, with his and Merian Cooper's Argosy pictures chipping in. James Kevin McGuinness, who'd written for Ford during the second World War, writes his last script from a story by James Warner Bellah, who wrote the other stories on which Ford's cavalry pictures had been based and who'd write the narration for *This is Korea!* the next year. The cast includes John Wayne, Maureen O'Hara, Ben Johnson, Harry Carey Jr., Victor McLaglen, Jack Pennick, J. Carrol Naish, and Grant Withers. Wayne's son Patrick puts in his debut for Ford, as do *Yearling* co-stars Chill Wills and Claude Jarman Jr.

It opens with the usual raft of stock footage of Monument Valley but there's a stupendous edit that...may have been accidental, so to speak. The rest of the film has a clumsiness, evidence of Ford treating this as work-for-hire, but this one works. Ford shoots a bunch of kids leaving a schoolhouse, edits to them on the street headed toward the gate at the edge of the street, then cuts into a dolly-in on the same gate a hundred feet closer. He takes the momentum of the previous shot and makes it literal in the answer shot. Very good way to get the story started and also show us just how important Wayne's character is as he rides back to the fort. Johnson is still Tyree, Big Victor is still Quincannon, and though Wayne's name is Yorke with an 'e' this time around, but he's playing the same decent man. He salutes the "Indian scouts" along with the rest of the regiment. Wayne's posture has calcified now. He's the Wayne of legend. The inimitable stance, the walk, the posture, he risked a lot on *She Wore A Yellow Ribbon*, got no reward, and was done risking. Now he'd just be John Wayne as everyone wanted him to be. "This coffee isn't as good as it used to be..." He muses to Naish, who's playing his native Irish for the first and last time, after a long time away from the fort. No, but it's still pretty good.

Jarman plays Wayne's estranged son, a recent Westpoint scrub coming to see his dad for the first time in more than a decade (Ford *hated* his own son in reality; Wayne was nicer to his boy, who starts showing up in Ford films with big parts soon). Ford introduces him cannily, in a roll call. McLaglen knows *Quiet Man* is on the horizon and is leaning into the brogue as he calls out the names of the new recruits. When Jarman responds to the roll, his voice is the only one with reverb. Wayne hears it like it's a gunshot and walks out on a meeting with eyepatch-clad Peter Ortiz to see the young man for himself. They're going to learn to love each other, especially once wife and mother Maureen O'Hara shows up. Wayne, for instance, is startled by the sight of his boy riding on two horses "like them ancient romans." Ben Johnson does it magnificently of course, and if Ford doesn't shoot it particularly well, you can't dent the spectacle. You just don't see something like that every day. Fred Kennedy makes fun of Wayne in front of Jarman, so they settle it with their fists. Wayne gains a little respect for his boy when he won't squeal on his opponent and McLaglen gets the last laugh when he finally socks Kennedy so good he falls out of the frame. McLaglen looks like King Kong here and he's broad enough for a silent film, eyes slowly shifting in his muppet head. He and Grant Withers, who plays a sheriff looking to arrest Ben Johnson, would die in 1959.

O'Hara and Wayne's reunion is beautiful, both have a shaky way with their voice and she seems like she might break down. O'Hara is the second coming of Katherine Hepburn; gorgeous and garrulous, red headed even in black and white. You can't hear young O'Hara without hearing old O'Hara in interviews later in life, waxing rhapsodic about the boys she tolerated as a starlet. "Number one you're a fine figure of a woman!" She was one of a small handful of golden age stars who lived long enough to become an interview subject for a hundred different Hollywood topics. Wayne meanwhile looks almost like a threat sitting across from her blowing cigar smoke out of the corner of his mouth, looking her over with erotic regret at dinner before the regimental singers, Roy Rogers old band, show up. I'm now starting to see where Walter Hill got his musical sensibility. The film's tenderness is the one thing Ford and co. didn't half-ass. The less said about its appalling treatment of the villainous tribes the better. It's nightmarish, fascistic stuff. You believe that these characters, these actors, care for each other, and Ford keeps a hushed and reverent sky of silence and longing over everything. Soon all could be well. Soon they could be allowed to be who they are, to love without fear, to be home once and for all.

### Wagon Master (1950)

Lindsay Anderson called it avant-garde, Bogdanovich called it Ford's masterpiece. It may never unseat *The Searchers* in the public definition of a Ford film but, per Dennis Lim, "This most leisurely and lyrical of westerns," ought to be what people think of when they think "John Ford." It opens with a bit of canny silent movie storytelling, with a wanted poster over the face of James Arness, one of the Clegg gang wanted for murder. Charles Kemper is their leader and he's so voluptuous in his operation of the criminal enterprise that he seems both disappointed and impatient with the idea he has to kill the bank teller who shoots at them. The film's treatment of violence is its most frequently noted feature other than its musicality. Tag Gallagher notes that the Mormons in the film, who Harry Carey Jr. and Ben Johnson must protect across potentially hostile territory, won't raise a hand in violence but have little trouble profiting from the fellows who will stoop to violence no matter how much it sickens them to do so. Ford was back from World War 2 but on his way to Korea. He was getting callous to the sight of violence. His Korean film is some of his most mean-spirited filmmaking (he had been accused of cavorting with Hollywood Reds and they threatened not to let him back into his old photographic unit, so his work during the war is especially bloodthirsty). The mirror image of *Wagon Master*, nearly his most gentle. Like *Four Sons* and *Pilgrimage*, this tries to make some accounting of the way violence blackens the soul. The war, so to speak, was out there. What happens when it refuses to stay out there.

Ford's Mormons don't want to use violence anymore than young cowhands Johnson and Carey; they're really Quakers but they weren't othered enough for Ford. Mormons were a weird enough species that Ward Bond could deliver a "I bet you think we're all crazy!" speech up front, demystifying them for the audience. Of course nothing he says is true, either. Real Mormons were famously violent. There were years in the South West where you couldn't hit a town whose sands hadn't soaked up Mormon blood from this or that family feud (read *Prophet of Blood* if you can track down a copy). But there was just no way Ford was ever going to make a movie glorifying Quakers, not so soon after a war and so soon before another one. Wyler would at the end of the decade in *The Friendly Persuasion*, and later Charles B. Pierce would make the best of the Quaker movies, *The Winds of Autumn* and your author would try the same thing with *Eyam* in 2012.

Bert Glennon is back after a decade away from Ford, and his images of the wagon train are as loud and sweet as any of the songs that make the montages of movement. A scene of Johnson happening upon the drying out Joanna Dru and her wagon train of performers is pure Bresson. She wants a cigarette, he lights her one in close-up, it almost burns his hand and she throws the cigarette away. She wants a drink, he kicks a blanket to the side and reveals a bottle, she smells it and throws it away. Sin and temptation are the villains as much as the gun-toting Cleggs. "Hell ain't cussin', it's geography!" snaps Carey at handsome Chuck Hayward. The ideas here are whose norms get to make civilization. Tellingly the first crime the Cleggs commit is to stop the singing and dancing when they get to the camp in the middle of the night; you can kill who you must but never ever interrupt a hootenanny, as Homer Simpson tells us. The zealots, the crooks, the laborers, or the theatrical? Ford's own personal moral DNA split into quadrants. You need them all to make one artist.

The film is marvelous for a laundry list of reasons but I think my favourite is the way it makes modernism out of tradition, like Joanne Dru vanishing into a thicket to bathe or a drunken doctor lying in a bed with ornate headboard next to the wagon train; the erotic promise suddenly alive and staring back at you in the everyday. There's singing and dancing and brawling, but every so often Glennon and Ford put the camera a hundred yards from the wagon train and let their song echo over canyons and mesas, filling the land with sound that doesn't fully make it to our ears except as a whisper. Music is like the sun. Without saying it, Ford says there is no life without it. You need it to make a new life. Ford wasn't making this with stars (just the usual gaggle of friends - Bond, Johnson, Carey, Alan Mobraw, Jane Darwell, Hank Worden, Mickey Simpson, and Frank McGrath) so he could just do what pleased him, as William Wellman did in the equally stunning wagon train movie *Westward The Women* (based on a story that also served as the basis for great Hugo Fregonese pictures), also about the creation of community through joined value systems. A robbery is expressed through motionless tableaux, a living painting. Glennon's camera follows Dru as she runs back to the safety of her theatre company, smoking a cigarette as she leaves Johnson and the promise of domesticity, like she's just slept with him. It's one of the more suggestive things in Ford. The Navajo and the Mormons agree on justice when one of the Cleggs tries to force himself on a native woman. People stand around scenes of motion like statuary, like the topiary in *Last Year in Marienbad*. Each still close-up moves at the speed of light. A gunfight is told in Eisensteinian futurist fragments. When it's done Johnson throws his gun into the dust. Violence may keep civilization but it doesn't make it. As he aged Ford would remember that.

## This is Korea! (1951)

Like the imminent *What Price Glory*, the opening hints at a kind of avant-garde tendency Ford infrequently nourished within himself. There's a solid minute of context-free combat. Soldiers feeding loud machine guns by hand, planes dropping bombs, great destroyers firing on land, a house going up after a bomb is dropped. It's wild and powerful to take in, even more so because it's just some stuff. There's a little of Welles' modernism in opening things this way. The Korean War was shorter than the second world war by a considerable margin and Ford was only over there for a short while working the documentary crews like he did in the last war. He only made two films about Korea, one of them almost a decade later when communism was ramping up again in South East Asia and America was starting to hear that the French were having trouble with the insurgency down there. There would be no third war for Ford, not really. His last film, which went uncredited for most of my life, would be a tribute to a Korean War general named Chesty Puller (featured here, looking absolutely deranged. His line, dubbed in afterwards. "Put some mo' FIRE down on those people" really drives home how completely ludicrous this war was) released after America had left Saigon. By then the country's attitude about servicemen had split completely. Ford's beloved Navy was under a cloud like every other branch of the service. It didn't help, I'm sure, that younger directors were making anti-Vietnam westerns left and right.

John Ireland, Alan Dwan, Ward Bond, and Irving Pichel split voiceover narration duties between them, each sounding a different degree of drunk. Ford starts the narrative by showing beatific Korea before "the red hand of Communism" messed things up. We're told these Koreans were homeless and hungry until we fed them...which again makes me wonder if anyone nearby had ever looked up "communism" in the dictionary. Ford's trying to turn Korea's story into *The Hurricane*. That doesn't quite work (Ford evidently forgot who the villain was in that film...), but the footage of Korea is pretty enough. The Americans celebrate Christmas in the first five minutes. Then it's combat for the next 10. "You could light your cigarette on that gun barrel...An Enemy Shell! DUCK!!!" says John Ireland (I think). I'm suddenly seized by flashbacks to Robb Webb narrating with *Fishing With John*. "When it comes to the shark, man is on his menu. It's a wonderful world we live in."

They name check the hospital corps here, which reminds me that somewhere nearby Bob Hope was doing USO shows with a young Larry Gelbart in tow writing jokes for him, taking notes for what would eventually become *M*A*S*H*. We follow an orphaned boy as he's dropped off at a nunnery, which is sickening for a host of reasons. "Little Babe Ruth DiMaggio," they call him, as a soldier pats his head just a little too hard for my comfort. Ford must have been mentally writing *7 Women* as he filmed. Sirk's *Battle Hymn* also takes place in this milieu, in a much less grotesque fashion. Ireland gets a real froth going describing the Americans literally taking a flamethrower to the Koreans. "Cook 'em out!" Sean Gilman wrote about this film's politics being given the negative image treatment by Dante Lam, Tsui Hark, and Chen Kaige with 2021's *The Battle of Lake Changin* and its sequel and watching this it's kind of a wonder we aren't hearing about retaliation for this thing sooner. It's pretty ghastly. Every few seconds there's a reasonable chance you're seeing two or three dozen people die. "What's it all about? You tell us!" Well...Mr. Narrator, maybe if you don't know what you're fighting for, then you shouldn't be fighting?

**The Quiet Man (1952)**

Republic Pictures was a B studio owned by Brooklyn-born maven Herbert J. Yates. Yates had risen quickly through the ranks of the American Tobacco Company and retired at 30 with enough money to own a studio that at its height offered credible competition to the majors, though it was never considered a prestige outfit. It was like a forerunner of Annapurna, in that directors who'd had poor luck being advertised by majors could look to them for few-strings attached budgets. They started in the mid 30s after Yates bought up some poverty row studios (including probably the most famous of the genus, Monogram pictures, the studio that kept Bela Lugosi's heat on in the 1940s) and a film development lab (and invested in 20th Century Fox for good measure). Yates didn't "get" art, so locked horns with the men trying to make it until they just stopped bothering. By the late 40s they were known for making eccentric competition to the majors, movies like Alan Dwan's *Sands of Iwo Jima*, James Edward Grant's *The Angel and The Badman*, and Edward Ludwig's *Wake of the Red Witch*, all three starring John Wayne. The late 1940s and 1950s saw them flirt most heavily with contender-status, funding Orson Welles' *Macbeth*, Nicholas Ray's *Johnny Guitar*, Frank Borzage's *Moonrise* and several films by John Ford, including the film that got Ford his final directing Oscar, *The Quiet Man*, a movie Yates almost ruined by arguing with Ford every step of the way. Their moment in the sun was the beginning of the end for the little studio; by the late 50s they were making nothing but bad genre films. No one would ever breathe the word "Oscar" and "Republic Pictures" ever again.

Ford traded money and better sets for complete freedom with the material. John Wayne thought he lost the wager on that score, that the sets looked like shit, but I'm guessing he wasn't complaining when his coach won his Oscar. This was an important one to Ford, he got his older brother in a prime spot in the cast list up front for the first time, he shot in his ancestral home where his parents had fled before his birth, and it's absent the major prejudices that so defined most of American genre films. The only thing suspicious enough to get anyone's hackles up in *Quiet Man* is that Wayne plays an American and he wants to marry an ornery man's sister. Big Victor McGlaglen is Wayne's rival, his sparring partner, and even though he loves Maureen O'Hara, it's *Vic* needs seducing.

If the film's flabbergasting visual beauty (to say nothing of the thickly laid local color) has, not for the first time, something of Walt Disney about it, Winton C. Hoch spent a decade filming travelogues before Ford snapped him up for the big leagues. With Hoch filming it like he was trying to convince tourists to move in and Ford just so happy to be home, *The Quiet Man* is a movie that threatens to be too beautiful every couple of minutes, but if you can get over that, there's even a little dramatic tension almost worth getting knotted up about. Wayne wants to buy a house that Big Victor has his heart set on, and tension gets worse when he wants to marry his sister, too. This turns into a war of words and petty deeds, with all the village taking part. Irish drama is reborn in its image (and not just). Wayne is, it must be said, a little lost in some of his close-ups, not knowing what to do with a role that's mostly him looking at profound beauty. I don't think Wayne was the kind of guy who got why things were beautiful. Certainly there aren't multitudes of quotes where he's rhapsodically recounting the Matisses he's seen. So he chafes a little at the idea of a movie without much plot, but he's still a joy to behold 80% of the time. The posture is great in a grey suit (though the bowler hat makes him look an early incarnation of Elmer Fudd), and heaven knows he can muster passion when he needs. The film's cartoonish sexism can't really offend anymore (says a male writer), it's too preposterous to resemble anything like reality, just as we know Ireland doesn't *really* look like that.

The falseness of the sets makes it feel even more like a gentle fable, especially during the love scenes. A healthy sense of theatricality is needed as well, or it helps, with the central conceit of Wayne and O'Hara's love life as drama for the whole village to take part in and observe. Their love life is everyone's business. McLaglen trots out in front of the whole town to announce he's gonna let Wayne court his sister. It's in the safety of the set, of Ford's home away from home (he was never truly an Irish citizen, spent too much time away from her), where love can flourish. In Ireland, in the square and on the fields it's all theatre. On a set it's cinema and it's love. O'Hara and Wayne gripping each other, soaked to the bone and silent, Ford had never let lovers linger so. A minute of silence, of basking in their feeling. Mocking them are the flashbacks to Wayne's last knockout, shot in a 30s style that was never quite Ford's. Scorsese takes it for *Raging Bull*, so seductive and wanton is it. That sickly spotlight, the faces staring at us in either horror or casual sadism. Wayne has seen what life looks like when you believe you're this close to having it all. So now he wants nothing. More veiled autobiography? Maybe, but then Ford didn't want to stop making pictures. When he did, he died. He was about to start saying goodbye to everything he'd loved.

**What Price Glory (1952)**

Ford returned from Korea in time to make another service comedy to help with the weirdness of the public face of the war (tellingly, as always happens with unpopular wars, the war about which he chose to make his comeback vehicle was not the one we were then losing). Supposedly Ford had done second unit work on a Raoul Walsh comedy in 1926 of the same title, based on a play by James T. O'Donohoe and Laurence Stallings. The film received a musical sequel in 1929 (presumably absent original stars Victor McLaglen and Edmund Lowe swearing at each other - something about which outraged lip-reading audience members wrote to the studio to complain, which is funnier than anything in the play. You literally have to squint to get mad) and then three sequels all starring the original leads. Ford directed the play in 1949 in Los Angeles during a ten second break he had between movies and so finally committed to making his own version. The only inexplicable thing is that Victor McLaglen isn't in this one.

It sure begins beautifully; against a swampy matte backdrop (gorgeous; right out of *Fantasia*) a faint trumpet and chorus of "Glory Glory Hallelujah" echoes on the breeze as battered doughboys return from a skirmish. Then...for some reason, Ford starts the credits over a chipper and insistent bit of Alfred Newman's score over bright technicolor blue and the opening credits. From the saddest thing Ford had filmed in an age to the happiest and most resolute. It feels like we're watching the film be re-edited in real time. At times this feels like the movie Kubrick was un-making when directing *Paths of Glory* five years later, which elides all the fun and romance and honor. The scene of a woman bawdily singing in a tavern is answered in that film's grim final scene.

Dan Dailey's back from *When Willie Comes Marching Home* and James Cagney makes his first appearance for Ford. They're nemeses. When first they meet they strip off their coats, draw a chalk line on the floor, and start ~~kissing~~ punching each other, picking up a fight where they left off like Conrad's Duellists. Corinne Calvet is back playing the exact same part as in *Willie*, too, the randy French chanteuse. She wants to marry Cagney but he's already married. Ford either had a thing for French girls or a thing for Corrine Calvet, because he didn't usually film women like this. Gene Tierney's the exception, but she always is! Marisa Pavan makes her debut here with a small role as a French villager and is wholesome beauty itself. She was Pier Angeli's twin and married to Jean-Pierre Aumont twice, and he'd already been married twice before then once to Maria Montez, so that guy must have been the freakiest and most magnetic man alive. He was later in *Castle Keep*, which this threatens to become when Dailey and Cagney return from the front and don't want to leave.

Cagney's really good in this, never tipping his hand that he's in a comedy. The funniest stuff is all Ford and the cast. Cagney demands to get clean by having his adjutant slap him with a wet towel so hard it starts to hurt. Cagney tells his unit not to play cards with Dailey and there is exactly one half a second of laughter from them and then silence and then Cagney continues. Cagney goes to Paris for a week and Calvet immediately starts fucking Dailey. Her dad, Cognac Pete (yeah, I know. For real - Henri Letondal plays him. Presumably Le Mask sang about him in the 90s), wants him out because Cagney's still paying for the room. Dailey doesn't mind that he's being swindled but he's not about to start meeting Calvet in alley ways. He starts to mind when Pete complains to HQ that his daughter's virtue is being sullied so Cagney demands they get married just to spite his old rival.

Robert Wagner, impossibly young in only his sixth role, thirty years before allegedly killing Natalie Wood, romances Pavan - they sing together. It's precious. William Demarest is also back from *Willie*, having conclusively shed his partnership with Preston Sturges (who was on death's door and making the similarly pitched *The French They Are a Funny Race* around then), with whom he was funniest on screen and whom the dyspeptic actor did not understand in the slightest. Presumably Ford was a little more serious-minded. Demarest gets one of the biggest laughs in the film. When he drives Cagney back to the village after their Parisian meeting, one of the young soldiers asks if he got tattooed while he was in the city. Demarest just stands looking at him in total silence for about five seconds. Ford's comedies from this era had the benefit of not being particularly madcap, which means that actors like Cagney and Demarest could be funny by being themselves. "Omit the poetry!" says Cagney. Ford agrees. It's just business. Dense plotting, good physical bits, musical numbers galore, stirring combat footage, and the muted technicolor makes everything unusually pretty. It really works. James Cagney saying "Folies Bergère" perfectly alone really ought to raise this film's profile. But then there's the really weird stuff. Wagner sees an angel. A doorway leads right into the red lights of hell as Dailey faces down death. It really does have everything.

PART 7

# LATE STYLE, THE BEGINNING OF THE END

1953-1959

With *The Sun Shines Bright* we have the first conscious re-hashing of an old scenario for some other reason than it fits the needs of himself and his cast. Doing *3 Godfathers* again with Harry Carey, Jr. or Dobe as Ford called him, and a newly great Wayne, was a victory lap, yes, but it made good sense. Adding another entry into his Judge Priest saga nearly twenty years after original star and friend Will Rogers had died was a deliberate look back, a nostalgic bit of self-mythologizing. It gets worse as you dig into it (also looked upon with nostalgic fervor: the confederacy) but it's proof that Ford was just about done inventing and was going to start taking stock. He would still try new things (he'd shoot in 3D as a lark on the Wayne-starring *Hondo*, he'd direct for TV, he'd make one of the great cinemascope movies in *The Long Gray Line*) but his movies were about to become revisions of the old texts. Monument Valley horse operas, movies about old paint sages dispensing political wisdom, lovers in far flung places, Irish folk stories and fiery polemics alike, and a movie about his one-time screenwriter Frank "Spig" Wead. He was certainly right to feel a little valedictory, he had survived two wars, bad reviews, and won many Oscars and made millions, but it becomes a little dispiriting that he'd stop really trying to invent cinema anew like he used to. Some of these movies are among his best (five or six career highs by my count) and some of them are his most troubling and uninspired. By now it's fair to say there was no other way it could have happened.

## The Sun Shines Bright (1953)

Jonathan Rosenbaum compares *The Sun Shines Bright* to Carl Theodor Dreyer's *Gertrud*, by showing that they're ultimately about people taking leave of a time and place with some finality, with the world moving past outside their front door. There is, also, though he doesn't get into this quite as much, a sense of experimentation in a hermetically sealed environment. Ford hadn't experimented the way Dreyer had been allowed to experiment. Imagining Ford making something like *Vampyr* is enticing indeed, though you could argue he got close a few times (*The Black Watch* is probably the closest and there's plenty of coherent plot in there), but the point is Dreyer went from melodrama to pure cinematic expressionism into a kind of rarefied gestural purgatory, a place of purposeful abstraction and perfectly manicured marble surfaces, where emotion escapes like a fleeting shadow falling across the faces of broken men and women. Ford was too steadfast a melodramatist to ever give in completely to the kind of experimentation Dreyer attempted, but there's no denying that in the 1950s, he was rangier than he'd been since the early days of talking pictures. Even the opening with its white on black credits recalls the opening of Welles' *Citizen Kane*, and the sound stages used for the bulk of the action allow for the human voice to come across like a bird song through the artificial stillness. Rosenbaum surmises that this became Ford's favourite film of his (though frankly Ford said that about 12 or so of the things) because it was like he was writing his own eulogy (like Peckinpah would later in the unfunny *Ballad of Cable Hogue*); the man everybody could learn from. If so, Ford's ambitions are curiously less empathetic than most of his best work, but then there is something essential about admitting that no version of America will be absent prejudice in need of correction.

Tough to put one name to the film's box office failure but it killed Argosy stone dead before the company had had a decade and a half of freedom. Maybe it was the return of Stepin Fetchit. Maybe it was having Charles Winninger playing the character of Judge Priest that Will Rogers had originated. Maybe it was the lack of stars. Maybe it was Ford's truly impossible racial potboiler plot. What I can say is that Alejandro G. Iñárritu apparently watched it on repeat as a child and it made him want to be a director and no movie that did *that* can be called a success, even if this movie didn't have regressive nostalgia baked into it like a dead rat in a cake. Priest is anti-racist, sure, but he is so for 1905, which isn't quite the same thing as progressivism as we recognize it now...or would have in 1955...or frankly, 1905. The film loves its black characters but it makes them dance for the amusement of the whites all the same, which is the kind of terrible, violent love that's been mistaken for equality since the Civil War. It's no love at all. And all things considered it is still an old white Confederate judge who decides good and bad here. Ford believed someone like Priest (and himself, by extension, if we take Rosenbaum at his word) was up to the task. By the end of the film, all of the town comes out in a massive parade (the kind that would stomp through *Gertrude* a decade later) to concur. Would be nice if life were always so tidy, don't you think?

Ford wasn't ever really a modernist, but there are modernist ideas and theories put forth across the immaculate frames of its busily idyllic town square, and that isn't just in considered camera movements (though, goddamn, if you could cut out all the dialogue and plot and a handful of characters this is a perfect movie). Ford was at a point in history when he could afford to ask questions about which parts of the past we were going to keep around when the future arrived (as it happened, many people have justifiably asked whether Ford should be brought with us in that bright future, which I have to assume he would have suspected). Priest's politics are boiled down to his care for the lowliest in town (whether that's the black defendants he stands up for while calling them "boy," or the sex worker whose funeral he attends in defiance of propriety during an election) and for his highfalutin ideas about everybody getting along. He goes to a Union soldiers' meeting to talk about sharing flags with his Confederates across town and mentions that he really does love what the United States had become because it means someone who fought against the people of this town could now preside over their legal affairs. And in fairness to this deeply weird film, that really was what counted for forward-thinking at the time. What's perhaps encouraging is that Ford does seem to dimly understand that no confederate should be deciding the laws for a free United States. He puts Priest out to pasture (like he would Ethan Edwards in *The Searchers*) but America didn't. We liked our hanging judges and sons of liberty filibusterers and still do. America will never retire a senator so long as he can spray the word "no" at a vote for protecting judges while striking down measures guaranteeing bodily autonomy. Maybe few saw it in 1905, but by 1955 the wind was blowing backwards to the time of Judge Priest. Throwing the "good confederate" a parade may have sealed him in a tomb for all time for Ford, but we ripped the doors off the mausoleum the second he was done. America gives our enemies the freedom to decide what freedom means. Ford grappled with this, and I think it's safe to say he lost. Against all odds he wasn't hard-hearted enough to see the worst of the future, even as he looked back to an ugly past. His life was the silent parade behind a casket. Wars came and went, mores changed, America went from darkness into still more darkness.

### Mogambo (1953)

John Ford taking Sam Zimbalist up on his offer to remake Victor Fleming's *Red Dust* does catch one off guard but once you see the end result it does make a kind of sense. Kenya is just a stand-in for a frontier fort, except without all the uniforms around Ford could get a little more intimate, a little more down-and-dirty, and I don't just mean the scene where elephants knock Ava Gardner into the mud. Still when you think jungle adventure picture, you don't think John Ford (which is why Tag Gallagher put a behind-the-scenes still from its production on the cover of his book – it surprises you to see Ford directing a line of Kenyans). Jungle movies were all the rage then. The B movie Eds, Cahn and Wood, Jr., were churning out exotic nightmares at a rapid clip, RKO had been in the business of gorilla pictures since head honcho Merian Cooper had sent King Kong up the Empire State Building and they were still going strong in the 50s. Tarzan movies were still popular, though they traded Johnny Weissmuller for Lex Barker when the former started playing Jungle Jim. Byron Haskin couldn't stop making the things. Ford's friend Ben Johnson had wrangled Mighty Joe Young in 1949. Arch Oboler, the man who hated TV (which he dubbed The Twonky in a very odd picture also released in '53) with a passion unlike any other, was out to give audiences thrills they simply couldn't get on the idiot box. He made the first wide released 3D movie, *Bwana Devil*, and it had lions jumping out of the screen and into your lap. Every American couldn't just go on safari. That's what the movies were for. Ford deciding to make one of them was at once a chance to get quit of his usual surroundings but also to see what the rest of Hollywood was doing while he was busy being John Ford.

Naturally it wasn't smooth sailing, but with Ford when was it? The Mau Mau tribe were rising up against the English settlers and so English hunters were placed on set in Kenya for extra protection. Problem was Ford was in a blood feud with one of the English, who of course had no idea. Ford and Gable hated each other; you can't have two alpha male drunks on one set and ultimately the one with the camera has to win. The Mau Mau supposedly put a hit on Gable, maybe because Ford paid them to, maybe because they heard he was sleeping with Grace Kelly and were mad they had to picture it. The shoot only lasted a few weeks and all the indoor stuff was shot safely back in studios, a continent away from trouble. Cinematographer Robert Surteees would later sociopathically describe running over local kids in their cars like it was nothing; just another little on-set snafu like the time Ward Bond unplugged the camera one day on *The Searchers* to power his electric razor just as they were about to do a take. Ford treats the Kenyans kindly enough, though they don't have anything like inner lives. Unsurprisingly this came out the same year as *The Sun Shines Bright*, though I don't have to watch *Mogambo* through my fingers. Indeed, I can scarcely pull myself away from it. The visual storytelling is exquisite. A few cuts, a dolly movement, and we have the world. Spielberg steals a goat trap set for an apex predator for *Jurassic Park*, another tale of tourists learning an important lesson. Ava Gardner shows up at Gable's animal export business like a refugee from Sodom and Gomorrah. He seems bummed to see a naked Ava Gardner in his shower (Ford gives her tight curls to de-feminize her, probably mad that the studio wouldn't let him cast his beloved Maureen O'Hara), but they eventually make real nice. Gardner struts around without a bra and her purred line readings could melt the change in your pocket.

That stops when Grace Kelly and boyish, sexless husband Donald Sinden arrive. Kelly's also a little neutered (Ford eventually makes this literal, starting a garish conversation about female circumcision that will be concluded in John Guillerman's *Shaft in Africa*), with her long arms and flowing button-down shirts, though of course Gable is smitten instantly, so he sends Gardner back to civilization with a boat load of animals (get it?). Unfortunately, it sinks so she's back by nightfall. Gable takes her back in on condition that she not be hussy in front of the lady. Chastened and spitting mad, she repairs to her room and tosses a snake out of her bed ("Oh get out of here, Joe!") then almost smashes a bottle in anger before deciding sensibly that she'd rather just drink the liquor out of it. Who needs the Bible? This is quicker. Kelly finally does come alive when Gable saves her from a leopard he was trying to capture. He has to kill it instead, and he's so mad he rips Kelly's scarf off her head and ties it around her neck. She looks at him as if sex has hit her like a high fever, uncertain whether to cry, scream, laugh, vomit, or jump the old drunk like a broken-down car. *Hatari!*, Howard Hawks' answer to this, wasn't nearly so coiled. Gardner needles Kelly and Gable both in front of cluelessly cuckolded Sinden and Gable looks at her, ruddy faced and hammered, with an expression that says "I may pass out." Gable had played the role in the original film, but that was 30 years prior. He was much closer to death than his glory days, but that kind of works in spite of itself. Somehow Ford outlived him.

The blocking here is some of his best. The camera moves like a breeze across the Kenyan planes. If they ever restore this the colors will put out your eye. The atmosphere is hushed and distant, exactly my vibe. Albert Lewin and *Apocalypse Now* perfect it. Our lusty heroes staring at each other through mosquito netting and bamboo blinds, the sun in perpetual purple free fall. The pinks and greens of Kelly and Gardner's wardrobe and vanity set, the reds on the Kenyan's clothes, they all stand apart from the oranges and browns of the landscape. It's all designed to make you feel adrift. Kelly and Sinden's first real argument happens in green and grey shadow in their tent. When the film can just glide it's hypnotic, up there with *Wagon Master* (there's even a covered wagon and the usual marches down the Z axis). The invention of a Hollywood paradise, a place real but not real; isn't that why we watch movies? To go someplace better than here? Somewhere far away? Somewhere hidden? Somewhere they'll never find you? By the end of the film Gable has proven himself worthy of the part, drunkenly admonishing Gardner for worrying so much just because he's bleeding from a gunshot. Their bastard camaraderie is enormously moving.

**The Long Gray Line (1955)**

There's a breed of Ford appreciators who call this his best. Not hard to see why, it's basically an autobiography of the aging director, even though it's based on the life of Marty Maher, the man who worked his way up from pre-WWI dishwasher at West Point to beloved fixture and athletic trainer (Ford loved a boxer). It's one of Ford's great works of modernism - Michael Cimino steals the opening for *Heaven's Gate*; hilariously all the symmetrical images of the cadets in their greys can't help but look like footage of Mao's China, which I'm sure the publicly commie-hating Ford didn't intend - and it's a movie about watching the best of us die. Ford was doing that every day in the 50s. Tyrone Power's young co-star Robert Francis died right after filming this at age 25, but most of Ford's old gang was dying left and right. Harry Carey, Robert Homans, Brandon Hurst, J. Farrell MacDonald, Donald Meek, Warren Hymer, and his brother Francis were long gone and the rest of the decade would take another dozen of his best guys. Twilight was setting. He had a decade of good movies left in him, then six lonely years of miserable retirement when friends, eager journalists, and old lovers would visit fleetingly, reminding him what he'd lost.

Ty Power is the goofy Maher, who has to prove himself in the kitchen before he can make his way in the social order and official hierarchy of the famous military school. He stands up for the guys who mean something to him and takes many a beating to do so. The comedy is broad, but when it works it is sublime. Maureen O'Hara first meets Power in a hallway and they're both paralyzed by different things, a little Rene Clair-style gag of off-kilter rhythm. He gets knocked sideways and lands on his ass just in time to see O'Hara leave, making the hurt even worse. O'Hara doesn't speak for her first twenty minutes of screentime. She determinedly ices a cake while Power professes his love for her. The shot of Power and O'Hara finally speaking is the missing link between silent comedy and the new wave. John Boorman's *Zardoz* re-uses a gag from Buster Keaton's *College*, but the shot in the later film is unthinkable without the symmetry and unmatched eye-line of the two actors here. You can see this kind of stylized gag in a lot of Jerry Lewis, and Power frequently cuts as deliberately absurd a figure, as when he dons his red swimming clothes. And this is just one scene in a 2 hour and change domestic epic. This is his Jacques Tati film; *Playtime* before *Playtime*.

This was Ford's first film in 2.55 : 1, an ultra-wide aspect ratio, and though he uses the wider frame for things like the choir singing the opening medley (heavenly stuff), mostly what he does is expand the domestic melodrama. The cluttered kitchens and parlors look very cozy indeed with all that added detail. Most of the guys Ford came up with resisted. Fritz Lang famously said it was only good for filming "snakes and funerals;" Ford said it looked like a tennis court. Howard Hawks, William Wyler, and Raoul Walsh all tried it at the same time as Ford, though Ford went back down to 1.85 for *The Searchers*, and got as far back as 1.66 (all this to say, he changed, but he wasn't happy about it). It was only his last film, *7 Women*, that got the full 2.55 : 1 screen after this (though the version that's available is in awful shape so you can't tell anyway) and the aborted Mister Roberts. Maybe he knew it would be his last. Unlike *Mister Roberts* and *7 Women, The Long Gray Line* feels like the work of a sprite-ly fellow, a guy who knew exactly how to experiment, who could move around the set with the bounce in his step Power carries into his old age in the part (Power only lived another three years). There's no combat here, just the years passing through Martin Maher's home, the songs change, the faces change, but Marty stays the optimistic and concerned mentor, husband, and friend. Its catalogue of football matches and dinners shouldn't feel so enormous, so all encompassing, so much like Ford captured every grain of sand in the hourglass, but he has. When this comedy changes gears at the scene of O'Hara going into labor and its complications, it knocks the wind out of you. These silly stubborn people, as pure to Ford as were the Joads, are good and decent and you do want them to find beautiful things in their lives. This is Ford's *Meet Me In St. Louis*. His *Mrs. Miniver*. His *Little Women*. Michael Powell would try to make a military melodrama like this more than once and never quite got this good. Ford just...got it all right.

**Mister Roberts (1955, John Ford, Mervyn LeRoy, Ward Bond, & Joshua Logan)**

John Ford had had it. No one is exactly sure what about this particular picture brought out his worst, especially because in the lead up, he did everything in his power to make it happen. He pulled some strings with a reluctant US Navy to secure their participation and approval. He cast Henry Fonda in a role meant for a much younger man, then staffed the film with the likes of William Powell, Ward Bond, and James Cagney to make him look like he was a junior officer, especially compared to the rest of the cast (Jack Lemmon, Harry Carey Jr, Nick Adams, and Robert Roark among them). He was in Hawaii, he had a huge budget, he was making a movie on a boat; he should have been in hog heaven. Then the shoot started. He took a swing at Henry Fonda, got drunker than he'd ever been before, and got pulled off the film before it was finished. Ward Bond had to help him direct some of it because he was too drunk to function. Mervyn LeRoy was flown in to finish it and Josh Logan, who'd directed the show on Broadway and was suddenly an in-demand director, oversaw reshoots. He would have been neck deep in his own troubled production, *Picnic*, around the same time. William Holden had turned down the lead role in *Mister Roberts* and was currently also very drunk indeed on the set of *Picnic*, so filled with visceral hatred for his inexperienced co-star Kim Novak that the movie almost didn't get finished. *Picnic* made 9 million. *Mister Roberts* made 20.

Ford just doesn't do his best work with theatre. He'd directed his first stage production in 1949 and never looked back. He'd directed stage show movies before - *Hearts of Oak, Thank You* [both lost], *Lightnin', The Brat, The Plough & The Stars, Tobacco Road* - but you can sense the struggle to turn the stage-bound cinematic. He hated it but *The Plough & The Stars* is a riveting, action-packed motion picture, successful because of what it shows, not tells. *Mister Roberts* can't really show anything because nothing happens. Ford fills the frame with criss-crossing boats and strapping shirtless detail when he can but there's a lot of business needs doing in cramped quarters. William Powell retired the second this wrapped. He couldn't keep up with the demand to have whole scenes memorized anymore, and the heat didn't help. He does a good enough job; everybody does. It's just not very interesting. Fonda *hated it*.

Fonda's Roberts wants off a docked tub sitting uselessly in the South Pacific. He's second in command under humorless Cagney, who hates everyone and everything. Every week Fonda sends a letter to Cagney for approval in which he requests a transfer to active duty, and every week Cagney gets madder than a hornet because *he* thinks *Fonda* thinks he's above working on his boat. Meanwhile the crew is always a few seconds from active, frat house rebellion against Cagney, lead by the especially lazy Lemmon, who's trying harder to sleep with Ann Girard, playing the head of a nurse corps on shore. Powell is the ship's doctor. Fonda, looking on with pride at his dopey crew, is almost Ford-esque in stature but then Fonda's *nice* to these guys. Ford wouldn't ever be seen publicly doing anything like that. Mostly this is a movie about guys talking about the stuff they plan to do, then showing the ways in which those things don't happen. Pretty standard stage comedy structure, and every 25 minutes or so there's a laugh. Lemmon drinks dishwater thinking it's soup. Not exactly Molière but appreciated when the alternative is so much more wretchedly sitcom-worthy. We ought to be grateful, I suppose, that this lugubrious light comedy exists - if Ford hadn't crawled out from under it, he might never have made *The Searchers* to prove he still had it.

**Rookie of the Year (1955)**

The last of the partially missing Fords make their appearance as he ducks his head into TV for a few projects. On the production of *The Long Gray Line*, Ford makes a 10-minute ad for War Bonds called *The Red, White & Blue Line* that isn't terribly distinguished, mostly made up of footage from the movie and Donald Crisp making dinner in newly shot segments. Ford shot some scenes for John Wayne's film *The Alamo* and another Wayne picture called *Hondo*, and then there's his first TV production, for Jane Wyman's *Fireside Theatre, Bamboo Cross,* which Tag Gallagher, and Joseph McBride both describe as the low point of Ford's career. It seems to be gone now. Wyman plays one of two nuns in China who are kidnapped by communists who are going to kill them brutally because they're suspected of poisoning Chinese children. Eventually a dupe, a low-born servant who joined up with the party for the wrong reasons, kills his commanding officer and frees the nuns. Sounds pretty grim. McBride describes a hideous and purple screed against communist China, whom Ford had signed a highly public petition to keep out of the United Nations. Perhaps mercifully Ford's second documentary on the Korean war, this time well after the fighting had subsided and America had good and ruined the place, *Korea: Background for Liberty*, is also pretty hard to find.

Ford's turn to TV was big news. The New York Times ran an interview with him and Merian Cooper about their working methods, how these two big picture makers were going to make the change over to the small screen. Ford pretty clearly lays out his disdain for TV (cheap little movies for TV, good and expensive ones for theatres was the ethos) but he was willing to try new things, as *Mogambo* clearly showed. *Rookie of the Year*, made for *Screen Director's Playhouse*, is a little easier to track down, probably because it stars John Wayne. It starts by putting down the medium. A newsroom is crowded around the ticker tape machine in the center of the room as it spits out the news of a Yankee game. This was what TV was to Ford, just a machine spitting out information. If only he'd lived to see the cell phone.

Wayne's in a corner office trying to get a Times writer on the phone, he's got a story that'll get him out of the Emeryville PA paper he's stuck working on and back into the big leagues. The crossover between journalism and baseball clearly tickles Ford. He loved a big easy metaphor; when it's the size of the room you can just move in instead of shooting around it. Wayne discovered that a rookie player with a sledgehammer arm (his boy Patrick, who's going to turn up in *The Searchers* the next year) is the son of a disgraced player on the infamous Black Sox, the team that threw the world series (John Sayles made a Ford-esque study of the team in *Eight Men Out*). The player (Ward Bond, quite good in his single scene) is living under an assumed identity. Such was the disgrace that met men who tampered with America's game. Everything was life or death for Ford except...well, life and death. Vera Miles talks Wayne out of running the story, but she needn't have, the majors call him up anyway; Wayne's going to be covering baseball in Asia for the Times. He throws Bond's lucky ball through the window of the paper on his way out of town. Economical direction abounds (it's mostly masters, as you'd expect) and it's nice to spend time with Wayne having palpable fun with his character - it's the kind of part he used to play in 30s movies where he had one or two lines. A quick game of catch for Ford and his boys before the big game.

**The Searchers (1956)**

*The Searchers* is about a man's transition from one period of brutal, sleepless doggedness and violence into another. He gives peace about ten seconds of a chance and then hops right back into what he knows best; killing, tracking with only footprints, instinct and the extra sensory powers his hatred gives him. There's no place for Ethan Edwards, and Ford knew his time was up, too. He hitched his wagon to the conservative establishment in Hollywood and he didn't even like their messaging anymore. Walking off of *Mister Roberts* was like saying goodbye to any notion of bravery, of doing the right thing. He didn't know anymore what "right" was. He wouldn't fully abandon the bromides of the military, the church, the Republican party, but he'd never make an uncritical movie about the machinations of all of this ever again (except once, as a favor to Harry Cohn, who was too dead to appreciate it anyway). His final documentary was about his friend Chesty Puller, but like Cohn he'd be dead before it got released. Richard Nixon came to salute him at the AFI. He knew what he looked like on paper, but he'd fight it on celluloid. When *The Searchers* opens with Dorothy Jordan standing in her doorway and the camera follows her out into Monument Valley, revealing that the film isn't in Ford's typical academy ratio but in 1.85 widescreen, it's saying "disabuse yourself of what you think you know. Outside, out here, things are different." Ford would never go back in. His youth was gone. His America, too. It would be wars fought for the "right" reasons, while men with scars and bad dreams just tried to squeeze back into civilian life like it was their dad's ill-fitting suit. America was no country, really. It was purgatory. Ethan Edwards wouldn't be getting into Heaven; he'd wander the wasteland forever.

Before starting this book, I'd seen *The Searchers* more than any other Ford film, I don't think that's uncommon. Seeing it now after having seen, in order, the previous 66 Ford films, *The Searchers* feels even more like a miracle. Ford had obviously been great before but this is like watching Van Gogh sit down and whip up *The Starry Night* for you in his den. The casual brilliance of the fulsome tableaux, the darkness hiding beneath Wayne's avuncular charm, the homey feel of the Edwards' home, Wayne giving up his war medals to a little girl for all they mean to him. Ford introduces Jeffrey Hunter, his penultimate discovery and a great one who never ever got more beautiful than he did under Ford's lights, like he's Peter Pan. He leaps from the saddle, in love with life on the prairie, and then Wayne, unshaven, voice like sand pouring against rusty metal, cuts him down to size. No one will ever be human to a man who's been taught to kill everyone who's different on the inside or outside. I've seen *The Searchers* more times than I can count. It's even better and tougher than I remembered. When Wayne strides into frame in his dungarees and his red leather and suspenders you forget for a minute it's the iconic image of Wayne, that he'll wear them to hell. He wears a black hat, but it doesn't show up right away. He's the villain of the piece, whether or not Ford knows it, but I guess we can be honest and say he does.

Everything in the film is a tug of war between dogs. Ward Bond shows up to deputize Walter Coy but Wayne stops him to take his brother's place. They scrap and Bond nearly threatens to arrest him but looks the other way when Jordan and Wayne share the most tender of goodbyes. Everyone knows everyone a little too well. Wayne will later give her and the rest of his family up as a fact, a hand on his horse and a face about to crack with tears if he'd ever let himself. He knows they're gone. He knows he can't save them. He had them back for a second only, and now he's alone again. He brought hell back with him, this time. Ford shoots the raid like a horror film. The view of the Comanche as inhuman, as worse than demons, is intolerable, unspeakable. A shade or two from how Ruggero Deodato treats animals and rainforest tribes alike in *Cannibal Holocaust*. Filmmakers and theorists will spend the next 70 years dealing with what *The Searchers* has to say. Sergio Leone avoids it. Walter Hill graffities it. Michael Mann rejects it. Peter Jackson takes from it. Gore Verbinski returns it to sender. No one's yet replaced it. Hollywood has done away with the scaffolding and equipment you'd need to do so. If tomorrow an indigenous filmmaker like Sky Hopinka or Elle-Maija Tailfeathers showed up to remake *The Searchers*, no one would know what to do with it. Good, ugly movies go right to streaming and as we speak right-wing no-talents (at best) are trying to take the western back from the revisionists, who've had it since Ford's death. "Don't let the boys waste their lives in vengeance" is the movie's message and no one heeded it because so few understood, and even fewer knew they weren't just talking about violence. The world is bigger than Monument Valley but you wouldn't know it.

The key thing *The Searchers* gave to me as a young moviegoer was the sense of time and distance. The image that matters, the one that stays with me, is of Wayne and Hunter in the snow in their thick winter coats, staring into infinity, the studio skies blue and mournful behind them. Getting lost in a quest away from civilization, into darkness, into nothingness. Chasing your hate to to the ends of the earth. Time just passes. Wayne sees the Jourgensens three minutes after Harry Carey Jr dies, but it's been a year in the movie's timeline. Single-mindedness, ignoring everything but what you think matters, it'll take the life out from under you. My brain internalized it until it was answered by *Apocalypse Now*, another colonialist juggernaut I'll never stop thinking about. What happens when you walk away from everything and for a minute consider that you might never have to go back. Time stands still. No responsibility but to what's always around you, which ain't much. Hunter runs away from Vera Miles to find his last living family member, sure, but also to arrest his boyhood. If he doesn't marry he doesn't have to grow up. Ethan Edwards font of playfulness, buried so far under the misery and prejudice is proof of it. The way he tucks Hunter in while using him as bait, the way he laughs at the man's accidental marriage. It's lasted to today, too. The things boys say when no one else is around, on their headsets, in their dorm rooms. Proof of the right kind of humanity to people who share the same outlook. That safety is away from civilization. It used to be that the idea was civilization was always around the corner. Now maybe it's safer to run away. The world has rules, after all. And has them for a reason. You might stay yourself out there, maybe. You might feel free having no purpose. You might feel free.

Watching *The Searchers* now, which I can still remember seeing for the first time on the big blocky TV in the living room in my grandparent's Jersey shore house, it's not the same movie just as I'm not 10 years old anymore. I have grown to love Ward Bond, the drunken fascist coward. I can't imagine movies without him. And Wayne? The draft dodging little boy trapped in the big bear's body, who maybe wasn't ready to play Nathan Brittles, but bitterness and years at the mercy of John Ford's harassment had more than prepared him to play Ethan Edwards? How do you not love this disgusting bigot? How do you look at the walk, the arm grab, the retreat into pre-sexuality and see the man hiding beneath the bluster? By the time of the playboy interview he was lost, probably, but Wayne was always the big kid trying to impress the rest of the school yard. So here he is! And he doesn't look he's trying to to impress anyone. He'd finally quit his body, flown clear away from himself. Free. My dad and I drove to Monument Valley, the picture I took is on my phone, every time I open it, I see *The Searchers*. History is ugly but art can be beautiful. For the first time in my life I saw John Wayne lift Natalie Wood into his arms, remembering him picking up her sister Lana Wood playing her younger self at the start of this picture, a lifetime ago, I cried. To cry at the *Cannibal Holocaust* of the 50s, for men who wanted us to go back to war every chance we got, for men who didn't feel *anything* for the rest of mankind, for Wayne, who memorized Harry Carey's body language, for men who were dying, for men who are dead. Maybe not my proudest moment, but I have no trouble confessing it. Art was the province of bad boys and bad girls, as Olivier Assayas reminds us, and now it's going, going, gone. I'll never forget driving to Monument Valley with my dad, who taught me about the world, talking about depression, talking about our family, talking about film, reminiscing about the made-for-tv movie *Gargoyles*, shot in barren deserts like Ford's, mentally researching our own projects for the future, a guy and the kid he raised to see the world through movies. He let me pick the music for the drive over; and we talked about how hard life can be, how hard it is to *talk* about how hard life can be. We watched the sun come up over the buttes, mesa, and plateaus, and knew what we owed each other in the shadow of the never ending horizon. He loved the son who had taken his interests to heart, who can still call him and talk about con artists and crime writing and horror movies and westerns, I loved the dad who'd given me everything from life to my political perspective to my zeal for movies. Tough to imagine making that trek without *The Searchers*. Tough to imagine a lot... without *The Searchers*.

## The Wings of Eagles (1957)

"This motion picture is dedicated to the men who brought Air Power to the United States Navy. One such man was Commander Frank "Spig" Wead. The flying records he smashed helped him win the lasting respect of his fellow Navy men. The screenplays he wrote helped him win the lasting respect of his fellow writers in Hollywood." There's Ford once again helpfully defining his political life. What was more important? Respect from the Navy or respect from Hollywood? Wayne plays Ford's old buddy Spig, who wrote *They Were Expendable* at his urging, who has to learn responsibility after weeks of acting like cock of the walk. We meet him taking Kenneth Tobey for a joyride in his baby; a terrible little plane he can't afford. Naturally he crashes it into a tea party pool when Tobey asks him to land on the water. Maureen O'Hara (who plays Wayne's wife) isn't amused. She needs him to take his responsibilities seriously. As for that, he loses a kid barely ten minutes in. Wayne's mission is to convince the Navy that they need to encourage their men to take risks, and Ford seems like he's trying to prove the same thing. His filmmaking is pushed an F stop in every direction, moving from absurd light comedy to terrible tragedy in a breath, the lighting deep and hot as possible to make this movie seem like a series of dreams. It doesn't seem possible, this cockamamy version of full metal comedy.

Wayne's wearing his own hair for once and he looks good! He's 50 here and Wead died in 1947 at the age of 52, he's meant to be about 25 when we meet him...so that doesn't really work, but for Ford's purposes (this is occasionally one of his comedies about overgrown boys that finds its final form in *Donovan's Reef*), he's just fine. His domestic combat with O'Hara isn't as magical as their work in *The Quiet Man*, but O'Hara is radiant - you can't take your eyes off of her. Her anger seethes inside her like a fever. Wayne's Wead keeps disappointing her until he finally sinks so low that he has no choice but to finally become who she needs him to be...and then war breaks out and they never get to try. Ford's playing with fire here; he has a comedy fistfight broken up by comedy cops where everyone winds up in the pool. All fun and games. And then three scenes later Wead breaks his neck. Consequences. Ford trying at last to give his ideal comedic cinema (of drunken barroom brawls and frenemies and silent movie marching) some edge, some gravity. To show you what happens when you go home after being a hero; one of the finest scenes in this very fine film is Wayne coming home to see his daughters, who mistake him for a salesman because they haven't seen him most of their childhoods. O'Hara watching news of her husband's aerial race success on the big screen is like an intrusion of post-modernism into the cozy upholstery – Ford's post-modernism is almost never remarked upon but he was ahead of his time in a dozen ways. This movie seems to be scratching at its boundaries, Ford aware (at age 63) that there was still work to be done, ground to be broke.

Speaking of that - Wayne and O'Hara have sex! They sleep in separate beds and Wayne pays for it with his neck, but they still do it. Wayne smokes a cigarette afterwards and everything. Took him 40 years but he did it. Refreshing, and shockingly not all that odd to imagine Wayne as a sexual being. O'Hara of course couldn't help but be a kind of sexual being - when she smokes a cigarette after Wayne tells her not to visit him in the hospital (in effect that she's on her own with the two girls) it's about the most beautiful sight in the world. Dan Dailey takes over as Wayne's wife after that, back from the other service comedies. He sings to him and feeds him while O'Hara stalks the hospital grounds like a wraith waiting for him to welcome her back into his life, which never happens. Ward Bond plays Ford here, which is kind of touching. Bond looks a million years old, allowing himself to have a little fun at his director/tormentor's expense. The movie does sort of become about the Power of Movies™ but Ford kind of discovers that doesn't interest him half as much as making myths out of everything else (*Liberty Valance* is a few years away). "Writing's just tellin' lies but they wrap it up in fancy paper..." He's better here trying to make use of the widescreen frame than he is telling the story of a movie writer in anything but shorthand. First chance he gets he sends Wayne out of his happy home and back to war and stock footage. It causes a little discomfort watching Wayne, who didn't serve, acting in between footage of real pilots going down. His heart gives out before he gets a chance to be a husband. Visions of Maureen O'Hara dance in his head, in one of Ford's finest sequences - silence, regret, and joy. What he could have just returned to but never felt he'd earned. "Home is the sailor, home from the sea."

**The Rising of the Moon (1957)**

Back in Ireland at last. It had only been 5 years since *The Quiet*

*Man*, of course, but an awful lot had happened since then. He'd made the film that would become synonymous with both his name and the Western, though he had no way of knowing that. He'd won Oscars and almost got run out of town on a rail for his behavior on the set of *Mister Roberts*. He had been brought low and seen incredible highs. I think it's perfectly understandable that he wanted to go back "home." There's even a character here named Feeney, his real last name. It's also equally understandable that this is mostly a low energy comedy. There are a couple of laughs but sometimes he turns the camera on, he lets the actors do shtick, then he turns the camera off. The man holding the camera was Robert Krasker, probably the most sought-after monochrome photographer in Europe after Carol Reed's *The Third Man*, so everything looks stupendous, but Ford was clearly resting his feet a little. Most of the movie takes place in cramped cabins. He cuts more than usual, his framing too rarely rises to poetry, and scenes go on entirely too long.

The movie is a triptych (never a good idea; they're never created equally, except by Kelly Reichardt) narrated by Tyrone Power, the one Hollywood name in the cast. The first one, based on a story by Frank O'Connor, has a man refuse to pay a fine for striking someone, instead resigning himself to jail, to the chagrin of his best friend the police inspector. The second one, based on a play by Martin J. McHugh, is about romantic misunderstandings on a train, complicated by money. The third one, based on a play by Lady Gregory, concerns an escaped fugitive on the eve of his execution. The cast is stacked with Irish talent who only ever made it to California to play freaks and drunks. Jack MacGowran doesn't look young exactly but when you know him from *The Exorcist* he certainly looks different here.

There's an element of kooky ethnography here - a shot of train passengers disembarking and heading for a drink resembles the similarly desperate comedy antics of fellow outsider Michael Powell's Australian comedy *They're a Weird Mob*. You'd think the station bar was heaven on earth...though in fairness it is. Beautiful stuff. He adds dutch tilts to the third and final political segment and I confess it's odd to see those in a Ford film, but why hire Krasker at all if you don't want a Dutch or two. This segment flirts heavily with greatness, but there's a disconnect between the Eisensteinian form and the featherweight tone. For a good 20 minutes every shot is perfect, and a push-in on a cop deciding to let the fugitive get away stops your heart. If only the rest rose to the occasion.

## The Growler Story (1957)

"Dedicated to that Dedicated Woman..." sounds like a Sammy Cahn lyric... "The Navy Wife." Ford's navy short subject starts with a little more consideration than these tend to. His camera's on the dock of a cruiser as it surfaces and men crawl out from her guts and take a look around. It's still shot on cheap stock, but he's got actors playing his seamen, so he could take time with this one. The boys all jump in (they're pre-stripped) and swim off the side of their mighty vessel. His first image of strapping nude sailors in almost three decades. Starting off with welcome flashbacks to *The Blue Eagle* and *Men Without Women* is a good start, let's see if he can stick the landing.

Ken Curtis, Ford's son-in-law, plays a real vet, Howard Gilmore, who died at sea. Ford must have really liked him because in *Wings of Eagles* he's playing a John Carradine-style misshapen clown, but here he's promoted to man of honor and family and duty here. He says goodbye to his family (kisses his young daughter right on the mouth, which I sure didn't love watching) and then heads into the documentary footage Ford collected off of Hawaii. The score sounds like Max Steiner but is likely some industrial copycat. For a minute we're adrift in the momentum of things, of boats leaving port, of bands marching, of people waving; it's almost modernist. Curtis' crew takes down an enemy craft and there's a deeply uncomfortable moment where you realize his actors are reacting to really torpedoed subs with the boyish glee of Archie and Jughead. There are always parts of Ford I can never wrap my head around.

Ward Bond is below deck keeping morale high. Ford films Curtis crawling in and out of the compartments of the ship with real gusto. Someone says "Hell." It's thrilling...! If you don't mind the implication, that is. Curtis' Gilmore quite excitingly gets washed off deck as the ship really sinks below surface with him aboard. Then he utters his famous last words "Take her down," the "Let's roll!" of the 40s. Gut shot and dying, he orders the rest of his guys to let him wash away in the murky blue, to save themselves. The next shot has a packed squad of his boys in angelic, nearly blinding white uniforms as they give his wife his medal of honor. Kids salute him nearby, too. Surely everyone can get behind *this*, right? That's the thing about Vietnam that must have really rubbed Ford (many vets, probably) the wrong way: there weren't any stories about heroism, about people doing the right thing for their men. War was about to get a whole lot more ambiguous than the national narrative could handle. Gilmore's laurels float away to sea in the penultimate shot, and the story of American heroism along with them. Nothing was going to be this easy ever again. Ford, against all odds, decided to do his part there, too.

## Gideon's Day (1958)

The story I always heard was that Ford returned to Ireland to make *The Rising of the Moon*, and stayed to make *Gideon of Scotland Yard* not because he thought it would be good but because he heard Akira Kurosawa was going to be in town and he wanted to meet him. Fun to imagine a time when someone like Ford could just pick a script out of a hat as a pretense to go get a beer with someone he liked, but also despite the film's dogged literalism and crowd-pleasing form, there's a lot here to get lodged in. Freddie Young and Charles Lawton Jr. shoot in color (it was released in black and white in America - I'd love to know why; maybe making it so would make it seem more foreign and respectable as America was primarily shifting to color) and so the film has a beautiful painter's palette of primary shades and Ford shoots in his usual classical style, adapted for the tiny lodgings in London. The effect is rather like if Ford had ever tried to make a Hitchcock movie (though of course the plotting has nothing on Hitch, nor would Ford have intended it that way). I like to think Ford brought Lawton over in his suitcase and Young was waiting for them when they got off the plane already. Together they make a mid-century modernism that Ford almost rejects. Young shot *Mogambo* for Ford, but he also shot *Lawrence of Arabia*, four years later, also featuring Jack Hawkins and Howard Marion-Crawford. Not hard to imagine that the funeral that opens that film isn't for Lawrence at all, but for Ford himself, whose last classic was released that same year. The world would spend the rest of the century puzzling over his legacy - even now it's easy to get lost in the reckoning.

When the movie starts Hawkins is doing his comedy Wayne impression - locked out of his own bathroom with shaving cream still on his face. It's a hair expected but charming. Hawkins barks like a dog and salutes the parakeet. He's always fun to watch, our Jack, one of the great cinematic drunks. The domestic bliss in the Gideon household is agreeable indeed. By the time he makes it to work, however... He gets written up for blowing a red light and goes in and just about kills one of his colleagues with his diction. He suspects a fellow detective of taking bribes to look the other way while someone sells drugs. When he looks closer he finds out he's also cheating on his wife. Very odd indeed to hear a Ford hero talk about "reefer." Wonder if Ford ever did drugs? Probably would have been a little happier a fellow. An 18-Year-old girl is murdered a few seconds later. If this is like a Hitchcock film, it's *Frenzy*; an acknowledgement of the derangement of the world. Drugs and corruption and murder around every corner. Even with the dreadful, major key score it's abrasive. There's a killing (a local loony kills a young girl off-screen with her mother just around the corner) that has the same sickly color tones and hushed discomfort of the late Hitch before and after. The apartment is a grotesque English purgatory; the body comes down the stairs draped in a red cloth. The whole movie feels like it's keeping hell (the second half of the century) at bay.

Gideon goes to a church to talk to a snitch and we overhear a local vicar (Jack Watling) who's being tormented by the local primary schoolers. He won't use his war stories to soften his image in their eyes so they'll stop making fun of him and laying traps for him. War was hell. He wouldn't wish it on anyone. Interesting. He'll later knock the shit out of some knife-wielding maniacs. A better kung-fu priest than Peter Jackson's; he makes the police take their hats off when they come to arrest the prone ne'er-do-wells. When Gideon's interrogating the office turncoat's wife she learns he's a crook, a slut, and then dead in the span of five minutes. He gets run down by his connections off-screen. She throws whiskey in Hawkins face to insult him. Why not throw a cigarette, a dinner jacket, a hundred bucks, and a lady too, really complete the insult? Every scene in the offices of Scotland Yard has impeccable blocking. Shadows and colors duking it out as the men pace this way and that. There's a scene where he and Cyril Cusack look at a slide projector - the room is green from one angle and red from another; he predicts *Peeping Tom* here and all but invents the Giallo. Wild. Just wild. The film may consistently stop short of ordinary greatness, but it is fascinating minute to minute, quite unlike anything else he made. Hawkins interrogates Dianne Foster, who's standing in front of a portrait of herself. When she hears the charges she stands terrified in front of her own picture and the serene expression painted on her portrait's face. A little Kuleshov, a little Chuck Jones, a little Wilde. Turns out the painting and the crime were both her husband's (Ronald Howard – who, like Foster, retired young and lived a long life) handiwork. He tries to explain himself to Hawkins with a gun in one hand and a paintbrush in the other. He's been knocking over payroll trucks to pay for painting supplies. Life is art. Later when they're using the loudspeaker to try and talk some bank robbers (mincing, gay-coded bank robbers) into surrendering, Gideon (who by now has had about six pints of whiskey) calls it a "concert." Ford seems suspicious of art here, and yet... 132 films and 40 years into his career, doesn't he agree? Doesn't he have to? *Gideon's Day*, rather like *Mogambo*, with its conservative ideas and liberal form, hints at different lives and careers for Ford, different directors living in his head with him all at once.

**The Last Hurrah (1958)**

Shockingly this film has nothing whatsoever to do with the 1944 Bette Davis movie *Mr. Skeffington*. I guess Skeffington was just a popular name. In his and Ford's second and last collaboration, Spencer Tracy is the aforementioned Skeffington, the fulcrum of a political machine in Anytown, New England. He's supposed to be one of those entrenched figures people just deal with because he's been in office so long (kinda like some filmmakers I could name). He's like the grocer or the postman, people's hatred for him is just part of their everyday lives. *The Last Hurrah* is the missing link between Capra's *Mr. Smith Goes To Washington* and Otto Preminger's *Advise & Consent*, still starry eyed about a handful of political tricks, but jaundiced enough to not treat Skeffington like Nathan Brittles or Judge Priest. He's as lovable as Will Rogers and just as wily. He's going to retire after his upcoming campaign for Mayor, and he wants his newspaperman nephew to come learn from him. He knows a good man when he sees one. Charles Lawton, Jr. shoots it in higher contrast than usual, which makes even more sense when you learn Orson Welles was Ford's first choice for the lead role (rumor had it Ward Bond fucked that up for him by calling Welles a commie, but Welles later said it was because the wrong lawyer picked up the phone when the call came in). It would have been Ford's answer to *Citizen Kane* with Kane himself floating through it like Baron Harkonnen the same year as *Touch of Evil*. That would have really been something.

Dianne Foster is back from *Gideon's Day* (guess she made her plane, after all) playing Mrs. Jeffrey Hunter and aside from Ford's beloved Jane Darwell, she's the only female presence in this sea of old white faces.

And what a sea! John Carradine, Basil Rathbone, Carleton Young, Edmund Lowe, Bob Sweeney, Wallace Ford, Frank McHugh, Donald Crisp, Pat O'Brien! Ricardo Cortez, Charles Trowbridge, and James Gleason all retired right after they wrapped. Skeffington's a friend to the Jews, so he pisses off former klansman Carradine, the head of the local reactionary paper and Hunter's boss. Carradine wants Charles B. Fitzsimons to win (funnily enough Ford directs him like a New Yorker cartoon version of Richard Nixon, complete with prop dog), and he's exactly the perverted creep Ford's cinema loathes. He cuts a figure like the fay bank robbers in *Gideon* (Skeffington's own son [Arthur Walsh], whom he despises, is a jazz fan, if you catch Ford's drift), some little toad that needs to be shown how the world works. Hunter does, too, but what he needs is a lesson in corruption. Hunter resents that a local man's wake turns into a campaign stop. He wouldn't last a day in the real world.

Skeffington (a creation of novelist Edwin O'Connor) was based on J.M. Curley, mayor of Boston, who settled with Columbia for a hefty sum because he thought them making this would prevent any interest in a real biopic. Now that's shrewd. The movie remains unmade, but Curley does have a downtown bar named after him, one of the few places you can get food after 10 PM in Boston. Curley was as corrupt as the day was long, but Ford's mayor is basically just crafty. His actual affiliations are nonsensical but that doesn't matter. He's a repudiation of the more difficult Ford heroes; born in the ghetto, against discrimination, chip on his shoulder about the rich. He lives to stick it to the inbred protestants still mad an Irish Catholic upstart and his Hebrew friends have muscled in on their white paradise. Rathbone's goose gets well and truly cooked when his nitwit son gets a public facing job, which will humiliate the old badger (their argument over this is a highlight, both actors at each other with everything but knives and bullets). Donald Crisp has my favourite line, though. When he finds out Fitzsimmons is being interviewed on TV he runs into the room to watch it. "Turn the thing on." It's nothing, really, just a throwaway line, but it sounds improvised, it sounds real. Reality finding its way, as it sometimes did, into Ford's films - the TV is still a dishonest thing to Ford. It puts the image of an all-American fool on TV so people can find him charming and cute. Crisp can't in good conscience vote for him, he sees right through him, sees through the TV. "Turn the thing on." That's all it is. A thing.

Skeffington loses his election, even though his opposition makes a Nixonian blunder (the real Nixon loved Ford, so I'm guessing he missed this in theatres); big money and "the thing" can't be beat. Tracy takes the defeat in good humor; he has plans, after all, it's only dying that finally stops him, though it doesn't rob him of his good nature. He awakes from his death's door stupor to say he wouldn't have changed a thing about his life. This would, I can't help but feel, be more successful a moment if we'd seen Frank enjoying himself outside of politics, but Ford still thinks men are the thing they do above all else - it was certainly true of him, even with his yachting voyages (guess what Frank, Jr. suggests for his dad after his heart attack?). Still, it's a magnificent performance, one of his very best. Tracy walking away from the victory parade by a fountain in a lonely park, the booming horns and drums, the spotlights, all of it in the back of the frame portending a life's work done, is as affecting as his tales of falling in love with his wife at age 6 and never looking back. He's had his parade. No more the victory march and the life of purpose. No more the common man. He gets three feet up the stairs in his lonely house towards the portrait of his long dead wife when his heart gives out. "Ya done grand things, Frank... grand, grand things. This is not the last goodbye, Frank." Indeed it wasn't, for Ford or Tracy.

**The Horse Soldiers (1959)**

1959 was the year of *Rio Bravo, Day of the Outlaw, Warlock, The Hanging Tree, Ride Lonesome,* and *Westbound*. Big demonstrative westerns that acted as states of the union. Howard Hawks, by letting in Ricky Nelson and his cheerful songs into *Rio Bravo*, was allowing the genre a little breathing room. Of course he'd spend the last decade of his career revisiting this to slightly diminishing returns. Turns out it wasn't the future because the western as men like Hawks and Ford knew it had no future. *Warlock*, the two Boetticher films, *Hanging Tree*, and *Day of the Outlaw* all see the writing on the wall and deal with the darkness in the human spirit and indeed in the idea of the western settlement. Warlock and Day bring hell to western towns. *Ride Lonesome* is about the destruction of the soul, playing out in a sleepless quest for vengeance. And then there's Edward Dein's *Curse of the Undead*, a little B movie about a vampire gunslinger. In John Ford's *The Horse Soldiers*, his last film of the 50s, John Wayne's steely union brigade has to put up with the addition to their ranks of an idealistic doctor played by William Holden. Holden makes Wayne deal with the realities of what they're fighting for while they plan to raid a Southern stretch to provide cover for Ulysses Grant. Holden delivers a black woman's baby in the first twenty minutes. 1959 was also the year of *The Beat Generation, A Bucket of Blood, Compulsion, Cry Tough, Gidget, The Rebel Set,* and *Teenagers from Outer Space*. The 60s were going to be here any second. Most of these directors wouldn't survive them. On the set of *The Horse Soldiers* Ford's beloved stuntman Fred Kennedy died on camera during a take. That alone must have told him his day was seeing its dusk. He'd never seen a good friend die on camera before. He vowed never to do it again, even as all around him they died off screen.

As John Wayne was hardening into an even worse arch conservative (his *The Alamo* was only a few months away) John Ford was turning away from him, away from the politics and the inherent and fascinating contradictions of his 40s and 50s films. What was on Ford's mind now was what to do with a whole life behind you and a few years of bewildering uncertainty ahead of you. The toll of making the "right" decisions become a fixation. Future Sam Fuller leading lady Constance Towers becomes Wayne's prisoner after she overhears their attack plans. She has a slave, played by tennis pro Althea Gibson, who helps her commit her acts of sabotage. Towers plays her character like a villainous stepmother in a kids movie by way of Scarlett O'Hara - it's marvelously loathsome work, though she softens by the third act. With Holden under arrest for insubordination (punishment for helping the black family) and Towers under arrest so she can't spill their plans to the Confederates nearby, they become of equal stature in the movie's calculus, which is quite the conundrum. Wayne's authority is only good until the war's over, after all, what happens then when people have to decide between a ghoulish southern princess and an idealistic doctor. America decided, alright.

Wayne's good here - he oughta be, he made almost a million dollars on this picture - when he's not just spitting out the dialogue (all the idioms are current, which is kind of distracting). He's got some very good little mannerisms and affectations. Ford was sober on this one, and it kind of shows: the compositions are wonderful but the drama's less tight. Ford did pay his black extras as much as his white ones, which evidently got the local's hackles up - the irony that the movie was set during the Civil War seems to have been lost on them, as it always is. Apparently Ford relented when Gibson demanded her character not speak in Mammy-isms (remembering, no doubt, what happened when he tried to direct Ethel Waters on *Pinky*), but he couldn't even bring her to Louisiana for location shooting because of the state's Jim Crow laws. The experience must have soured the idea of movies for her because she didn't make any more despite being quite good here. People complained about the premise back when - wouldn't these guys have just killed Towers instead of taking her hostage? Grim. Being in Louisiana must have reminded Ford that what he was doing was important, and he'd better start acting like it. We got two more near-perfect films out of him but in general his burgeoning liberalism (as it would be understood today) softened him considerably, which had the odd effect of stopping him from making his usual kinds of picture. Even the beloved *Liberty Valance* in '62 (not coincidentally his movie about society's "need" for violence and lying), was probably his darkest movie since *The Searchers*.

Ford perhaps dug a little hard into the southern stereotypes with this one between Towers and the two hicks, played by Strother Martin and Denver Pyle, his men ply for information before beating them up and tying them together. They're foul creatures - even the amputee prisoners they pass don't cut the most sympathetic figures (the score sure seems suspicious of 'em). It was time for people to wake up and realize that the face of racism hadn't changed. Would you be shocked if I told you this film flopped? Americans weren't interested in John Ford trojan horsing 60s idealism into their westerns. It is gorgeous though; Louisiana looks cold and off as the setting for a Western. This has to be Ford's bluest movie, taking cues from all those union duds in the frame. Its visual splendidness makes up for the slack pace. There's an amazing scene where a man on horseback rides into a barroom and Wayne knocks him down, pushes the animal out the door, and then throws the rider out after him. One take. It's like something from his earliest pictures – and it was something Harry Carey used to do on stage; this gets an even darker retread in *Liberty Valance* as we'll see.

PART 8

# APOLOGIES, REGRETS, DEATH, AND DYING

1960-1973

Ford never looked forward in his last ten years as an artist, only backwards in the hopes that he could mold a better future out of the past. His crew would mostly die, and he watched as violence and sex took a more central role in his beloved pictures, as the wars he fought became unpopular, as the world looked more and more foreign and unknowable and it just kept leaving him behind. He would give interviews where he could say out loud what we'd suspected about his political leanings and his sympathies. In 1928 he had written a piece in the New York Times that called for less of a search for universality in film language; "for the director who strives too hard to represent humanity by rubbing down the rough edges of racial and personal traits is likely to make his work drab and colorless." Which explains somewhat why he saw no compunction about his occasionally vilifying Natives, Englishmen or Germans. Some other picture would correct him down the line. Well Ford started to try to make those movies, and met with, as he himself predicted, vastly varied results. In one of a few interviews with Peter Bogdanovich Ford confided that he "killed more Indians than Custer, Beecher, and Chivington put together...Let's face it, we've treated them very badly – it's a blot on our shield; we've cheated and robbed, killed, murdered, massacred, and everything else, but they kill one white man and God, out come the troops." The trouble is Ford still believed America had a shield to blot, and not simply a spear stained red, the symbol of this country's crooked heart. Ford could not now have an unbiased look at the place he called home, and indeed his part in creating its image. He was too far upriver. You can sense in Ford an attempt to get back to basics, to try and rebuild but you can't do that unless you tear everything down first, and you cannot unmake a movie. In this last period as Ford grew back into helplessness and prepared to die, the words of the school teacher in *How Green Was My Valley*, looking at young Huw Morgan reading an adventure story from his sick bed, creating his own world with each turn of the page. "I could almost wish I were lying there in your place – if it meant reading this book for the first time."

**Sergeant Rutledge (1960)**

James Warner Bellah (whose books inspired Ford's Cavalry trio) and Willis Goldbeck (*Freaks*) went to Ford with the idea for *Sergeant Rutledge* which explains why the film is such an outlier in his movies in a few important ways. Obviously it was his first film with a black lead (though Woody Strode was fourth billed by a very nervous Warner Bros.), and it brings back his expressionistic moral fog from his early 30s films. In a piece for RogerEbert.com the late Sergio Mims points out that it was exceptionally nervy to make a movie about a black man falsely accused of raping a white woman five years after Emmett Till, though he's wrong in saying that Ford's humanism was just a quality that emerged in the 60s, it's just that he was finally taking stock of what his work had implicitly and explicitly said and brought back his attitude intact from the 20s. As we've seen he looked out for union men and sacrificed narcs, but his treatment of black characters hadn't yet risen above respectfully misguided (to put it mildly), with the possible exception of Clarence Brown in *Arrowsmith*. Althea Gibson's part in *The Horse Soldiers* is a good example; her performance is naturalistic and Gibson gives her dignity missing from, say Stepin Fetchit's work in the Will Rogers movies, but she's nevertheless defined by her relationship to Constance Towers, whose character owns her, even if she weeps when Gibson is killed. Ford's liberalism was not dissimilar to many from this period - he wanted to champion the causes of the oppressed but didn't do much work to understand those same people. *Sergeant Rutledge* is the one successful film where his lead has nothing in common with Ford beyond a military record.

Strode, like Ward Bond and Jeffrey Hunter (who, in a funny coincidence, also got his first role in a Henry Hathaway film like Strode), had been a football star, responsible for integrating the NFL with a few others, which is probably why Ford liked him. Actors drove him crazy. Strode also looked like no other movie star on earth (only Lance Reddick has emerged since as a man who possesses Strode's absurdly chiseled physique and uncommon good looks). His insanely muscular body, his stern figure; he was born for the pictures. He'd been making movies for almost twenty years when he made *Rutledge* and had his iconic supporting role in *Spartacus,* which made him as close to a star as a black man was allowed to be in the 60s (both Harry Belafonte and Sidney Poitier's stars were on the rise, too, though they'd only get to make the movies they really wanted in the 1970s), finding much success as a character actor, a few of those times for Ford, who put him in three more of his remaining ten films, though only once more as a black character. Unsurprisingly his best movie roles weren't in Hollywood. Valerio Zurlini put him in *Black Jesus* in 1968, which ought to tell you how the film treats him, and while he was out of the country he got his small role in *Once Upon a Time in the West*. He plays a convict capable of beating up a half-dozen guys in William Lustig's superb *Vigilante*, which works because even by 1982 he was still in better shape than most people half his age. He, Constance Towers, Chuck Hayward, and Maureen O'Hara outlived everyone else in the Ford stock company, and he finally appeared in Sam Raimi's *The Quick and the Dead* before his death the year of its release. His Rutledge co-stars Hunter, Willis Bouchey, Sam Harris, William Henry, Jack Kenney, Cliff Lyons, Jack Pennick, Jack Perrin, Jack Mower, and Ford's *Birth of a Nation* co-star Mae Marsh (unsurprisingly and un-sentimentally cast as a bloodthirsty rubbernecker to the trial of a black man) would all be dead long before Strode, some before the decade was out.

Rutledge is an inventory of the many kinds of injustice and prejudices that assailed non-whites in the new frontier. Even though Strode is our noble hero, there are still Natives to be fought. Juano Hernandez, born in Puerto Rico, plays a character who doesn't know when he was born because it was in bondage - they do the math with him on the stand. And then there's the matter of the trial. Hunter defends Strode in his rape and murder trial, and while Strode didn't do it, someone did. The lynch mob that attends the trial doesn't care one way or another if he's guilty, they want him hanged. It's tough to survive here, no matter who you are. The US Government wanted the west. Everyone would suffer 'til they got it. Barbed wire was invented right before Rutledge takes place. Writer Aaron Gwyn surmises that that is what ended the Wild West as we understand it, because it allowed people to say this or that piece of it was theirs, after most indigenous people were slaughtered and the rest put in reservations, fenced off from white society. Ford's only real mistake here is that in showing Rutledge's panicked actions when he fears white justice, he doesn't afford the Apaches the same courtesy. Just why is it they're so anxious to kill the cavalrymen stealing their territory?

Towers is the first witness. She arrives at a deserted train station by herself and finds that Apaches have killed everyone - the red blood on the corpse she discovers is pretty wild for Ford. Bert Glennon photographs once more, his last time before closing out his career on TV, and the colors of every garment are like lightning strikes in the frame. The interplay between the past and present is curiously unemphatic. There are no fades. The two timelines intersect, sometimes jarringly. It's almost Godardian. Otto Preminger had introduced Americans to a much more frank discussion of sexual violence in *Anatomy of a Murder* the year before. Ford hadn't shied away from the horrors of life before but the idea of working through the jockeying perspectives about what constitutes civilization as horrible violence hangs over it is a new one for the director. The law never really interested Ford; his outlaws usually saw the light or died, or weren't really bad sorts to begin with. Rutledge's presumed guilt is already a death sentence in this America. Rutledge ironically appropriates slave-owner slander ("we heal fast") to goad Hunter, much like the talk of "contraband" in *The Horse Soldiers* digs a knife into the distance we're meant to have from history (the two films represent a binary, just like *Fort Apache* and *She Wore a Yellow Ribbon*). The shot of Strode taking full stock of the shiny handcuffs Hunter slaps on him is a powerful one, the fear, the shame, the anger in his eyes. Ford lets us into Rutledge's head in disquieting ways. The line that stands out as much as any of Ford's images is "I walked into something none of us can fight ... white woman business!" delivered mournfully by Strode to his fellow black soldiers. It's shocking for 1960, yes, but it's still kind of shocking now, maybe more so than Strode's use of a slur to describe himself, one of the first times the word had made its way into American movies.

The courtroom scenes and the many scenes of people failing to read relevant passages in law texts hint at the thorniness of determining Rutledge's guilt at every turn. Give people the chance and they'll use protocol over what is practical or intuitive, but protocols can be easily misunderstood. A shot of Hunter looking at Strode through a window highlights the failure of perspective. He knows in his heart Rutledge couldn't have killed and raped the young woman, but he wasn't there. He's just looking in on Rutledge's state of mind and heart and actions, same as the opposing counsel who wish to see him die for the crime. Rutledge impugns Lincoln's promises, which applied to every President after him who failed to do right by black America in a way that promised real change, real safety, real freedom. "Like Rutledge says...some day..."

**The Colter Craven Story (1960)**

Ward Bond lucked into a pretty sweet gig as Major Seth Adams on *Wagon Train*, a hugely popular NBC series in 1957. Bond died in the saddle and the show changed networks to ABC and found a new star in John McIntire, another Ford player. Bond had been in the two films that influenced the series, Ford's own *Wagon Master*, and Raoul Walsh's *Big Trail*, which featured that week's special guest star John Wayne in the lead. Wayne plays General Sherman in this, though he's winkingly not correctly credited. *Wagon Train* was such a huge phenomenon at the time that it was enough for Gene Roddenberry to pitch *Star Trek* as "Wagon Train in space" to get the greenlight at NBC. The idea was Bond would push the wagon train a few miles every week and they'd run into some high profile actor who played a traveler with a story to tell and a lesson to impart. Ford likely did this as a favor to Bond, and just to ensure he didn't work too hard they re-used some footage from *Wagon Master* to pad the runtime, but he did bring a whole mess of his favorite actors with him. Wayne, Anna Lee, John Carradine, Ken Curtis, Chuck Hayward, Cliff Lyons, Paul Birch, and Hank Worden. Quite a group.

The eternally busy Carleton Young (who was becoming a Ford regular) plays drunken doctor Colter Craven, whose own wagon broke down. He's one of Ford's poetic drunks. "Tomorrow comes regardless of which way we're headin'..." he says to Bond, a far off look in his eye. He did the right thing the wrong way so he isn't welcome at the nearest fort, which means he has to hitch with Bond and co. for. a few extra miles. Bond's got business with some local hooligans (he kicks some ass and looks pretty credible doing it - gotta hand it to him!). Ford confirms what I suspected about his fondness for Ken Curtis - Carradine plays his dad. Perfect casting. Carradine's hoarding water and Bond needs it for his horses. Young needs booze but can't drink it on the train despite its abundance for medicinal purposes. Real "water, water everywhere" situation. Young has to prove himself by getting sober and doing basic surgery for the train like Thomas Mitchell in *Stagecoach*.

Ford directs in a far less exacting style than usual. Lots of uninspired shot-reverse-shot for conversations, mostly he does everything in functional single takes. Bond and Young's heart-to-heart about why the doctor can't perform (surgery) anymore is really gripping. Bond always did really good work for Ford but this feels different, more open, more of a raw nerve. Young sweats and fumbles and cries and Bond has to just soak it all up. The horrors of working slaughterhouses and doing surgery come alive in his pinched face, his taut string voice. "It wasn't enough. They should have given me a sword instead of a scalpel." For 8 minutes it's Eugene O'Neill. Then it jackknifes into a comedy flashback about a different drunk played by Birch. Bond's a little sillier here, naturally, even if the subject is still the darkness of alcoholism before and after the war. Bond was dead before the episode aired, which puts the whole thing into even starker relief. He was a great actor, a great utility infielder for Ford, and a great friend to the ornery director. He struggled all his life with drink. His epitaph, this pretty excellent hour of television, is a cautionary tale about just that. Ford would steal another 15 years on Earth drinking just as hard. Tomorrow comes. Tomorrow always comes.

**The Alamo (John Wayne & John Ford)**

If you ever needed any kind of proof that Ford was an artist (at this point in this project I'd hope you're basically on board) watch *Hondo*. Ford dropped by the set of the 3D western starring Wayne (who, absent Ford's direction, is terrible) and directed one shot of cavalry troops. It's the only good shot in the picture. The rest of John Farrow's movie (which Wayne claimed he directed most of) might as well be a radio play, complete with inert Wayne performance (if you've ever wanted to see John Wayne in drag as John Wayne [and what is *Hondo* but a cheap burlesque of *Shane*?], here's your chance; his fuck-me swagger is turned up to 11). It took Wayne very specific circumstances (like, say...a good director) to give performances you could stand to look at. His *Green Berets* - an appallingly lumpen, hideously pitched mess - is a good example. Why is it that Wayne is so rakishly appealing, so easy to watch in *True Grit* a year later, and when looking at him in *Green Berets*, you long for someone to lead him out of the sun and into a chair to gently expire and stop playing soldiers in the yard. His nose looks like something he grabbed off the Burbank ground and stuck to his face with mud. His skin looks like the end result of a long experiment in radiation poisoning. The dynamic is like if Wayne was an unreliable dad and Ford was a night without drinking. Wayne, under Ford's direction, is one of the most heartbreaking and dignified performers in the American cinema. Without him you don't know what state he's coming home in after work.

When Wayne went to Texas to film *The Alamo*, his passion project, Ford showed up uninvited and started directing from about ten feet behind him. Wayne realized unless he got Ford off his back they'd have to call it a film by John Ford, so they sent him off to shoot some second unit footage. Joseph McBride asked Wayne about the things Ford did or didn't do on the set of his movies and Wayne, ever the diplomat, croaked "Christ can't you people give me credit for anything!" Far be it from me to impugn the directorial chops of John Wayne, but if Ford had ridden him harder the movie might have had a livelier pace and a tighter, more appealing mise-en-scène. Scenes frequently just end and the edits take us from wides to mediums with no rhyme or reason. The dynamic between Laurence Harvey and Wayne is preposterous. It never stops being weird that Harvey is here hobnobbing with Richard Boone and John Wayne – he's even more wrong in Welles' unfinished *The Deep* but I guess it's good he had friends who trusted him. The dynamic between the country bumpkins and effete, by-the-book Harvey a retread of the flirtatious dynamic in Ford's *The Brat*, with the worldly professor trying to make a society lady out of the uncouth rebel. I suppose it's fitting that the man who wanted to tell the story of America was a drunken, philandering, fascist hypocrite. This kind of thing comes out more honest when it's a hired gun like Richard Fleischer making something swampy and grotesque like *Mandingo*. Wayne gives himself a beard (Linda Cristal, 24 long years younger than he), who comes with interminable flirtation scenes (Chill Wills notes that he's glad Wayne's taken an interest in Cristal. "Last few years he had me worried..."), fist fights he wins handily, fay (but married) counterparts in Harvey and Widmark, and 160 minutes in which to build himself a shrine.

"Some words give you a feeling. "Republic" is one of those words that makes me tight in the throat." No frankly I don't buy that Davy Crockett said this to William Travis. I don't frankly believe any of these guys were the idealists presented here, what with their suicidally deciding they'd rather kill themselves and take hundreds of Mexicans with them over some property (which included slaves) than go home. John Lee Hancock was given the reins of Ron Howard and John Sayles' gritty, Sam Peckinpah-style remake after Disney got nervous about the idea of an R-rated movie about a pretty important piece of the conservative national narrative, and in hedging about the nature of the men at the Alamo's politics but going hard on the hellish personal lives of Bowie and Travis, it pleased no one (except me. I like that movie a lot) and lost hundreds of thousands of dollars. This was a huge smash with a ubiquitous Oscar campaign. The difference is all attitude. Here we watch the masculine ingenuity that led a hundred guys to die. The new one has an air of loneliness and desperation which helps a movie about stupid idea it was to defend The Alamo in the first place, even if the guys did ultimately find camaraderie in their weaknesses. In Wayne's movie you'd never guess all these hearty tactical geniuses all bit the dust together a few days into this heroic struggle.

**Two Rode Together (1961)**

Jimmy Stewart is introduced here kicked back in an old chair on a porch, deliberately framed like Henry Fonda in *My Darling Clementine*, just to let you know you're in for a bitter disappointment. Ford and Fonda did eventually get back on speaking terms, but after *Mister Roberts*, they'd never work together again. Fonda is in *How The West Was Won*, but not in Ford's segment. It's an unflattering comparison; *Two Rode Together* is no *My Darling Clementine*, indeed it seems like a greatest hits collection at half-speed, a softball after the more rigorous *Sergeant Rutledge*. Ford did it as a favor to the very dead Harry Cohn who had wanted him to make it but he felt like he'd covered the same material in *The Searchers*, but hey sometimes you gotta do your dead friends a solid. Speaking of which, Ford had to pause shooting to plan Ward Bond's funeral, who died before their episode of *Wagon Train* aired. Long time editor Jack Murray died right after completing the film, so did Edward Brophy. That makes this not just one of Ford's worst films but a lousy epitaph, too.

Stewart and Richard Widmark, whom Ford called "two deaf hairpieces" spend a lot of the first act lounging around a gambling hall with glasses of beer - the movie basically follows suit. Not much verve in Ford's images - there's an infamous two-shot of the leads sitting in a river chit-chatting (mostly improvised, and you can tell) that seems like Ford trying to avoid moving onto another set-up. It's a shame because it is a good idea, even if it is the *Searchers* clone Ford complained that it was - he even brought back absurd looking Henry Brandon to play one of the chiefs. Widmark's been tasked with ransoming people kidnapped by Comanches over the last decade or more, and he asks Stewart to come with him on this particular errand. Before he became a Marshall he had a lot of dealings with the local indigenous population - they might listen to him. He's anxious to get out of the house - his business partner wants to get married and he's not in the mood. Also on hand are Andy Devine, Anna Lee, Harry Carey Jr, Ken Curtis, Woody Strode, O.Z. Whitehead, Mae Marsh, Jack Pennick, Cliff Lyons, and Shirley Jones.

Stewart has to explain to a lot of the bereaved parents and siblings of the kidnapped what likely became of them - the whole movie could have been this, it's a great scene idea and Stewart handles it ok. Shirley Jones is looking for her brother - she's quietly the best thing in the movie, the usual brash tomboy Ford likes so much, but still terribly hopeful. She keeps a music box from her childhood that she listens to in private. Widmark doesn't have the heart to tell her to manage her expectations. Their courtship almost plays, but it's never not weird that Richard Widmark is playing a hopeful young lover. He's Richard Widmark! Even when he was young he couldn't have pulled that off. He looks like a well-done roast and he's obviously bored being so squeaky clean. That's not half as bad as Stewart romancing Linda Cristal (so good in Fleischer's *Mr. Majestyk*, still uncertain on her feet here) as Wayne had the year before. Cristal looks about 14 years old and Stewart was now so old that his voice shook when he spoke. It's like watching a man shotgun-marry his daughter. Really bad, creepy decision. Curtis and Carey loathe Widmark because he's a Union officer and they're proud sons of the South. They see him and Jones spending time together and it makes them crazy. Stewart has contempt for basically everyone, at least at first, until Cristal softens him up a little. The comedy fist fights, for the first time I can recall in a Ford, badly jibe with the more serious aims of the movie, to say nothing of Stewart's rantings about rape and murder. George Dunning's *Blazing Saddles*-style score doesn't help any. This is basically as close as Ford got to the spirit of exploitation cinema. His own version of the Italian westerns that were about to replace his.

I'm still blown away by Ford even pretending to buy into frontier politics - Mae Marsh says she's dead now because she's been living with the Comanche for so many years now, even though she can speak English (playing out an eerie what-if scenario vis-à-vis her death in *Birth of a Na-*

*tion*). Ford's softened just enough since *Rio Grande* to allow his natives a fuller range of emotions and understandable tribal conflict, but the script believes the American way of life is preferable to theirs. Ford subverts this by just not directing it very well and *Cheyenne Autumn* was a few years away, but even that's a paltry offering. The Cheyenne don't have souls in that either. This movie allows for a little greyness between the idea of bringing people home to lives they don't know anymore, but there's no doubt in the movie's mind that removing them from the Comanches is the preferable choice. Linda Cristal is a Mexican who was kidnapped and then married to Woody Strode's brave (people forget Strode was part Cherokee). Stewart uses her as bait and kills him as a favor to Brandon, and then takes her for himself. I'd kill to know if Ford or screenwriter Frank Nugent understood just how ugly the optics were if they so despised the idea of the movie that they didn't care one way or the other. The one boy they bring back (David Kent, who looks like Eddie Munster) kills his white mother. So much for that.

## The Man Who Shot Liberty Valance (1962)

Of all of the Ford films that get called great, *Liberty Valance* is maybe the one that seems to be obviously, demonstrably great from the jump. It's Andy Devine who says it. The garrulous coot has grown old. Very old indeed. His voice is no longer the cartoon squeak of greasy wagon wheels. He needs a minute to get up. He speaks with such tenderness, such softness and warmth when he sees Vera Miles again since their relative youth. He has such overwhelming dignity, the first time Ford had ever allowed himself to say that he loved the chubby actor, whose life he made hell every chance he got. Ford wouldn't have let him play this part if he didn't love him. Wouldn't have let him anywhere near it. This is in the running for Ford's most romantic movie, and yet it's also got his darkest and most unforgiving ending. He loves these people. He lets them destroy themselves, to ride into a lying eternity. "Print the legend," and die a fraud. Nothing strips you bare like a lie.

John Wayne is introduced as a void in a coffin, which could have upset some people. He's already passed into oblivion, to myth, and even so he was about to get buried without his boots or his gun. Tom Doniphon was his name and he made and unmade our hero in the same pull of a trigger. If the funeral in *Lawrence of Arabia* is also Ford's funeral, so is this. Of course he went in a fashion much closer to his heroines in *7 Women*. A drink in one hand and contempt in the other. He'd made heroes out of right wing maniacs like Stewart and Wayne and Bond and Fonda and watched as they became landmarks like the Statue of Liberty or Monument Valley itself. Doniphon died of old age and left a gaggle of ashen-faced mourners behind; Miles, Devine, Woody Strode, and Jimmy Stewart's Ransom Stoddard, one of cinema's greatest names...probably better even than Liberty Valance. Carleton Young, who took to Ford's world as quickly and intuitively as anyone had a few years back, is a newspaper man who wants to know why a big shot senator like Ransom Stoddard has come to bury a man no one ever heard of. Time for a story.

*Two Rode Together* was a lesson for Ford, never too old to learn one, despite his stubbornness. He focused up and his next movie, written by *Sergeant Rutledge*'s Willis Goodbeck and James Warner Bellah, would be better. He gave Stewart another chance, the role of a lifetime, and he'd already had a few of those in his day. William Clothier, the film's cinematographer said that shooting on black and white in cramped Paramount studio backlot sets was a matter of the studio being cheap. Ford gave a more poetic answer; black and white meant you had to be careful. And he wanted to be more careful. Of course, he cuts more frequently to get around the set. He's learning. When Hitchcock made *Psycho*, it was an experiment in making a movie like he might an episode of television. *Liberty Valance* is much the same. How to find poetry in so much obvious artifice. Well if anyone could find it, it was Ford. The domestic character of most of this movie's dramatic scenes (five or six characters sharing cramped kitchens and the like) bring us back to the boarding house in *Upstream*. DeVine and Edmund O'Brien and Jeanette Nolan and John Qualen all slapping on the periphery of Wayne and Stewart's disagreements like angry waves.

Stoddard gets held up by Liberty Valance (Lee Marvin - together with his sidekicks Strother Martin and Lee Van Cleef, like the 70s were turning up early for dinner) and left for dead. As he's recovering, he romances Miles, who's Wayne's girl despite their distant dynamic, teaches her how to read (Stewart is so deeply affecting during these passages), and tries to set up his law practice so he can throw the book at Valance next time he sees him. Wayne tries to explain to him that this far out in the territory, with the ineffectual Devine as marshal and criminals making their own luck, the best thing to do would be to shoot him dead. Stoddard can't agree. A world without law & order is chaos - Roland Joffe's *The Mission* restages this debate less efficiently a few decades later. Nothing has changed except the argument for the law's become poisoned by the kind of people who uphold it. The dynamic here is introduced when Valance trips Stewart and Wayne rises to his defense. He spends half the scene on the floor watching them like a kid. "Just try it, Liberty." Bellah and Goldbeck gave Ford the damndest treatise on America, a place that'll rise to a taunt before it'll rise to an example. Stewart tries to give the people enlightenment, words and culture, but he's no match for the silver whip and the gun. Ford would have understood that, he fought it in himself every day.

Absolutely no one is who they're supposed to be here. A cast of geriatrics playing 20 year olds (O.Z. Whitehead is supposed to be 15 or something in most Ford films and Denver Pyle, who plays his dad, is younger than he is - it's like *Bonanza* around here) shouldn't work but it does. It especially does if you're excited just to be back in the company of Sam Harris and Jack Pennick and Mae Marsh and the rest of the Ford players. Cyril J. Mockridge's music is one of the better scores in a Ford film (there's a heaping helping of the leftover Young Mr. Lincoln score in there too), but crucially Otho Lovering edits it down in the mix so it doesn't overwhelm the important stuff. Wayne is so damned good in this, finally old enough to play Nathan Brittles and behaving younger than ever. His teenage courtship with Miles brings out his best. He's a jock protecting a nerd from his bullies, and he cares so much he can't protect himself in the process. He has to let people do as they please, even if it means breaking his own heart to do so. Ford gave Wayne hell all the way through. He called out his failure to make it as a football star like Strode had, his refusal to fight in World War 2 like Stewart. Maybe the rancor helped him, he may never have been better, or maybe it was just business as usual. Ford the secret socialist giving his hard right star, the public face of his art, the hard time he knew no one else would give him. Ford could still torture his people. If we remember Wayne tugging his arm at the end of *The Searchers* like Harry Carey used to, that gets a wrinkle when a horseman rides into a rally to drum up support for the corrupt candidate up against Stewart for state representative. That was the same thing Carey did to become famous in his first stage show, the thing that led to his being in pictures in the first place, the thing Ford had him do in several of their earliest collaborations. Everything was fair game. Everything could be revised. Everything could be changed in Ford's backwards glance at who he was.

Critics loved the movie but hated the ending. They didn't want to be told what to think about Stewart and Wayne's understanding, about the nature of things, about the truth. Of course it was the ending that made the film a classic. People still remember "print the legend." It's the title of more books than you can count on one hand. And without it, there's no movie. Stoddard has to walk towards respectability, towards myth, knowing he's a liar, knowing that the help Doniphon tried to give him was for naught. It bought him his career, his life, his marriage. But it took his soul. He profited from violence, the thing he spends the whole picture saying no society can brook. He missed Liberty Valance and yet wears his body like a topcoat on every press stop and flesh pounding for the rest of his life. The ghost of Tom Doniphon's nobility will haunt him and the legend of Liberty Valance will drag him down every timid step of the way to the grave, like the steps he took towards the gunslinger on the night he died. He wants to finally expose himself, he wants absolution from the press but they won't grant it to him. This brutal ending, like *7 Women*'s final seconds... that was what lived in Ford's heart. He betrayed it over and over, but there it was, like the blinding sun on red sands. He was a soldier once but now he made pictures, images like songs, like thread that spun itself around the souls of his audience and hung there forever. "I'll be around..."

**Flashing Spikes (1962)**

The Alcoa Company a Pittsburgh based aluminum manufacturer, still the 8th largest in the world, I'm told, was founded in 1888. When Aluminum foil was becoming de rigueur in post-war American kitchens, Alcoa, needless to say, became a huge deal, and thus had money to burn. This led to their buying up lots of TV ad space and indeed producing two of their own anthology series. NBC got *The Alcoa Hour* in 1955 and ABC got *Alcoa Premiere* in 1961, hosted by Fred Astaire. Ford directed an episode of the latter, and the plot is very similar to that of *Rookie of the Year*, Ford's first episode of TV. It also involves a disgraced baseball player. John Wayne makes another appearance as he did in that, along with Jimmy Stewart, Vin Scully playing himself and a young-ish Jack Warden (Jack Warden was never young). It'd be fun to think of Ford directing Astaire but I don't believe that happened; the prologue was clearly filmed elsewhere. Saul Bass did the titles for Alcoa and John Williams does the music, which is a real changing of the guard moment; he and Spielberg both had dealings with Ford. Ford was becoming a living museum piece, and his next few movies would make this seem like something he was encouraging, stately and airless on the one hand, goofy and stakeless on the other. If not for *7 Women*, he might have just passed gently into legend.

John Wayne's son Patrick is back as Bill Riley, a baseball player marred by his association with Jimmy Stewart's Slim Conway. Slim was drummed out of baseball decades ago in disgrace, another Black Sox type scandal. Warden is marvelous as the lead investigator of Wayne's case, he's got big Dick Miller energy – Wayne is accused of cheating just like Stewart and now their association makes his guilt seem like a sure thing. Ford shoots the baseball scenes with tightness - lots of cutting, which makes this sort of a piece with *Liberty Valance*'s cramped grammar; William Clothier's back as cinematographer, too - and makes the plays seem genuinely exciting. Stewart's doddering Slim Conway is an easy performance to like, right down the plate for the natural comedian. Stewart and Wayne bond over a farm team game until someone recognizes Stewart in the outfield. Suddenly he's a pariah, the opposite of his *Liberty Valance* hero. Wayne knocks into him pretty good when he next hits first base, cutting him with his cleats (the flashing spikes of the title). Stewart just takes it, which gets Wayne thinking he was too hard on him. When a mob comes up to him after the game, Wayne, out of pure reflex, rushes to his aid, bat in hand.

Stewart tells his old friend Tige Andrews that Wayne's gonna be the next big thing in baseball, so he recruits him. Unfortunately the Korean War breaks out - time for some stock footage, which Ford may have shot himself for all I know - so he joins the Marine league and becomes a star. Wayne's dad shows up to referee one of the games and then Stewart happens upon him, having evidently been called up to active duty as well despite being a hundred years old. Back in the states he starts lurking around Wayne's games and the press (or...well Carleton Young anyway) start taking pictures of them together, which makes it appear as though he's taking a payday from Stewart to throw games. Stewart's very good, of course. Seeing him hear the baseball game over the radio is more interesting than the game itself. Eventually everybody's name gets cleared and Bill wins the world series. A little anticlimactic, but it's good to see Ford's old morality on display. This is an anti-blacklist drama, pure and simple, Ford finally giving into his better angels. Stewart gets back to the game just as the old commies were getting their jobs back at major studios.

**How The West Was Won (1962, John Ford, Henry Hathaway, Richard Thorpe & George Marshall)**

Just as 3-D was being revived to combat flagging movie attendance due to the increase in the purchases of televisions, an inventor named Fred Waller came up with another blockbuster idea to get people out of their houses. It was called Cinerama and though it sounded big and special, it was really just filming a movie with three cameras and displaying the completed images with three projectors. Unsurprisingly this costly and unwieldy process didn't catch on. A few documentaries were produced using the format, the first by RKO producer and John Ford collaborator Merian C. Cooper. It was dead by 1974. Waller was dead before his invention was ever used. Very few movies were shot and exhibited in true Cinerama and ultra-widescreen stopped being something directors wanted to shoot in. As you might expect John Frankenheimer gave it a whirl, John Sturges did too (and so did the Russians, filling in the Cinerama gap), but who wants to wait on three different loaders to get a take? *How The West Was Won* is probably the most successful of the Cinerama movies taken on the terms of the distribution format itself (there were only a handful of theatres equipped to show it and it still tripled its money at the box office) and well...it just isn't very good. Four directors, as many cinematographers (William Daniels, Milton Krasner, Charles Lang, and Joseph LaShelle), every white star money could buy, and it just kind of sits there. Ford's segment is the best of them but only because it looks so damned odd.

Richard Thorpe was mostly on hand to shoot the luminous exteriors for cut-aways, so it's unfair to judge the frequent Tarzan movie director's chops based on this lugubrious white noise. Hathaway's a good director so his segment is fine from an image and sound perspective, but the politics are paleolithic. Spencer Tracy narrates, opening by talking about how settlers like Jimmy Stewart's Linus Rawling are "More Indian than Indian." Rather underlines the warped sensibility of the project. The West was "Won" from... *who, again*? I don't think Mother Nature was playing. What did "we" "win"? Traffic choked highways, the movie argues in its final minutes. I've been to Monument Valley, it's abject poverty for hundreds and hundreds of miles in every direction. We go ten minutes before Stewart's talking about how attractive Indian girls are if you've been away from white women long enough. Mostly the movies that people point to as being examples of the cut-and-dry black-and-white sensibility of the Old West as Hollywood wrote it don't exactly fit the profile. This? This is as bad as people say. Shame because if Hathaway had simply intended it as a landscape study (caves and rivers are things of impossible splendor in his hands) it would have been quite something, but then again Hugo Fregonese did this in '66 when he made *Old Shatterhand* and that has much less terrible ideas in its head.

An episode with river pirates led by Walter Brennan and Lee Van Cleef is energetic but belongs in a Disney film. A bit with Debbie Reynolds and a dragged-up Thelma Ritter on a wagon train is dull but for Ritter's incredible presence (she saved even her worst movies). Reynolds fends off a marriage proposal from Robert Preston with a whip and then very eventually Gregory Peck wins her over instead. Reynolds sings and dances for a bit and it looks ridiculous in the endless widescreen frame. Hathaway had no clue what to do with all that space if it wasn't full of streams and trees. Reynolds promotes herself from frontier bawdy shows to steamboat finery in no time at all. The score plays "Green Sleeves," which if I don't miss my guess is the inspiration John Williams took when scoring *Last Crusade*. All this musical elephantiasis will recur in Joshua Logan's *Paint Your Wagon*, which is, against all odds, less objectionable than this in every way.

Raymond Massey is Lincoln, who makes his fourth appearance in a Ford film, having been respectively a lawyer, a figurehead, and a martyr for the director before he can now combine all three. Massey would play Lincoln something like 100 more times through the next few years. Like Walter Huston, who had been Griffith's Lincoln, Massey was Canadian. Ford moves the camera for the first time in the picture when he re-introduces Carroll Baker after an intermission. We get the exciting sight of Andy Devine in three strip technicolor jutting from the three axes like the starchild in *2001* (an actual Kubrick connection: Sue Lyon, his Lolita, is in *7 Women*). Ford's form is stunning, made awkward but compelling by the anamorphic warping. He didn't care that it looked weird and he was right not to. Steven Soderbergh (who made his own *Grapes of Wrath* in *King of the Hill*) does this again in *No Sudden Move*.

George Peppard plays Carroll Baker and Jimmy Stewart's son despite being three years older than his mom. Stewart dies in the war, Peppard goes to follow him, and then Baker dies off screen of grief when she hears this. Ford fills the frame with business, which is a nice change of pace. He has lines of cannons going off in sequence, surgeons operating revolving door field hospitals like something out of *Metropolis*, mass graves being dug, corpse dust filling the air, lavender flowers blossoming to keep the back of the frame separate from the front. Russ Tamblyn, a disillusioned confederate, and Peppard have a heart-to-heart about all this butchery right as Generals Sherman (Wayne, playing him for a second time) and Ulysses Grant (Harry Morgan) walk up and have the very same confab. Tamblyn decides he deserted too hastily and tries to shoot them both, so Peppard stabs him to death. Suddenly he's back in the fight, if only there were anything waiting for him back home when it's over. There's a few seconds of battle footage which has Ford detonating explosives near horses, which I believe was a first for him. It's pretty jaw-dropping spectacle, so of course it lasts about ten seconds.

George Marshall's up next, one of the only directors who had the distinction of working longer than Ford, starting in 1915 and directing right up until his death at age 83 in 1975. Peppard heads west and tries to keep the peace between railroad settlements and local Arapaho. Richard Widmark is the tycoon who keeps making things worse. Marshall straps his three cameras to a wagon to film Henry Fonda riding on horseback dead center of the frame, accidentally creating the halfway point between Muybridge and the 360 camera of the 2010s in the process. The rest is about what you'd expect, briefly enlivened by Fonda's frontier scout and a scene of buffalo stampeding through the railroad. Hathaway returns for the final segment about outlaws. The first shot is a riot. A man proudly surveys his huge herd of sheep before a gunshot fells him and some guys ride in and steal the herd. Don't know if Hathaway meant it as a joke but it's funny. Most gallingly, he uses rear projection for a scene aboard a wagon soon after. It teases a better movie when it becomes clear that the hero and villain of the piece are Lee J. Cobb and Eli Wallach, but alas. Hathaway's cartoon physics and abuse of the frame are James Wan-esque. Ford walks off with the movie and it never comes back.

## Donovan's Reef (1963)

*Donovan's Reef*, which Ben Sachs once called "John Ford's The Tempest" was seen as so peculiar for Ford that he had to explain himself a little when releasing it. He called it a "spoof, a whammy crazy thing" which was the wrong word but there also wasn't a word for what he was doing. Comedy that begged for a negligible plot so there could just be jokes. The Marx Brothers movies are good examples. They were so distinct they're still called "Marx Brothers Movies." The plots of *A Night At The Opera* and *A Day at the Races* are so unimportant that even fans could be forgiven for not knowing them. By contrast *Pillow Talk* or *His Girl Friday* have very simple conceits and the comedy is all plot related - everything funny is a result of the mechanics that keep the romantic leads together or apart. Rock Hudson lies to outsmart Doris Day, Cary Grant lies to outsmart Rosalind Russell, and every time someone walks through a door they're here to complicate those lies. The same is not true of, moving forward, a few choice Rodney Dangerfield movies or *Step Brothers*. I like *Donovan's Reef*, it has plot points, but between viewings I forget them. The important thing is Lee Marvin and John Wayne beat the hell out of each other in the most beautiful place on earth. Take out the dim treatment of the Polynesians and it's the perfect hang. Marcel Dalio's here to remind us of *To Have and Have Not*. Caesar Romero's here because everything's better when he's around.

When you break down the important stuff, it's two guys who have, for twenty years, gotten together on their shared birthday (which is December 7th, for some reason) and beaten the living hell out of each other. It's a tradition. They *like* doing this. They have to pretend they don't but they do. Is there other stuff in the movie? Sure. Romance, a matter of inheritance, family. Does any of that matter? Absolutely not. The meat here is Lee Marvin and John Wayne drinking and embarrassing each other and punching each other every now and again and generally getting shabby treatment from everyone, including the gods, who dump rain on them and break down their buildings and stuff. It'd be ludicrous to claim this was the first movie that was about drinking first and fun last (*The Thin Man* movies get close, but the solving of mysteries is fun), but it's part of an important continuum that includes *Mikey & Nicky, Last Night at the Alamo,* and *Withnail and I*. Every scene comes with the sound of bottles being thrown across barrooms, jalopy engines misfiring, and men shouting at each other. It's like supervising a shift at the drunken brawl factory.

Ford intended the movie to be about curing racial prejudice. The actual plot involves hiding the illegitimate children of Jack Warden from his American daughter Elizabeth Allen. Warden's out of town, Allen's going to beat him to the Polynesian beachfront he and Wayne call home, and Warden's never told her about her half-sisters. Lee Marvin's answer to the problem is to drug Allen and throw her on a ship leaving town (Marvin himself appears to have had the same fate befall him before arriving on the island, kind of the silly flipside of the fate of Thomas Mitchell in *The Long Voyage Home*)? It's unclear, but everyone knows it's a bad idea so Wayne does what he imagines to be the gallant thing and pretends the kids are his. He and Allen hate each other like cats at first sight, so naturally they'll fall in love before too long. The natives are a little broad for Ford's message of tolerance to hold much weight, but it always was. Perhaps the most American thing about him, the most neoliberal, is that every single time he tried to say something for tolerance he put his foot in his mouth in the doing. Ford apparently knew enough Mandarin to direct a few actors here and on *7 Women* in their own tongue. He should have let them re-write their dialogue. The constant pageantry of the islanders singing welcome for everyone reminds me of a criticism I once heard about Stanley Kramer's *On The Beach*; Australians don't just sit around singing "Waltzing Matilda" all day. The attempts to cover up the miscegenation reek of Ford looking backward with a sidelong glance at his own history of racism. He should have been forthright. He should have just said what was in his heart rather than kowtow to deranged times. Bond was dead. He could say it all now.

"As Shakespeare said..." "Quite." This is based loosely on James Michener, making this the only good movie to ever come from anything he ever wrote. Most Michener movies are a goddamned snooze. Michener was born in Doylestown, same as me, there's a very cool museum he founded before he died in the center of town, across the street from the Henry Chapman Mercer museum, containing all of Mercer's trinkets - it's like a cross between *Raiders of the Lost Ark, The Haunting,* and T.G.I. Fridays. I always liked going both places as a kid. Michener wasn't interesting enough for his house to turn directly into a museum but if you've ever read him, you already knew that. The best thing you could hope to do with him is something like this, where it's light jazz and sexual antics for two hours.

Wayne complained that Allen was way too young for him and tried to get Maureen O'Hara but Ford refused, probably just to needle him. Allen's good here, the right air of mid-Atlantic sexlessness to combat Wayne's leather strap boorishness. I thought it'd be more gross watching him romance anyone but I think because the atmosphere of the movie is itself so unthreatening, there's a harmless burlesque quality to this. He does absolutely look like one of Tolkien's Ents, but movie star charm transcends just about everything, hence why so few of them ever go to jail. Warden is very dignified here, hardly suggesting that he'd spend the last twenty years of his career playing coots and codgers. He and Allen have wonderful familial chemistry on screen, the slow thawing of their own expectations, their uneasiness at their relationship being what it was giving way to the possibilities of what it could be. It's right out of *Rio Grande*. Really the only odd part about this movie is that Ford's next film was *Cheyenne Autumn*, the film after that is *7 Women*, and then he was done. A hell of an offbeat way to end one's career. But still one of my favourite Christmas films.

**McLintock! (Andrew V. McLaglen [& John Ford?])**

It's tempting to call this shapeless fiasco the most sexist film of all time (all the box art has some version of John Wayne slapping Maureen O'Hara around the corral, spanking her with a fire shovel, dragging her this way and that, knockin' her around) but that'd be giving the film more credit than it deserves in any direction. My mom used to watch it sometimes when I was a kid, not, I suspect, because she thought it was good, but because my mother had a finely honed sense of kitsch. She loved John Waters, saw him speak a few times, and enjoyed, for instance, the bit in half-assed dayglo satire *Predator 2* where Danny Glover tries to calm an old woman by saying he's a policeman and has the situation in hand. The lady, having just seen the monster, says "I don't think he gives a shit." She appreciated when "too much" reared its head and still does. I think she appreciated that *McLintock!* was the western finally parodying itself into uselessness ten full years before *Blazing Saddles*. She liked John Wayne's absurd walk and the joke in Mike Nichols' *The Birdcage* about it. To me *McLintock!* is a crucial text because it's got two connections to my beloved *Mystery Science Theater 3000*. Ford's third important leading man Victor McLaglen's sporadically talented son Andrew directed it, and he later directed the great cop movie *Mitchell* with Joe Don Baker, the subject of one of the best episodes of the show. And in keeping with the film's proscriptive sexual politics at the end of a sex-ed short Mike and Bots start naming other titles for short subjects that include *"How much affection?"*, *"Oh no, pleasure!"*, *"Procreation not Recreation"*, and finally *"McLintock!"*

Wayne is a cattle baron who is king of all he surveys except his unruly wife and the local political class. Not for the first time in a Wayne western the archetypes are Shakespearean - this one is *Taming of the Shrew* and boy does he have a shrew to tame. O'Hara is Wayne's estranged wife and she's exactly the kind of frigid castrating harridan you'd expect.

All that's left for someone like this is for Wayne to knock her around til she cries uncle. The story goes that McLaglen took ill or something and couldn't direct for a few days so, as if on cue, Ford drove up drunk, staggered out of the car, and said to cinematographer William Clothier "Let's go to work, Bill!" McLaglen denies this ever happened, but I wonder if he'd have changed his tune if the movie hadn't been a hit. Still, it's funny to watch this and think of Andrew watching the scene where Jerry Van Dyke dances like a jackass and thinking "I'd like to see that John Ford do better!"

Patrick Wayne is in this. Never turned into much of an actor or a star, shoulders too big for his lean body. He punches the camera like Clint Eastwood will do in his superlative chimp comedies. "When I called you a reactionary, that's merely my generation's term for your generation, nothing personal, sir." Yeah, we believe all this. For sure. McLintock's daughter thinks her beau's being crude to her so Wayne shoots the young man with a blank cartridge, all in good fun, then when Pat goes to spank the young woman, Wayne gives her a shovel to do it. In the movie *Den Of Thieves* Pablo Schreiber and Curtis "50 Cent" Jackson intimidate a young man out of dating one of their daughters with their bulging muscles and it only seems faintly like the poor boy happened on a ten-man porn shoot. That doesn't start here, but its success reminds us that this is how the old boys and real men do it and if you don't like it, take it out on the arches. Wayne and O'Hara's slapstick courtship is as good as Shakespeare to this town. Some women need to be tracked across town as if by the Terminator to have the independence spanked out of them. You couldn't make *McLintock!* today because who the fuck would want to? Wayne always gave hilarious interviews about his projects where he'd say "This is a movie that reflects true old fashioned American values! Justice! Liberty! Pride!" And the movie is just old men grousing about everything until they get their way and punching women and eating entire cows. At the same time Wayne gamely jumping over upturned desk chairs and asymmetrical ladders, chasing his wife through town like he's making the world's slowest copy of the "Beat It" video does have a dusty, bitchy charm. How can we say no this retrograde bullshit? Handily and unequivocally, I suppose, but this absolute garbage has its "virtues", in the abstract. As Sean Clements says, it's like a dispatch from the planet Zeebzorb.

**Cheyenne Autumn (1964)**

The first image in *Cheyenne Autumn* is of a statue of a Cheyenne man on horseback. He's mute and dignified and there's a kind of beauty to the carving. Get used to that level of interrogation because it's about as deep as *Cheyenne Autumn* gets when telling the story of Wounded Knee. Yes it sets precedents for other westerns to be about the experiences of Native Americans but it's for movies like *Dances With Wolves* where the white characters learn from the example of natives, who are peripheral and whose identity could be swapped out easily for any other culture. William Clothier and John Ford take their time in showing the beauty of the Cheyenne way of life, its people, their clothes, their customs, their music, but there's an airless museum quality to it. Furthermore some of these natives are played by white men or Latinos, as was by now custom in Ford's technicolor westerns. Maybe Ford was too old, maybe he just still didn't get it (Native depictions were long his Achilles' heel, though he pumped money into their communities and wished them no ill will), but it's always going to be that Cheyenne is a tangle of useless contradiction. A frequently beautiful film about the plight of the Cheyenne that has no interest in who they are, where white actors are top billed and speak most of the dialogue. The Cheyenne stand in mute defiance and judgment of the white heroes and of white viewers. But the movie ends and the western continued, and then the 70s saw the US Government kill and imprison and frame hundreds of first nations activists because they didn't behave like the natives in this movie. You'd need something stronger than art to pry the fingers of the US Government from the throats of every tribe.

Right in a row are two scenes that play nicely off each other. Edward G. Robinson talks Denver Pyle into supporting the Cheyenne by reminding him they fought at Gettysburg together and neither of them had met a black person before. Right after this a newspaper editor says that stories of bloodthirsty natives are old hat. This paper, from now on, is for the Cheyenne! You can pick which one you think best sums up Ford's attitude, which is kind of him to acknowledge. Ford finally realizing the tide had changed enough that he could make a movie like this also airs out how ill-equipped he was to make it in the first place. Symbolically it's important, but that's about it. That Ford, the man everyone loves to remind us described himself one time as "John Ford and I am a director of Westerns" (good god how I'm sick of that quote. No one ever gets it right, either), made this movie about the lying equivocations of the white men in charge, and brought the last surviving members of his company along with him. Notably absent: John Wayne. Here as far as I can tell in good faith: Widmark, Robinson, Carroll Baker, John Carradine, Carleton Young, John Qualen, Judson Pratt, Bill Borzage, Ted Mapes, and Ben Johnson. Here because Ford asked them to come: Mae Marsh, Jimmy Stewart, Patrick Wayne, George O'Brien, Ken Curtis, Arthur Kennedy, Harry Carey, Jr., and Bing Russell. I don't know about Arthur Kennedy, Sam Harris, William Henry, or Chuck Hayward. Good to see them all, anyway. Jack Pennick died the year before filming started. I'll miss that crooked smile, those haunted eyes. Handsome George O'Brien only hung in this long because the old man loved him and he loved the old man; the last bit of tissue connecting Ford to his hero F.W. Murnau.

The structure doesn't allow much of anything to gather a head of steam. A few minutes with the Cheyenne, a few minutes with Widmark's platoon tracking them down as they leave their reservation, and then a scene with some more white people we may never see again, ranging from Jimmy Stewart as Wyatt Earp to Robinson as the Secretary of the interior. Stewart's tangent is probably of the most interest because it's a career capping check-in with the heroes of *My Darling Clementine* though it's about an hour and a half too long. Stewart's playing cards with Kennedy and Carradine and all three of them are wearing fun hats. Nothing else about the segment really works so you take what you can get. The slackening pace and the elaborate sets start to look less like older Ford and more like *Once Upon a Time in the West* or *Heaven's Gate*. Carroll Baker is good in this, playing a Quaker who keeps up with the Cheyenne on their march - that bit really does work in the context of the story that the movie should be telling. Baker wound up making Italian movies because she wouldn't stand to be taken advantage of by American producers and watching her in the Ford films you feel for her. She's good and she's magnetic! She deserved better than the sex symbol status they tried to foist on her, and that she sued to get quit of. Wild to think that working for Umberto Lenzi was a better fate than working for Paramount.

There's a well-acted conversation between Richard Widmark and Mike Mazurki, who was about to play the marauding Mongolian in *7 Women*, where the latter complains that he's not used to killing people because of what they are, what they can't help, rather than because they're trying to kill him. His comparison point is cossacks, "who wear furry hats and kill the Polish because they're Polish", which meant "communists" to most Americans in the 60s. This movie can't decide if it's coming or going. There's always someone to lead by negative example. When Karl Malden next appears he's wearing a furry hat and speaking in a German accent. He admires the natives but sells them out when he gets his orders because "orders are orders." This is about as uncomplicated as Ford got. Mazurki sees the natives getting rounded up and put in a warehouse. "This time we're the cossacks..." The Cheyenne get tired of waiting and just as Malden's being relieved of command for being a drunken functionary who won't see reason they flee. A shootout ensues and the payoff is a doozy. Malden, back to the camera, striding emptily into the corpse-strewn cinemascope frame, snow on the ground, fog in the air. It's like hell as envisioned in Nobuo Nagakawa's Jigoku. It predicts the aesthetic of J. Lee Thompson's *The White Buffalo*.

Evidently Edward G. Robinson couldn't make it to the location shoot for the ending because the troops are rear-projected when he arrives to talk to the Cheyenne and they use a double for his approach to Victory Cave, which is a set. It's eerie. Living breathing people as wallpaper. Remind you of anything? A scene later the chanting of the Cheyenne is captured in flanger-fied false stereo. Ford just can't make anything real here. The ending should mean more, all of this should, but it ends and at least the feeling of a heroic journey culminating in a dreadful, ambiguous future is appropriately emblematic of how things really went. They walked all that way to prove a point and were followed every step of the journey for a worse one. That's our history. That's how we tell it, without shame or guilt.

**Young Cassidy (1965, Jack Cardiff & John Ford)**

Jack Cardiff's turn to direction had the same trouble as many a technician's first outings behind the camera. The opportunities were scant and thankless to begin with, especially in England. Like his *Things To Come* director William Cameron Menzies - it didn't matter to studio heads how talented he was, they had money to make and they thought they knew what audiences wanted, and mostly that meant undistinguished thrillers. He was a camera operator on fiction and cinematographer on documentaries and wound up a camera operator on *The Life & Death of Colonel*

*Blimp*, and so impressed director/producers Michael Powell & Emeric Pressburger that they promoted him to cinematographer on *A Matter of Life & Death*. For the next few years no one alive was better at shooting technicolor. But as is always the way of these things, that wasn't enough. He wanted to direct. He made the switch in the late 50s with two now forgotten thrillers and then his "big break" was the D.H. Lawrence adaptation *Sons & Lovers*, which premiered at the 1960 Cannes Film Festival. It looks creaky indeed next to the big prize winners that year; *L'Avventura* and *La Dolce Vita*. Still if I had to guess it was that rustic drama that told producers he'd be a suitable replacement for John Ford when he fell ill about a week into production of his Sean O'Casey biopic, which was to be Ford's last film in Ireland. He'd adapted *The Plough & The Stars* already (and Lady Gregory's *Rising of the Moon*; Edith Evans appears in this as Lady Gregory) and had O'Casey's approval before shooting started, but then Ford fell ill and O'Casey fell even iller. He died before the thing was finished.

Cardiff does a perfectly fine job (he says four minutes of Ford's footage wound up in the final product, Tag Gallagher estimates that it's closer to ten), which is about what he was capable of as a director. His thriller *Dark of the Sun* is good value. *My Geisha, The Girl on the Motorcycle* and *The Freakmaker* are not. The opening is beautiful, one gallery-worthy image of Irish streets and children after another, but the movie must eventually start. Cardiff has a more modern edge here than Ford would have brought to it, but it's still tempting to imagine what he'd have done with it if he could have lurched from his sick bed, might have really been his *Frenzy*. Rod Taylor is our young poet, starting riots like those that assailed the release of Synge's *Playboy of the Western World*, and romancing both Maggie Smith and Julie Christie, the lucky devil. Christie stokes his passionate side, Smith the bookseller brings out his inner intellectual. We meet the strapping young lad digging ditches as the wealthy elite ride by in fancy carriages. It's not long before he's throwing punches and hopping beds.

Ted Scaife was a camera operator on *Black Narcissus*, which Cardiff had photographed and on *The Third Man*, which *Rising of the Moon* photographer Robert Krasker had photographed, so he was a logical promotion on this. After this he suddenly did a run of incredible, legendary movies; *The Dirty Dozen, A Walk with Love and Death, Play Dirty,* and *Hannie Caulder* among them. He and Cardiff restage *Battleship Potemkin* on Dublin cobblestones. The film tantalizingly threatens to become something gorier and wilder every once and a while. He uses his zoom lens, which Ford would never have done, and his split diopter, which I'm not confident Ford knew existed. All this trickery though, it's pretty plain that it's because Cardiff doesn't really know how to tell the story. The best stuff is functionally covered, like Cassidy haggling with a grocer to get provisions for his sick mother after the English bank refuses to help him. The ending would be powerfully upsetting, Cassidy realizing the life of an artist is a life lived alone, except that the next second he's having a cheery moment with a kid. Way to pull a punch.

It's never easy to try and turn a writer's search for prose and success into something cinematic. Terence Davies managed, but he's in the pantheon along with Ford. Cardiff falls quite a bit short of that standard. The truth is the movie lacks the immediacy of the six line poem Yeats (played by Michael Redgrave here) wrote about the riots surrounding the release of *Playboy*:

Once, when midnight smote the air,
Eunuchs ran through Hell and met
On every crowded street to stare
Upon great Juan riding by:
Even like these to rail and sweat
Staring upon his sinewy thigh.

### 7 Women (1965)

If *Cheyenne Autumn* and *Sergeant Rutledge* were apologias (which is perhaps a debatable point) for Ford's previous treatment of the people relegated to peripheral or villainous roles in his movies, *7 Women* seems to be the same thing for the women whom John Wayne had hoisted onto his knee over the years. *7 Women* has male characters, but the dynamics between the women are the same as that which applied to all of his pictures. Eddie Albert's zealous priest indeed has the hysterical willfulness of someone like Grace Kelly in *Mogambo*. Margaret Leighton has the staunch pragmatism and situational blinders of Henry Fonda in *Fort Apache*. The way she looks at Sue Lyon (the film's Jeffrey Hunter analogue), with stuttering regard, with tenderness that tears her apart inside, like Dorothy Jordan touching John Wayne's coat in *The Searchers*. Betty Field has the hysterical nature of Boris Karloff in *The Lost Patrol*, Mildred Dunnock the sideways but steadfast gallantry of Victor McLaglen in *She Wore a Yellow Ribbon*, Anna Lee like Richard Widmark in *Cheyenne Autumn*, Flora Robson like John Carradine in *The Grapes of Wrath*, Jane Chang like Carradine in *Stagecoach* ...and then there's Anne Bancroft, who's maybe more John Wayne than John Wayne. She struts into the film with sexual certainty and no patience for Leighton's god. She touches Lyon without the fear that Leighton has. She smokes like a chimney, constantly bringing up the specter of sensuality. She wears trousers and claims she's better than any male doctor they could have found. She's a reckoning on two legs and my favourite Ford hero. Astonishing to think she was a last minute replacement for Patricia Neal. This is as iconic a part as Mrs. Robinson.

Husband and wife John McCormack and Janet Green wrote the script from a story by Norah Lofts. McCormack has a considerably smaller resume than Green. Green wrote *Sapphire* and together they wrote *Victim*, both for Basil Dearden, both about the prejudices of the English. Lofts was very concerned with witches as a stand-in for women deemed useless or problematic, writing both *Jassy* and the Hammer horror film *The Witches* with Joan Fontaine. Bancroft's Dr. Cartwright is another of her modern witches, suspected of turning Sue Lyon atheist by Leighton. People like to talk about the confusion between the title and the actual number of women. There's two explanations; the movie means the 7 white women or the 7 women are the ones Bancroft sacrifices herself to save. There is much talk about the demands and expectations placed on womanhood. Robson needs to have a baby to feel like a woman. Leighton can't give in to her desire for either Lyon or Bancroft, and the more Bancroft defies her the worse her obstinance grows. "I hope your god is merciful!" Every utterance has an edge to it, like everyone's a good scare away from upending their entire worldview.

Bancroft's woman of science and vice is here to rip their god out of the sky. Taken with the bleak ending that actually supports Bancroft's heathen solutions to problems of the spirit and the flesh and it's no surprise this flopped. Audiences were wrong. This is good. Ford doesn't get much in the heads of the Chinese and Mazurki and Strode playing Chinese is appallingly silly stuff (especially because the actual Chinese talent on hand is so good - Hans William Lee is very good indeed, probably scoring the most emotional line read in the piece), but this is one of his best and most forceful films. He doesn't treat it with the stateliness of the apology films, he just gets lost in the dramatic currents and interpersonal dynamics. These gals are wound so tight that even the appearance of a bottle of liquor is enough to send everyone into a fit of pique.

When Mazurki the Mongolian and his men arrive all that thrashing subtext becomes text. They press Chang into sexual slavery, they kill the Chinese women and children the missionaries had been helping (pre-saging *Apocalypse Now* and Kurtz' story of hacking off inoculated limbs), which of course throws into pretty stark relief the treatment that Natives received at the hands of Americans. Leighton retreats further into puritanical derangement, chastising Bancroft for making a deal on behalf of the other 7 women with her body and their captors for making her. Bancroft, however, cuts a nevertheless rational and dignified figure after sleeping with Mazurki. She's unbothered by the judgment because she made the decision that kept her in good with her values, her own god. You can feel Ford trying to do the same thing time and again. It's only after she knows that the other women have been safely led away that she gets revenge on the man for his murder of the innocents. "I've never been home to England," says Flora Robson, dreamily, realizing she may die without ever seeing it. Which means that she never found a home. The film is populated by the forever lost, the people who couldn't simply be themselves. Lyon doesn't quite realize what she's asking when she asks Bancroft to try and bargain for the safety of Field's baby. "That sounds like a text, Mrs. Andrews, but you made it up. We chose a lonely life to help others. What right have we to shout abuse behind our celibate walls?" All the others can offer Bancroft is prayer. She can actually do something for them. One final kiss for Mildred Dunnock, the film's one real allowance, and then the greatest last line in all of cinema.

**Chesty: Tribute to a Legend (1976)**

Not, as I initially assumed, a profile of Chesty Morgan, the stripper and softcore actress, this, Ford's posthumously released final film is a tribute to Lieutenant General Louis B. "Chesty" Puller, who looks like a schizophrenic's drawing of Edward G. Robinson. Ford finished it in 1970 but it wasn't screened until '76, three years after Ford died. John Wayne narrates, but first introduces himself, drunk if I don't miss my guess, still wearing his cowboy get-up (he must have been on the set of one of those dreadful Mark Rydell or Andrew V. McLaglen westerns when they caught up with him). Then it's off to Virginia Military Institute. Ford once more photographs the rituals and dancer-like movements of soldiers with a certain degree of awe.

Wayne takes us back to the start of Chesty's career, joining up in time for World War I, then (jesus wept) joining the American backed Gendarmerie of Haiti, who actively hindered the local's governance of themselves. This is all rendered in stock footage; I guess it's possible Chesty's in those pictures, but you can't really see him. Then it was off to wreak more havoc. Woody Strode would have been playing Patrice Lumumba in *Black Jesus*, the kind of guy Chesty would have been sent to kill, right around the time Ford was shooting this. Chesty proposed to his wife sight unseen (normal stuff) and she said no so he kept working at her 'til she relented. Their wedding photo is insane; both grinning like zealots, their expressions offering metric tons of inscrutable inner workings towards completely distinct goals. Pearl Harbor was next. Ford led Puller into battle in the pacific.

We finally meet Chesty (who officially died in '71, though might actually have gone during this interview) and he looks furious to still be breathing through that flapping flounder's maw on his face. Wayne tells a bewildering story that I truly wonder about where apparently Ford had Wayne come visit him in Guadalcanal and dressed him like a cowboy and sent him to go mingle with the troops like he was Bob Hope or Marilyn Monroe. Cosplaying for freedom. Another hilarious anecdote has Chesty being shown a flamethrower for the first time and wondering out loud where the bayonet is supposed to go. It takes little imagination to picture this amphibian psychopath stabbing people and incinerating them in one go. Then it's off to Korea.

Chesty led the charge at Inchon during Korea, where they fried communists indiscriminately and started using chemical weapons. Amazing to think Wayne had just made *The Green Berets* two years earlier and we were desperately losing the Vietnam war when this was shot. There's some pretty ghoulish footage of American soldiers' bodies being dragged out of frost-covered combat zones on sleds. To the bitter end of his military career Chesty said he'd give everything up if he could just get a gun in his hand again and go kill some more. He still visits the grave of Stonewall Jackson and Robert E. Lee, the lunatics who inspired him to get into the army to begin with. Seeing Chesty Puller standing framed in Ford's camera (quite nicely, it must be said) I think about the arguments I've gotten into with other socialists about the relative usefulness of Joseph Stalin to the modern cause. I think it's time we got rid of statues to old war "heroes". Ford's heart is not in this, which is a bit of a relief. Wayne keeps fucking his lines up and he doesn't go back for second takes. He made it fast, this distasteful little number, then let it sit on a shelf. Then it was someone else's problem.

Ford's last movie was met with boos when it played its one posthumous premiere screening and then was shuttled back into a vault like the rest of his war pictures, only emerging to complicate the legacy of his fiction. In truth, however, it needed no further complicating. "Staining" might be the better word, but Ford had already stained his own work plenty without the horrific sights and sounds in his war-time non-fiction. Ford had lived his way, stumbling through Hollywood history like King Kong, laying waste to the emotions of the people closest to him, leaving a trail of beautiful ruin in his wake, an American portrait that all but replaced the truth of American history. Ford created America as much as any general or president or any other uniformed killer, and it is his America that now must be broken through in order to reach the truths it protected. Ford lived his life, as much as he could, with the dictate uttered by Nathan Brittles in *She Wore A Yellow Ribbon*, "Never apologize, Mister, it's a sign of weakness" a mantra, as we've discussed, that became the title of Lindsay Anderson's collected writings. But Ford did apologize. He needed to be loved, he wanted badly to be understood, and with every step closer to his death, at age 79, surrounded by the dozen or so admirers he had left, he knew that he was going to leave wreckage behind him, as well as a life and a body of work. He'd thrown punches at friends, ruined lives, chased women who wouldn't or couldn't love him back, turned away from the people who did love him, and finally in giving a parting gift to a friend, made a documentary about the righteousness of the American imperial project. It had to be so. Nothing Ford ever did was uncomplicated. And no work of art, no line of a poem, no gesture as profound as John Wayne grabbing his arm as he retreats from the family he loves with his head but hates with his heart, nothing John Ford ever gave to us was merely a gift. There were strings attached, and now, 50 years after his death, we remain tangled in them. It's our job to live with his contradictions. It's our job to take John Ford out of America and see them both for what they were, what they failed to become, what they wanted so desperately to be. America was John Wayne and John Ford, and though it may become something greater, but we must never forget what it was.

PART 9

# THE MODERN FORD CANON

Ford's influence was felt long before he stopped making movies. In helping to create the director's guild and end the studio practice of team filmmaking – two directors assigned to a project as on his movies *Salute* and *Born Reckless* – which in turn helped directors finally hone their own style and become brands long before American critics had taken up the French Auteur theory about film authorship. Were it not for the work of a handful of directors in setting up their union, Ford might have been the last American auteur. The truly remarkable thing about Ford was that, unlike many of his peers, he was one of the first directors whose influence could not be subtly applied. If you were paying tribute to Ford, with, say. dolly shots at Monument Valley, everyone knew what you were doing. The sum total of cinema became an evolving thing, but Ford and a few others kept their images above the fray. People knew when you were cribbing from Ford. They didn't know or cared who stole from even directors as good as Tay Garnett, John Huston, or Robert Siodmak. And certainly without Ford most of what follows is unthinkable...

Lindsay Anderson started directing acidic, concupiscent wonders even as he was still a critic taking stock of Ford's evolution as an artist and interviewing him when possible. Anderson, like Jean-Luc Godard, started a small revolution in his local film scene with his critically minded peers. The British New Wave isn't as celebrated as the one the French created but the great works are still stunning (though funnily enough the ones most people have seen and remember, the ones starring The Beatles, were directed by an American). Anderson's two real contributions to this new kind of English picture were *This Sporting Life* (which Ford liked), and *If....* (which I don't think Ford saw). What Anderson, who understood Ford's films with a certainty and just enough distance that he frequently seems like his most fair critic, took from Ford's films is a poetic perspective. There isn't much that links Ford's work and Anderson's pictorially but what Anderson prized in Ford's films was that the subject was never more important the experiences of his characters emotions. *This Sporting Life* likely appealed to Ford because more than a movie about a man's sexuality or his profession, it's about the fact of his blinding passion, the things he *wants* that in turn destroy him. *Young Cassidy*'s script has a very similar arc, which if Ford had finished directing, would have likely flattered Anderson. *If*…., one of the finest films ever made, by contrast is the inverse of Ford's military pageantry movies. Malcolm McDowell and his gang are given entryway into a world of military order and religious discipline and overturn it, becoming like the hated other tribes whom the cavalry are sent to destroy. They fight back and become, from within, the undoing of the making of the next class of vicars and generals and schoolmasters. It's a queer melding of Ford's interests – the rejection of a status quo unwilling to make room for you, and the finding of one's inner mettle to prove yourself through collective, disciplined action. Anderson's teenagers, like the men of *They Were Expendable* and *Fort Apache*, break the rules as much to protect each other as to prove themselves. He saw Ford just before he died, aware that whatever they had been to each other as student and teacher, then as peers, and now as men who would never again mean the same thing to their public, was inevitably changed. Anderson was not sentimental, something he learned from the best of Ford, but in 1987 he made *The Whales of August*, set in Ford's birthplace, Maine, starring D.W. Griffith's leading lady Lilian Gish and Ford's old friend Dobe – Harry Carey, Jr - one final look backwards at the men who made movies into dreams of escape, of cruelty and love. He said goodbye to Ford with a film that Ford himself could have made. He died in 1994.

The French critic Bertrand Tavernier also had admiration for Ford, and got even closer to him. Rumor has it he actually bathed the ornery director when he asked him to during a visit to Paris. Tavernier's own movies had a musicality right out of Ford's movies, from the jazz scores of *Round Midnight* and *Beatrice*, to the delta stylings found in *Mississippi Blues*. His interest in military ceremony and chivalry seems right out of Ford's cavalry films, and movies like *Life and Nothing But* and *Captain Conan* could very well have spilled from Ford's camera pen; similarly the breezy, near angelic goings on in *A Sunday in the Country* recall his Judge Priest movies ambling pace and lovingly created milieu.

In 1961 TV director Sam Peckinpah makes his first feature film, *The Deadly Companions*, starring Ford's leading lady Maureen O'Hara and co-starring Ford regulars Chuck Hayward, Chill Wills, and Strother Martin, and shot by Ford's cinematographer William Clothier. He begins to build up his own stock company to rival Ford's, many of his favored actors right out of Ford's rolodex including Ben Johnson, Emilio Fernández, Edmond O'Brien, Cliff Lyons, and William Holden. Slim Pickens (the thinking man's Andy Devine) also started appearing in Peckinpah's movies and never stopped. Like Ford, Peckinpah was a terror on set and a famous drunk, and his movies dove even deeper into the waters of the homoerotic historical than Ford's. *Ride The High Country* (released soon after and transfixed by a lot of the same sexual paranoias as *Two Rode Together*), *Major Dundee, The Wild Bunch, Pat Garrett & Billy The Kid, Bring Me The Head of Alfredo Garcia* all have a world-weary erotic longing, movies about men who destroy themselves and try to destroy the world because they can't simply be with the men they love. Peckinpah's romance of male bonding is right out of Ford and his melancholy seems to be at once inwardly representative and also a comment on the world of Ford's movies. Those beautiful lies no longer possible. The west was not a sacred place of reckoning and discovery, it was a necropolis. By the time of Cormac McCarthy's *Blood Meridian* trying to look at the west and see only its beauty wasn't merely naïve it was retrograde, a purposeful twisting of the knife in the backs of the tribes and historians who did so much to bring the crimes of cavalrymen to light. And still Peckinpah embraced something of Ford's lyricism in describing the destruction of these old tales and what they were meant to cover up. They must die, but he's sad to see them go. He'd restage the departure of Ethan Edwards in *The Searchers* over and over again and surely there's no greater Ford line not in a Ford movie than Joel McCrea saying "All I want is to enter my house justified" in *Ride The High Country*.

Ford later obliquely complained about *The Wild Bunch* but we know him to be a tellingly jealous man prone to using insults to cover up affection. It's possible he recognized too much of himself and his own desires to compliment the film, especially because Peckinpah was freer with his characters sexuality and the violence. The effect of *The Wild Bunch* was felt right away in other corners of a panicking old Hollywood as Ford's old friend Howard Hawks made *Rio Lobo* in 1970 and it features bright red squibs out of Peckinpah's make-up kit and a scene involving a train heist. A scene of William Holden shooting a woman in the stomach and screaming "Bitch!" must have set off old-timers used to wrapping everything in innuendo, to say nothing of glorifying the cowboy and the old fashioned values he was meant to symbolize. Peckinpah also made oddball comedies about male bonding (*The Ballad of Cable Hogue*, *Junior Bonner*) and even made an extremely perverse riff on *The Quiet Man* in his 1971 rape revenge movie *Straw Dogs*. In that a repressed young American returns to the old country (in this case England, which frees Peckinpah up to be less romantic than Ford) with his beautiful native wife in tow, and she immediately fires up the libidos of every creep for miles who must have her. The film's climactic donnybrook is an insane home siege gun fight instead of a fist fight between two simpatico chums. Peckinpah's politics were more openly anarchist than Ford's, revealing a void in the heart of his cinema where Ford's beating heart should have been. It is possible to walk away from his body of work believing that Peckinpah made movies because he couldn't kill people.

What's unsurprising is that Peckinpah's *Cross of Iron*, his movie about a marauding gang of Nazis during World War 2 didn't wind up having much in common with Ford, but a similarly designed movie, Michael Mann's *The Keep* does have a little more in common with Ford. Centering at first on a Nazi platoon invading a Romanian village, their commandant (Jürgen Prochnow) must call in reinforcements in the form of a Jewish scholar (Ian McKellen). Soon an unlikely band of allies has to come together to face a crisis of faith behind enemy lines. The conflicting approaches to the spiritual evil recalls Thursday and Kirby's conflicting tactics in *Fort Apache*. The men of *The Keep* have to combat their foe and also deal with the waning regard of the villagers, which is right out of a Ford frontier picture. Mann's *Last of the Mohicans*, his version of *Drums Along The Mohawk* (which it resembles more than previous adaptations of the James Fenimore Cooper novel it's taken from), has some of Ford's stiff upper lip rugged masculinity (to say nothing of his visual poetry) and his *Miami Vice* movie and TV series center on the kind of male friendship that was key to Ford's films and his life. *Ali*, his biography of the great boxer, has a little second-hand Ford taken from *Raging Bull* and the same imperfect but noble hero who marched through Ford's films all his life. Mann's code of honor broadly recalls Ford and the perimeters are wrapped up in critiques of the kind of institutions Ford used. He never had much use for the police, the job most of Mann's heroes have, because his life was so far from the rigors of everyday struggle. His lifestyle was so far removed from most of urban American life, so he never dealt with cops like most people and so couldn't develop much of an interest in them as anything but figures of fun. However the ways in which he deconstructed the purpose of the cavalry and both the union and confederate armies has very much the wary respect and fascination that Mann has for the police. Al Pacino and Robert De Niro's single-minded pursuit of one another brings to mind Thursday and York in *Fort Apache* but also Wayne in *The Searchers*, except of course that Ford could never give a movie over to the interiority of Scar the way Mann does De Niro's bank robber or indeed the way he does Wes Studi's Magua in *Last of the Mohicans*, who gets monologues that are tersely constructed but revealing of the history of horror visited upon indigenous tribes by the conquering Europeans.

David Lean became something like the British John Ford, following his subject matter to the letter (he even worked with Katharine Hepburn in *Summertime*, a movie implicitly about Hepburn's refusal of Ford and the rest of her famous suitors and what life looks like when you're trying to reconnect with the world after losing it). He made domestic comedies and movies about men at war before becoming a specialist in doomed romance, and then finally making his epic historical pictures. *Lawrence of Arabia* and *Doctor Zhivago* are self-investigating looks at the purpose of warfare and the bitter irony of becoming skilled at it. T.E. Lawrence understands the Arabian people he's embedded with and he understands his native English masters but he can't help but sabotage the former's chances of independence from their colonizers. Still the movie soft pedals Lawrence's sociopathy and has as much brown-face as any Ford movie, which continues to make its classic status an awkward thing indeed. However, I'm of a mind that it's a good thing that people are made uncomfortable by the movies that used to make billions of dollars at the box office. Look what we just *accepted*, indeed applauded*!* What else do we just deal with? What of our tendencies will we be shocked by in the rearview mirror, and have we artists as good as Lean and Ford were to nestle them comfortably in work that will still follow us? One that *hasn't* is Lean's penultimate film *Ryan's Daughter*, his riff on *The Quiet Man* (*Straw Dogs* followed it by only a year, really separating the classicists from the modernists). Pauline Kael told Lean to his face that she thought it was awful and he was so hurt by it he stopped directing for almost 15 years. When he returned it was with *A Passage to India*, his own *Cheyenne Autumn*, which attempts to give back to Indians what Ford attempted to give back to the Cheyenne. Their success rates are equal, though I'd sooner watch Ford's pictures than Lean's in this case. Lean and Ford both were just too wrapped up in both traditional filmmaking ideas and their own identity to fully divest themselves of either. In the end they could only be themselves. Now their one-time popularity is our problem and our legacy.

The first movie that appears to have been made in conversation with the Ford body of work and indeed his life may be Cy Endfield's *Zulu*, about the siege of a British hospital by warriors in 1879. Endfield had been blacklisted in America for his politics and moved to England to start over, making the intense working class trucker movie *Hell Drivers* as a farewell gauntlet to America's censoriousness. When he gained control of his contract and money, it was in a partnership with actor Stanley Baker. Together they made *Child in the House, Sea Fury, Jet Storm, Zulu* and the magnificently depressive anti-epic *Sands of the Kalahari*. Because of Endfield's open political leanings and his intimate interest in the working class his movies resembled the work of directors like William Wellman, Raoul Walsh, or Jules Dassin more than they did Ford, which is what makes *Zulu* such a fascinating exception. The socialist Endfield has to justify a movie in which a tribe of black, othered warriors are his villain. He does his best to give them humanity and space and life you can understand – certainly the great chanted songs and charges linger well after the movie is over and are not simply acts of menace, their voices are beautiful – while also trying to make something between a siege western a la Hugo Fregonese and Val Lewton's *Apache Drums* and a cavalry picture like Ford's *She Wore a Yellow Ribbon*. As in Ford's cavalry films we meet a rogue's gallery of loafers who need to make good, strong silent sergeants not looking to be heroes, and at the center of it all are two officers at loggerheads like Fonda and Wayne in *Fort Apache*. Endfield's photography is less self-consciously beautiful (he couldn't glorify the brutal and awful necessity of survival – "*You think I could stand this butcher's yard more than once...*" says Baker's beleaguered Lieutenant Chard after a whole film putting up with the cavalier attitude of Michael Caine's younger and brasher Lt. Bromhead, who got his post because of his well-connected family) but his pacing and characterization is up there with the best of Ford. *Zulu* asks the average colonial subject to rise above and beyond the call of duty and finding that it is small men, sick men, weak men, and strong, noble men alike who weather the horrors of conquest when it's ironically visited upon them for the first time. Kings make commands, ordinary men follow them, with no particular feeling for who is at the expense of that order. You feel tired when the movie is over. An epic at war with itself. Baker would later star in a six-part remake of *How Green Was My Valley* in 1975 for television, just before his death at age 48.

At the same time as *Zulu* another young director was painting his own Ford impression in a whole new palette. Sergio Leone was a vocal

Ford fan and after years as an apprentice director in the Italian film industry (he worked under Vittorio De Sica among others) he struck out to change his fortunes and wound up changing the history of film. With a borrowed American star (Clint Eastwood, who like Ward Bond had been on American TV westerns and had the swagger and intense eyes of John Wayne) he made *A Fistful of Dollars*, the first successful Italian Western, an unexpected international crossover hit. Soon after he followed it up with a sequel (*For A Few Dollars More*) starring *Liberty Valance*'s Lee Van Cleef and soon the whole Italian film industry was devoted to making cheap westerns in Spain with American movie stars, many of them former Ford heroes like Woody Strode and Henry Fonda, who both starred in Leone's 1968 *Once Upon A Time in the West* playing against type. Leone's value system was about as far from Ford as you could imagine. Indeed part of the charge of seeing Henry Fonda in *Once Upon A Time in the West* is that Leone has him doing such outwardly villainous and dreadful things that a relaxed censorship board (the Italians were always pioneers in the art of cinematic torture) allows Leone to really show. Leone's world is full of crooks, cowards, bandits, and murderers and he turns their trespasses into Botticellian compositions, chasing Ford's more considered pacing over a more fashionable New Wave-indebted montage.

Leone's star Clint Eastwood would turn to directing in the early 1970s but wouldn't start truly showing the signs of his Ford appreciation until later (though he almost immediately courted the kind of controversy Ford movies stir now by making movies about runaway female sexuality and the men who must tame their urges). His 1973 film *High Plains Drifter*, is like Leone in that its value system is the opposite of Ford's. A stranger comes to town to save them from bandits and they reveal themselves to be just as crooked as any outside force. Eastwood's interloper is like a gun-toting variation on Terence Stamp's character in Pier Paolo Pasolini's *Teorema*. He forces everyone to reveal and then destroy themselves. By contrast his 1976 western *The Outlaw Josey Wales*, is much more gentle, and continues Ford's work of challenging the assumptions of western tales of bravery. His 1977 film *The Gauntlet*, in which Eastwood must protect Sandra Locke from cops and criminals alike, has the same coiled chemistry as the Ford films with Wayne and O'Hara. Eastwood began styling himself like Wayne as well, a beer drinking My-way-or-the-highway loner who got results and beat the hell out of anyone who stood in his way. His Dirty Harry character softened up to become more Wayne-like in the later entries of that film series (especially the Eastwood directed *Sudden Impact*) and his role in the boxing comedies *Every Which Way But Loose* and *Any Which Way You Can* have the damaged pride and hard-bitten spirit of Wayne roles in movies like *She Wore A Yellow Ribbon* and *Donovan's Reef*. Replace Lee Marvin with a chimp and you've got the vibe.

Later Eastwood movies like *Honkytonk Man, Bronco Billy, Heartbreak Ridge, The Bridges of Madison County, Absolute Power, Million Dollar Baby, Changeling, Gran Torino, Invictus, The Mule, Richard Jewell,* and *Cry Macho* all bear the hallmarks of a Ford's technique and humanity. There's the lonely heroes rediscovering themselves in the reflection of a community out of *Grapes of Wrath, She Wore a Yellow Ribbon,* or *Wagon Master*; the creation of a new Irish boxing legend to rival *The Quiet Man* in *Million Dollar Baby*; the slow unearthing of and eradication of inner prejudice in *Gran Torino*. When racist old Walt Kowalski learns, like Ethan Edwards, that the world is moving in a direction he cannot follow in *Gran Torino*, he sacrifices himself so his surrogate family can continue in his absence. The slow begrudging love and respect of individuals is a theme shared by Ford and Eastwood, from the central illicit pairing in *Madison County* to the adoption of an old man by a cartel in *The Mule* to the white man who discovers paradise in a Mexican kitchen in *Cry Macho*, and perhaps my personal favorite Paul Walter Hauser's title role in *Richard Jewell*, pitched somewhere between Thomas Mitchell and Andy Devine's honest Falstaffian second fiddles, who is slowly exonerated by a lawyer who learns there is no more honest man than Richard. Eastwood took Ford's thematic concerns and his filmmaking economy and brought them as far as he could into the 21st century and met with a surprising amount of success, even though Eastwood has been painted as a rabid conservative in his private life (and like Ford his films tell another story). Eastwood's heroes frequently, as Ford did in his own life, find more connection with the men thrown into their lives through circumstance than they ever did with their flesh and blood family. Eastwood's own favorite director from his early leading man days, Michael Cimino, made two films about the struggles of immigrants old and new, in *The Deer Hunter* and *Heaven's Gate*, which share Ford's acknowledgement of the essential violence of history and the care and attention lavished on ceremony and ritual (the dances in *Wagon Master* and *My Darling Clementine* and the election in *Liberty Valance* recur throughout Cimino's work). Eastwood's most famous revisionist western, *Unforgiven*, is dedicated to Sergio Leone and Don Siegel, but there's no mistaking its dusk-lit compositions and Eastwood's monologue about violence as homage to anyone but Ford. "It's a hell of a thing, killin' a man.

You take away all he's got, and all he's ever gonna have." It's ridiculously easy to picture those words coming out of Wayne's mouth. Eastwood was burying them even as he was praising them, a tricky thing to pull off but he more than manages and created one of the best American films in the process, a new *The Searchers* for a new world.

Clint Eastwood wasn't the only director to repurpose and reconfigure Ford's Westerns into something for the late 20th and 21st century. In Nancy Kelly's *1990 Thousand Pieces of* Gold a woman sold into marriage breaks free and becomes her own person on the frontier in the 1880s; a woman finally allowed the full independence Ford dangled in front of his frontier wives and finally gave to Dr. Cartwright in 7 Wo*men, on*ly to then cruelly take it away. Michael Apted's *Thunderheart* has a Martin Pawley-style part-native cop head to an over-policed Native reservation to solve a murder and find himself among the tribe. Kevin Costner tries to make something as profound as Ford with *Dances with Wolves* but ends up in *Cheyenne Autumn* territory. He tries again in 2003 with *Open Range* and finally succeeds at Ford's full bore sentimentality without looking back over his shoulder to make sure he got the politics right. John Lee Hancock makes his best film when he's asked to remake John Wayne's *The Alamo*, taking over from Fordian Ron Howard. Hancock did add back the darkness of characterization Ford would have brought to the original *Alamo* if he'd been in the director's chair instead of Wayne. Howard himself made the very fine and very traditional *The Missing* around this time, his only real Western but far from his only Ford film. From the *Flesh*-inspired *Cinderella Man* to the reverse *Quiet Man* narrative of *Far and Away* to his own accidental *Tobacco Road* in the inexcusable *Hillbilly Elegy*, the men-at-sea theatrics of *In the Heart of the Sea*, and the men-under-sea theatrics of *Thirteen Lives*. Chris Eska's *The Retrieval* splits the difference between the brilliantly spiritual western work of Charles Burnett (whose own cop movie *Glass Shield* is something of a Fordian morality tale) and Ford's own myth-destruction and self-loathing. Tommy Lee Jones' exquisitely depressive *The Homesman* combines *7 Women* and *Wagon Master* with quiet fervor. Jeremy Renner's alignment with a local tribe, like Wayne's cavalry commanders in *She Wore a Yellow Ribbon* and *Fort Apache* make him uniquely qualified to catch a killer of a native woman in Taylor Sheridan's *Wind River*. Sheridan has since become a household name for his lightly Fordian *Yellowstone* TV franchise, starring Costner and pitched specifically at an audience who does not want their symbols of western masculinity and conviction challenged. Kasi Lemmons' *Harriet*, a biopic in the Ford mold, tells the story of the abolitionist Harriett Tubman in terms Ford was coining in the late 30s. French director Jacques Audiard came to America to make his oddball western *The Sisters Brothers*, which features a very Wayne-and-McLaglen-style love between the title characters. Andrew Stanton's sci-fi marvel *John Carter* begins as a Monument Valley western (Carter's back-story is much like John Wayne's in *The Horse Soldiers*) before heading to Mars, where Carter inserts himself in tribal conflict right out of *Fort Apache*. Gore Verbinski's *Lone Ranger* is shot conspicuously in Ford's Monument Valley and combines elements from *The Searchers*, *Fort Apache, Once Upon a Time in the West, The Iron Horse, Heaven's Gate, Young Mr. Lincoln, Deadwood, The Wild Bunch, Looney Tunes* and finally Buster Keaton's *The General*. In other words the ultimate Western and though it was instantly unfashionable and has only gotten *more* unfashionable thanks to its cast's personal lives, it's one of the finest motion pictures made in my lifetime.

George Roy Hill was one of a handful of directors who rose to (further) prominence making westerns in the broken mirror image of Ford's. Just as Peckinpah's westerns were like Ford movies that traded soldier's honor and cute codes for boozy vulgarity and gore, so was Hill's *Butch Cassidy and the Sundance Kid* an even cuter modernized version of the Ford concerns, amplifying his sentimentality while gently testing the waters of a relaxing concerns about morality on screen. Butch and Sundance have a woman between them to prevent their longing for each other to grow too large and they're hunted by faceless riders out of a horror movie. Hill's movies were usually too giddy and clever and plot-driven to be much like Ford's but they met in the middle on the ultimate hang out movie, *Slap Shot*. Like *Donavan's Reef* meets *Salute* meets *The Long Voyage Home* meets *Stagecoach* meets *The Last Hurrah*, *Slap Shot* has a million Ford concerns and one of the best instances of an attempt at creating a real-world Ford hero. Ford's men as played by Wayne, Fonda, Stewart, are sometimes too legendary to seem real. *Slap Shot*'s hockey players and their crooked coach played by Strother Martin, even the team captain played by matinee idol Paul Newman, are all exactly the kind of hate-filled, go-nowhere, beer swilling rejects you might actually see in real life. Like they took one of Ford's cavalry regiments and tossed them at a bus station and told them to get jobs. Newman began moonlighting as a modern Ford hero, perhaps most memorably in Sidney Lumet's *The Verdict*, a superlative movie about alcoholism and not knowing how to do anything other than what you're good at as your life otherwise falls apart. Lumet's stoic form occasionally yielded Fordian touches, as in his Larry McMurtry adaptation *Lovin' Molly* or his E.L. Doctorow adaptation *Daniel* and his last film *Before the Devil Knows You're Dead* but Lumet's deliberately lacerating concerns and high modernist form kept him energetically far away from Ford for the most part. Newman's cantankerous old timers in Robert Benton's great *Nobody's Fool* and Martin Scorsese's *The Color of Money* are Wayne/Fonda-esque, the way they want to impart some of what they know to the younger people around them while aware that the time when that information could be useful is fast coming to an end.

Scorsese of course is one of cinema's most unrepentant Fordians. His debut for Roger Corman, *Boxcar Bertha* is like a full metal *Grapes of Wrath*, complete with crucified Tom Joad in David Carradine's Big Bill Shelly [his father John Carradine, Ford's Jim Casy, rounds out the cast]. It's fair to say that there's a little Ford theory in everything Scorsese does but it most especially rears its head in *Raging Bull*, a movie he says he was inspired to shoot in Black and White because he saw how ludicrous Wayne's *Quiet Man* boxing trunks looked in color. *Raging Bull* is of course the noisy b-side to *Quiet Man*, a movie not about what happens when you successfully pull yourself out of your boxing career to settle down, but what happens when the rage and strength it took for you to kill a man in the ring follows you everywhere you go. The tangled web of local customs and ingrown ethnic feuds from Ford's Irish pictures informs *Mean Streets, Goodfellas, Gangs of New York, The Departed,* and *The Irishman* (amazing how many movies about Irish Americans he's made considering his feeling for Italian life). And of course his gansters catch the end of *The Informer* in *The Departed*, a story about cannibalistic Irish crooks narcing on each other in modern day Boston, the setting of *The Last Hurrah*, with Martin Sheen filling in for Spencer Tracy as the benevolent government godhead. In *Hugo* we have Scorsese's *How Green Was My Valley* in which a young and infirm boy sees the world through movies and the people closest to him, imagining life beyond the train station he sleeps in illegally following the death of his parents and uncle. Like *How Green is My Valley*'s Huw Morgan, Scorsese and Ford both spent some of their childhood locked away from the world because of medical maladies, reading in Ford's case to get a sense of the world, and watching old movies in Scorsese's. He would rent 16mm prints and screen them on the wall of his grandmother's house, which becomes Hugo's way of finding himself and his purpose after it's taken from him. Interestingly Paul Schrader, Scorsese's frequent screenwriter, remade *The Searchers* twice as *Taxi Driver* and *Hardcore* but has never really found much of a common ground with Ford (despite his occasional overlap with Schrader's hero Bresson, whose movies *Pickpocket, A Man Escaped,* and *Au Hasard Balthazar* have Fordian atmosphere and ideas, though Bresson's style is much more arch, disciplined, and haunting), preferring a humorless austerity that erupts into either carnality, violence, or the occasional joke. Ford loved life more than Schrader does which perhaps explains the traces of *The Fugitive* (his most hated film) and *The Informer* (one of his most beloved) in his studies of men who lock their souls away in journals. Tragically Scorsese's first western is still in post-production at the time of this writing and so its relative Fordian characteristics cannot yet be judged.

One of the great stories of cineaste serendipity is that when Scorsese was trying to rent a print of Michael Powell & Emeric Pressburger's *The Tales of Hoffman*, the other kid in the neighborhood who kept trying to rent it was future genre icon George A. Romero. Romero also had a little of Ford's romantic fatalism, but of course his movies had very high body counts and they were all the people on his block, so to speak, which already give them more humanity than Ford gives the Apache in *Stagecoach*. The zombies in *Night of the Living Dead, The Crazies, Dawn of the Dead, Day of the Dead,* etc. weren't ethnically othered or distant, they were the neighbors and loved ones of the heroes. A scene of an injured man screaming at his commanding officer in *What Price Glory* is repeated over and over in *Day of the Dead*, but the body count must be reckoned with here in a very different way from the Ford war and cavalry movies. Romero's own Western, the gruesome *Survival of the Dead* is a William Wyler tribute but the framing, lighting, and shot length is much more Fordian than it is late Wyler (as are the feuding Irish anti-heroes). *Knightriders*, his 1981 movie about a band of roving renaissance festival performers on motorcycles, is perhaps the most Fordian film Romero ever made, with its study of a fringe community and their nervous leader trying and failing to keep them together despite outside interference and changing mores, it's like *Wagon Train*. You can all but hear Danny Borzage and Ken Curtis rhapsodizing Ed Harris, the Henry Fonda of the 80s, as he leads his charges into false battle.

Another independent filmmaker, Eagle Pennell, the man whose work helped Robert Redford (who made his own attempts at Ford-style films in *The Milagro Beanfield War, The Horse Whisperer,* and *The Conspirator*, his neo-liberal take on *The Prisoner of Shark Island*) start the Sundance film festival, combined elements of classical movies into his new, improvised-feeling movies about working class losers. *In The Whole Shooting Match* (1978) and *Last Night at the Alamo* (1983) men try to survive their days and nights as they sense the days of the cowboy are coming to an end. Pennell is gentle and perceptive in his depiction of Southern masculinity. His characters *may* think they're John Wayne style heroes, but they're much closer to the real John Wayne – posers who can't imagine not being on top, who can't imagine a world where men don't rule everything just because they feel entitled to it. Pennell filled his movies with old country standards just like Ford and became among the first filmmakers to use a radio's playlist as a Greek chorus in the way most movies very lazily resort to needle drops today.

He wasn't the *first* to do that, of course; Peter Bogdanovich, one of Ford's many straight men and patient interviewers hoping to strike gold, had started using modern media as a foil for his action as early his proper narrative debut, 1968's *Targets*, when the action in the 1963 Boris Karloff movie *The Terror*, produced by Roger Corman, as a compliment to Karloff stopping a crazed killer at a drive-in. In 1971's *The Last Picture Show* (a Larry McMurtry adaptation), the movie that won Ford discovery Ben Johnson the Academy Award for best supporting actor, Bogdanovich uses early pop music as an ironic comment on the action, and he sends his young heroes to the movie theatre to see things like Hawks' *Red River* and Ford's own Johnson-starring *Wagon Master*. Bogdanovich became a filmmaker with more in common with Hawks than Ford (he saw *everything*, one of the first directors whose brand and legend were tied to his herculean viewing habits), but Ford's touch is felt in the despairing prairie setting of his grifter comedy *Paper Moon* (1973), a tribute of sorts to *Grapes of Wrath*, and there are the tell-tale hints of *Donovan's Reef* and *Mister Roberts* in the laconic *Saint Jack* (1979), another movie produced by Roger Corman. Perhaps even more crucially is the scene in his underseen 1976 comedy *Nickelodeon* where Burt Reynolds, playing a novice stuntman, winds up riding a horse in Klan robes for an appreciative crowd like Ford did in *Birth of a Nation*. Ford was dead before Bogdanovich shot the movie (which flopped), which is probably what gave him the confidence to do it in the first place. By the time Bogdanovich gets to *Texasville* (1990), his sequel to *Picture Show*, Timothy Bottoms' Sonny has become something like a Hank Worden character from Ford's 50s films and Jeff Bridges' Duane Jackson has aged into a cantankerous Wayne stand-in (complete with estranged wife in Cybill Shepherd's Jacy), surveying a kingdom he doesn't understand and onto which he can barely hang.

A much more *real* kingdom is watched over by a Fonda-like seeker in Lindsay Anderson's fellow New Waver John Boorman's *Excalibur*

(1981), one of a handful of Ford-like films the Irish filmmaker made. *Leo The Last* (1970) picks up in the boarding houses left behind in Ford's *Upstream* and spends its time among the forgotten poor of London. Marcello Mastroianni is the deposed prince who learns to love his fellow man. Lee Marvin is back in the tropics for Boorman's *Hell in the Pacific* (1968), which is a little like *Donavan's Reef* without any jokes, and then Powers Boothe heads down to join him in *The Emerald Forest*, a movie with the colonial hangover from the night of drinking provided by *The Searchers* and *Fort Apache*. In the latter Boothe has to rescue his son, who's been taken in by an Amazonian tribe like one of the captives Wayne sees in *The Searchers* or Stewart and Widmark have to "save" in *Two Rode Together* (avowed Ford fan Paul Greengrass also tells this tale in his own western, *News of the World*). *Hope & Glory* (1987), *The General* (1998), and *Queen & Country* (2015) resurrect Ford's interest in Irish life, from the people wasting away on military bases (a Ford perennial) to the folk heroes doing the dirty work for the cause. Boorman had no illusions about the nature of humanity, his fealty wasn't to "people," necessarily but to the search for the self. *Zardoz, Excalibur, Deliverance,* even *Exorcist II: The Heretic* are about challenging your assumptions, about searching for truth, about looking directly into the mind for the secrets of the world it creates. As Anderson said of Ford, Boorman's movies aren't about their erstwhile subjects but rather the experience of humanity. Lee Marvin strutting through *Point Blank* isn't a man after revenge, he's a man discovering life after the death of the ego. His world is a fragmentary abstraction in Boorman's telling, and as he stalks closer to his goal the world vanishes around him. He's a psychedelic Ethan Edwards pushed further and further into the wasteland.

Dušan Makavejev, born in the former Yugoslavia, started his life as a filmmaker in a Godardian vein, using footage of his country's former glory over footage of the confused ruin it had become after World War 2. Yugoslavia wanted to exist without acknowledging its debt to Stalin's Russia (Makavejev used footage of the uncovering of the Katyn Massacre in Poland in his blistering 1974 opus *Sweet Movie* as his critique of Soviet style communism while also admitting that Yugoslavia's overtures to capitalism were no way forward either. Yugoslavia under Tito tried to stay in the middle of all things, which was no solution to its continued problems). Makavejev's movies hit too close to home and he moved abroad to keep making his art. When Tito died in 1980, it freed Makavejev from his earlier conception of his artistic self and out came a trio of gently Fordian studies of community. In *Montenegro* (1981) a fraying American housewife is taken in by a group of Yugoslavs who enchant her with their combination of sensual rituals. She kills the man who would seek to free her from her life of domesticity. As in Ford the two worlds of the natives and the interlopers are not able to mix, though to Makavejev, that's squarely on the conditioning of the capitalists. In 1985's *The Coca-Cola Kid*, Eric Roberts is sent to Australia to handle a sales crisis at one of the plants his company manages. The former marine is charmed by a local woman and her children. In 1988's *Manifesto*, a town prepares for a visit from the king while a group of revolutionaries plans to kill him when he arrives – though the tone is as gentle as anything in Ford's Irish comedies (it is set in 1920, right around Ford's visit to Ireland as they were fighting for independence).

And speaking of awakenings and breakthroughs, Ken Loach came out of a relatively fallow commercial period with the thriller *Hidden Agenda* in 1990 about a woman whose human rights lawyer husband is killed in Belfast. She tries to divine the cause of his murder with the help of a briny police detective, like a marriage of *Rising of the Moon* and *Gideon's Day*. Loach would continuously make movies in the Ford vein moving forward after his initial career as something close to a neo-realist (a la Leone's old mentor Vittorio De Sica), he became a gentle dramatist with a Fordian sense of humor and a sharp sense of injustice in every imaginable setting. Movies like *Raining Stones* (1993), his Spanish civil war movie *Land & Freedom* (1995), his Irish independence, anti-Black and Tan movie *The Wind That Shakes the Barley* (2006), and his Irish dancehall drama *Jimmy's Hall* all boast a Fordian social concern and gorgeously deliberate form, as well as a love of the specific grace notes of a collective culture. Ford, we can assume, would have especially liked Loach's *Land and Freedom* as Ford once donated an ambulance to the fighters against fascism in Spain during the conflict. *Jimmy's Hall* (2014) is considered minor Loach but its Fordian sentiment emboldens its formal restraint. The movie wants us to remember, and indeed you can hear Loach telling himself this all through his lifetime of pointed political cinema, that we must make time for the things we fight *for*. Ford's films were filled with dancing and singing and humor and so in turn were Loach's, who, like Ford, considered retiring many times but can't seem to stay off of movie sets. There are always people who need a champion and Loach cannot help but try to be him.

Loach's countryman Mike Leigh also waited a long while to start showing the signs of his alignment with Ford. Leigh was always fearless about the issues in his movies (far more so than Ford was 9 times out of 10) but Leigh's vision of the working poor was very close to Ford's, though

Ford went further out of his way to romanticize their struggle and Leigh doesn't want sentimentality to get in the way of the reality of, say, living on the street. In films like *Vera Drake, Mr. Turner,* and *Peterloo* Ford's social concerns can be seen through Leigh's classical form; he renders the horrors of the human condition, especially in JMW Turner's landscapes in the 2014 biopic, as simple yet stirring tableaux. Turner's paintings of action highlighted the social inequality Britain fostered and Leigh's films have the same urgency and truth. Leigh wants you not to be blinded by pictorial pastoralism but rather to see the simplicity of a social struggle through purposeful composition. The ending massacre of *Peterloo* recalls Ford's combat scenes, except it's meant to be casually horrifying. In broad daylight this happened. It happens now. John Sayles, who was, at his best, America's answer to Mike Leigh, also favored the texturally dug-in feeling of *Grapes of Wrath* and *Long Voyage Home* in his labor union drama *Matewan*. There's also *Eight Men Out*, the film that dramatizes the Chicago Black Sox scandal that rocked baseball and inspired both *Flashing Spikes* and *Rookie of the Year*. Later Sayles efforts like *Lone Star, The Secret of Roan Inish, Silver City, Amigo,* and *Go For Sisters* all have analogues in Ford's canon, from Edward James Olmos' Wayne-like presence in *Sisters* to the colonial cavalry plot of *Amigo*. Like a more disciplined Ford, Sayles doesn't want overt stylization to stand between his audience and his true-life (or simply realistic) tales of the history of colonialism and warped masculinity. This has made it easy for Sayles to fall out of favor with the critical establishment who initially praised him, but his movies remain steadfastly *his* and bristle with the charge of decency and dignity. I think Sayles is still one of the most consistent and enjoyable filmmakers we ever got.

American genre maverick John Carpenter was always more of a Hawksian filmmaker (as seen in his *Rio Bravo* homage *Assault of Precinct 13* and his stated but abandoned goal of remaking *Only Angels Have Wings*) but in his romance *Starman*, in which an alien (who becomes like a parody of Wayne or Fonda in his inability to communicate with her in plain English) takes the place of a dead woman's husband, and his polemical comedy *They Live*, which features the longest fist fight since *The Quiet Man*, he taps into his inner Ford, from the earnest treatment of opposites in love and the working class struggling to stay vertical. The scenes of widowed Karen Allen explaining her love for her husband to Jeff Bridges' clueless alien have the gentleness of the reunion dinner in *Rio Grande*, some of the best work either filmmaker ever did. There's also a little of Ford's Cavalrymen in the stranded, abandoned men at the end of the world in Carpenter's *The Thing*. James Cameron similarly was after some of that Hawksian bravado but he found time to pay homage to Ford, from the estranged spouses out of *Rio Grande* in *The Abyss* to the shock of Maureen O'Hara-red hair on Kate Winslet in *Titanic*, to the Wayne homage essayed by Arnold Schwarzenegger in *Terminator 2: Judgement Day* (which is also a nod to Alan Ladd in George Stevens' *Shane*). Then there's *Avatar*, which wraps up a classical western binary in space alien flora and fauna. Sylvester Stallone, Schwarzenegger's friendly rival at the box office, became something like the modern John Wayne, down to the reactionary politics in his personal life and his use of his own family in his movies. In James Mangold's *Cop Land* he delivers a performance worthy of Wayne's work in *She Wore A Yellow Ribbon, The Man Who Shot Liberty Valance,* and *The Quiet Man*. Stallone's own *Rocky* movies never seemed in conversation with much else but his own life and image, but Ryan Coogler's sequel *Creed* does have a Fordian sturdiness and melancholy. Rocky himself must say goodbye to his past glory and the people who gave his life meaning out of the ring, as Ethan Edwards does, as Ford himself did. Mangold himself would keep making movies situated squarely between a couple of golden age directors like Ford, Hawks, George Stevens (who gets an extended shout-out in Mangold's *Logan*) and William Wyler with his love of male bonding, old fashioned love stories, and his digestible fatalism. His very enjoyable remake of Delmer Daves' *3:10 to Yuma* has much more to do with Ford and Wyler than it does the original film's director.

When Ford made *Rising of the Moon* he had considered adding a fourth segment, based on James Joyce's short story *The Dead*. It turns out that John Huston, who shockingly lived nearly into the 1990s, did ultimately film it, beautifully, in 1987. It was his last feature and it's probably his best work, tied at any rate with his 1972 boxer's story *Fat City*, which is as bleak as *The Quiet Man* is romantic. Ford and Huston had both served in World War 2 but parted ways over matters of politics, guilds, and unions. Ford wrote to his cousin to look out for Huston when he moved to Ireland because he was a Red and needed to be avoided at all costs. Huston paid Ford the same compliment by styling Albert Finney's perpetually drunken diplomat in his adaptation of *Under The Volcano* after Ford. Huston's dreadful ethnic comedy *Prizzi's Honor* owes a little to Ford's treatment of hermetic second-generation communities and their foibles. *The Dead*, like Ford's treatment of other Irish writers, has a commanding simplicity, an elegance of style that doesn't get in the way of the demands of the text. Huston could be a stubbornly literal filmmaker (he tried adapting the Bible in the 60s) but at his best he had a sensuousness, a sensitivity, and an unparalleled understanding of how to draw out and convey the inner workings of the heart on the faces of his performers. Like Ford, Huston was privately sadistic and was responsible for as much heartbreak and real, terrible damage to people as any artist who ever lived.

Unsurprisingly considering how much more desert it possesses than America, Australia had its own school of expert Ford admirers. Gillian Armstrong, who can truly do anything, made movies with Ford's stately beauty about coming of age (1979's *My Brilliant Career* and 1994's *Little Women*) that each owe a bit to *How Green is My Valley*. Peter Weir, the titan of the Australian New Wave, made his fair share of Ford-indebted works, from *Witness*' re-staging of *Wagon Master*'s culture clash (trading Mormons for Amish), to *Master & Commander: The Far Side of the World*'s depiction of duty and comportment in battle and *The Way Back*'s group of dogged, hated people on the run right out of *Grapes of Wrath*, and under pressure as in Ford's submarine pictures, and then there's Jeff Bridges' religious anomaly strutting through *Fearless* like the negative image of Fonda's priest in *The Fugitive* (Scorsese also paid homage to Fonda's journey in his 2016 film *Silence*). Russell Mulcahy was always a little too flashy and surface-obsessed to be a true Fordian (though that did make him one of the great filmmakers of the 80s and 90s) but his 2018 Errol Flynn biopic *In Like Flynn* brims with Fordian blarney and aquatic male bonding. Jane Campion, who for so long styled herself as an alternative to the male directors that both her homeland and America produced, finally made a movie with a deliberately Fordian sense of landscape to go with her lonesome cowboys in *The Power of the Dog*. It takes the homoerotic subtext of Ford's westerns and his life and makes them explicit, though not crudely. Her western landscape is like a sun-bleached print of the ones in Ford and George Stevens, where the cruelty of cattle barons can drape itself across sprawling acres like a massive cloud.

Kathryn Bigelow's doomed men-on-a-submarine movie *K-19: The Widowmaker* obviously owes a debt to *Men Without Women* and *Submarine Patrol*, but for more than the obvious reasons. Bigelow's men of war have the same curt, duty-calls mentality as Ford's, though after *K-19*, their perspective shifts because the character of the wars they were fighting changed. In *K-19*, the men fight for the glory of their nation, certainly, but they fight for their families, for their homes, which is always implied in Ford (some of the cavalry movies even have the families of soldiers come with them to drive home the purpose of every mission). Her movies about the quagmire of the Iraq War, *The Hurt Locker* and *Zero Dark Thirty*, lose the connection to home as men begin to identify themselves as soldiers instead of human beings, the thing that finally destroys Ethan Edwards. There is no home for them anymore, they deliberately turn away from it. They become stranded in their own hatreds and desensitized view of the world through the purposefully honed didacticism they use to stay alive. These movies are curious because though the farce of the organization and commitment of the Iraq War has been thoroughly documented and called out for the war crime it was, there was enough interest in their inner workings that both of those movies were very popular. As the beginning of the war recedes from view and joins Vietnam as one of the great stains on the legacy of America, how will these movies, their search for impossible objective truths about warfare, age?

Ermanno Olmi's religious allegory *The Legend of the Holy Drinker* shares an angelic view of alcoholism with many a Ford film, with Rutger Hauer doing his best Thomas Mitchell impression. Olmi's films were split, in a rather Fordian sense, between Marxist tales of working class life and the difficulty of maintaining your humanity in a culture of materialism, and overbearing and beautiful documentations of religious life in Italy. A true modernist when making the former kind of movie he saw humans become pieces of machinery that were starting to rule Italian society's production of goods and thus to stand in for the idea of identity and personal fulfilment. Reductively: money replaced god. Which perhaps explains why Olmi the radical was always willing to make movies with such reverent attitudes towards their religious subject matter. With Ford's light quality shining the way, Olmi movies such as *A Man Named John, Camminacammina, Genesis: The Creation and the Flood, One Hundred Nails,* and *Vedete, sono uno di voi*, Olmi attempts to link divinity to human beings, to show religion not as the perverted thing it becomes under dialectical materialism, but rather the ways in which people themselves create the divine through individual belief. Ford would never gotten into the weeds like this, but deep down his convictions about the world weren't very different. Like Hauer's holy drinker, he found the divine in his joys, in the things men give each other, and rarely made movies specifically about his faith (the big exception, *The Fugitive*, flopped which taught him to never do it again). Olmi did it for him.

Actor Paul McGann recounted stories of being directed by David Fincher on the set *Alien³* that usually included Fincher always being sure to vocally tip his hat to the directors who inspired him. "Here comes John

Ford," he'd say when lining up a shot with movement out of *The Searchers*. It may be funny to think of Fincher now as a Fordian director with his unyielding pace and 10,000 takes on every shot, but then you look at *Alien³* and see it's like the inverse of *7 Women* with the same considered air of apocalypse, hell on earth preceded by the arrival of a fearless woman. *Fight Club*, which could also be called *They Were Expendable*, is like a parody of Ford's tales of men in uniform, and *The Curious Case of Benjamin Button* actually becomes *They Were Expendable* for a reel. Fincher is a radical behind the camera but his values boil down to something rather like Ford's. Even pipsqueak anti-heroes like Mark Zuckerberg get the fullness of his consideration, and a movie as boundlessly dark as *The Girl With The Dragon Tattoo* has a happy ending. Knottier works like *Gone Girl, The Game,* or *Zodiac* clearly don't fit at all into a classical mold like Ford's but the disappointing *Mank* tries to recreate the studio system Ford occupied and *Benjamin Button*'s plot may be closer to the fabulism of Portrait of Jennie but it's in classical legible handwriting, Fincher's default when making crowd-pleasers. *Benjamin Button* also features a very Fordian turn from the great Jared Harris, who would later play another Ford hero, Ulysses Grant, for Steven Spielberg.

Spielberg is probably the most obvious Ford disciple of the post Ford years, maybe even more so than Eastwood. He met Ford when he was just starting out – a scene he replicates in his 2022 Roman à clef *The Fablemens*, perhaps the director's finest work. David Lynch (who made his own spin on Ford's westerns with *The Straight Story* in which a horse is traded for a riding mower on a cross country trek) plays Ford and instructs Spielberg's surrogate on a few of the facts of life, or filmmaking, which are the same thing to both men. Lynch captures Ford's unpleasant mannerisms perfectly and he aged into looking quite like the man. Spielberg listened to his mentor well. From the get-go the famous Spielberg face, the wide eyes, the marvel, the golden light dancing across the faces of his heroes as they cross the threshold from the possible to the magical, is a play on the face that Dorothy Jordan makes when she sees John Wayne riding onto her property in *The Searchers*. Spielberg found his own Wayne in Harrison Ford's Indiana Jones and styled Sean Connery, who plays his father in *The Last Crusade* after the likes of Donald Crisp, John Carradine, and Thomas Mitchell. The Spielberg light quality is right out of Ford's 50s movies, and indeed when Richard Dreyfuss gets to heaven in *Always*, he finds himself in *The Quiet Man*'s rustic expanse.

If *Jurassic Park* is a cross between author Michael Chrichton's

*Westworld* and Hawks' *Hatari!* then its sequel *The Lost World* is *Mogambo* with dinosaurs, a comedy of remarriage with bloody violence lurking behind every tree. Well-meaning but incomplete visions like *Amistad* and *The Post* both recall *Cheyenne Autumn* in their liberal aims, scenes of white men doing the right thing while sidelining their ostensible heroes. *Saving Private Ryan* dramatizes the D-day landing (which Ford was famously present for, shooting it with his crew) with uncommon brutality and clarity before becoming exactly the kind of soporific "duty calls" film Ford could churn out in his sleep. The hero of *The Terminal* is the kind of character John Qualen would play for Ford given his own solo outing, the lonely, dopy outsider you cannot help but love. As the legendary thinker Steven Boone says, *The Color Purple* is a violent pastoral made in the image of *How Green Was My Valley*, and, not coincidentally *Empire of the Sun* also centers on an English boy experiencing the hardships of adult life for the first time. *War of the Worlds* finds a family like the Joads heading into the unknown to survive an alien invasion instead of the great depression or the paranoid climate during the Iraq War (its actual target). *War Horse* may indeed be a better movie of *The Quiet Man* than *The Quiet Man*, with echoes of *How Green was My Valley*, *Kentucky Pride*, and *What Price Glory* for good measure. It's almost a shame the horse doesn't voice its thoughts like the one in *Kentucky Pride*, but Spielberg is actually capable of restraint, not that anyone gives him credit for it. *Lincoln* is the culmination of his love for Ford (beyond of course Ford's cameo in *The Fabelmans*). Ford made many movies with Lincoln as either focal point or uniting texture and so Spielberg had to make a Lincoln movie for his own time, 2012, the thick of the Obama presidency, and though its message of compromise won't age any better than D.W. Griffith's movie of Lincoln's life as apologia for *Birth of a Nation*, the filmmaking and the performances will. The thoughtful compositions and scientifically perfect camera movements designed to land us right inside the minds of its titanic presences (whether Daniel Day-Lewis' honest Abe or Tommy Lee Jones's Thaddeus Stevens) represent Spielberg at his best, channeling Ford while making a movie with emotionalism cranked even higher than Ford would have managed. *Lincoln* is a movie about people slotting themselves into a historic context in a moment that they understand will outlive each of them and deciding to become the person they want to be remembered as. It's a rewrite of the final scene of *Fort Apache* in which York lies to the press about the noble deeds of each dead man under Thursday's command. Here a roll call of otherwise forgotten men places their goodness on trial and even after repeated watches it is *thrilling* to watch as each man wrestles with their soul, with the goodness clawing to get out of them, to become who they know they can be. Maybe it isn't the most important story of the civil war and its unyielding attendant horrors, but it's the one Spielberg was qualified to make, and no one on earth is ever going to do better with this particular story.

The Lincoln movie is indeed something of a tradition tied to Ford, which is why A.J. Edwards' debut feature *The Better Angels* is so interesting. As in *Young Mr. Lincoln* he finds a passage of Lincoln's life that hadn't been much dramatized, his boyhood years, as he loses one mother and gains another. The setting recalls *Tobacco Road* with its hovels in the woods, but the form is a beautiful compromise between Ford's breathless care for his characters and Terrence Malick's blinking eye formalism. This is, of course, because Malick was Edwards' teacher, to put it more simply than their relationship deserves. Edwards was Malick's editor on a number of his films including the Ford-esque *The New World* (another revision of *Drums Along the Mohawk* somehow even more magnificent than *Last of the Mohicans*) about the first white Europeans to settle in Virginia. *The New World* is able to be honest about the conflict between its white and Powhatan characters and though it follows the story to its logical end and treats the romance between John Smith and Pocahontas with suitable warmth and respectfully chaste eroticism, it knows that this is, must be, a tragedy. It ends with America born and that's no happy ending.

Ford's fellow Irish director Martin McDonagh's *The Banshees of Inisherin* has the barroom picaresque quality of *The Rising of the Moon*. Irish Neil Jordan tipped his hat to golden age Hollywood craftsmen like Hawks, Norman Z. McLeod, Edward Dmytryk, and Leo McCarey in his choice of remakes and subjects, but occasionally tipped his hat in Ford's direction as well, from the hot button *The Crying Game* about Irish revolutionaries waging their war in peacetime, the lovely fable *Ondine*, about a lonely fisherman who gets a mermaid in his net, to *The Butcher Boy* about Huw Morgan-like figure growing up in 1960s Ireland, which Ford haunted during pre-production on *Young Cassidy*. The then-new star of *The Crying Game* was Jaye Davidson, who was chosen by Roland Emmerich to star in his desert adventure sci-fi hybrid *Stargate* shortly after. Many stories of men with guns sent to the end of the world find their inspiration in Ford films like *She Wore a Yellow Ribbon*, where danger is met with good humor and dignity so perhaps it's a stretch to make much out of *Stargate*'s resemblance to Ford films but make no mistake, Emmerich is a dyed-in-the-wool Fordian. Emmerich's movies have been shabbily treated by critics over the years, indeed like Michael Bay he can at times be one of the most unimaginative critics' favorite punching bag, but in adopting a pictorial and dramatical style out of Ford he has ensured that his movies will always find purchase with a swath of international audiences. He knows which buttons to push in his audience's emotional reactions, his compositions are clean, handsome, and functional, and his scenes of destruction have the mightiness of old school spectacle. His movies also have a very winning belief in the decency of people. He learned quickly that audiences don't like complicated art, so he brought them easy victories wrapped in beautiful packages (like Ford, his experiments in a more pessimistic worldview have always wound up his worst selling products). His white elephant *The Patriot* is another rewrite of *Drums Along the Mohawk* complete with unfortunately naïve political formulations about the participants in the Revolutionary War. The father-son relationship between Dennis Quaid and Jake Gyllenhaal in *The Day After Tomorrow* (which, like *Stagecoach*, features a group of people at the end of the world who have to stave off hostile elements) recalls many of the damaged father-son pairings in Ford's work. In his 2011 *Anonymous* Emmerich's Edward De Vere cuts a tragic and overbearing figure like John Wayne in *The Man Who Shot Liberty Valance*, trying to get a cowardly admirer to fight a war his way. His lonely death, having lost control of the empire he once loved and the love of the woman who mattered most to him, recalls both Doc Holliday's abortive romance with Chihuahua in *My Darling Clementine* and Frank Skeffington's final days in *The Last Hurrah*. *Stonewall* has the same misguided liberalism as *Cheyenne Autumn* and then there's *Midway*, a story of navy pilots that happens to include John Ford as a character (played by Geoffrey Blake), filming the battle of Midway from the deck of a battleship as he really did in 1941. More recently the Naval pilot movie *Devotion*, directed by J.D. Dillard attempted a similar kind of a story with success, though this time the famous celebrity the pilots encounter is Liz Taylor, played unconvincingly by Serinda Swan. It didn't help the movie that it starred Glen Powell as a pilot so soon after Joseph Kosinski's thrilling *Top Gun* sequel *Maverick*, which beat it to theatres by half a year, did the same thing.

Tony Scott, the director of *Top Gun* wasn't much of a demonstrative Ford fan, though his submarine movie *Crimson Tide* is naturally indebted to some of Ford's, and Denzel Washington (who also leads the Scott films *Man on Fire, Déjà vu, The Taking of Pelham 123,* and *Unstoppable*) is the modern John Wayne we deserve. He would later lead *The Book of Eli* by the wonderful Hughes brothers, Albert and Allan, which has a

Fordian sense of humor and centers on a man striking out to an inhospitable western landscape. Tony Scott's brother Ridley was more expressive in his admiration for Ford. His creation stories *1492: Conquest of Paradise* and *Kingdom of Heaven* have at once the indescribable beauty and the same perfidiousness of Ford's historical epics, but at least come to the merciful conclusion that missions to colonize other countries are doomed to folly and murder if in a very roundabout way. *Black Hawk Down* has the same attitude about combat, about helping the man next to you, as any Ford war film, and the same attitude towards the humanity of its faceless villains. *G.I. Jane* weaponizes the recruitment comedy antics of movies like *The Wings of Eagles* and *The Long Gray Line* while *The White Squall* dramatizes Ford's own approach to life; teach people the meaning of life from your yacht. Somehow Scott, like fellow Ford antecedents Spielberg, Emmerich, Spike Lee, Terence Davies, Tim Burton, James Gray, and Francis Ford Coppola, has never made a western. Unsung Fordian Thomas Vinterberg *nearly* has in the post-modern curio *Dear Wendy*, but that shows the fewest hallmarks of his Ford adulation. Ford's touch can be felt in the gentle alcoholic comedy *Another Round* starring a very Wayne and Fonda-like Mads Mikkelsen, the submarine drama *Kursk*, and his adaptation of Thomas Hardy's *Far From The Madding Crowd*, which adopts Ford's nostalgic view of a community in transition.

Spike Lee's kinship with Ford is in the earnest emotional pull of his work derived from his feelings of the communities he makes his movies about. The love for the Irish immigrants in America that Ford managed every time at bat is met by Lee's depictions of his people in New York in movies like *Malcolm X, He Got Game, Crooklyn,* and the uncommon war film *Miracle at St. Anna*, which of course greatly resembles Ford's own very strange war films. And of course Lee indicts the comedy of Ford's friend Stepin Fetchit with his incendiary film *Bamboozled*. Lee's movies are so often revisions of previous movies told from the perspectives left out of the first hundred years of populist filmmaking. Directors like Griffith and Ford are his frequent targets but he was canny enough to take from the theory needed to ensure that his movies would speak to the audiences who actually needed to learn the lessons American cinema refused to teach them. Lee used the ideas of America's artistic monoliths as a weapon to attempt to deprogram the people weaned on those same foundations. Naturally people resisted all through his career and rejected his broad strokes approach to identifying white supremacy, but as in all things the idea *must* be acknowledged before it can be met with and Lee has done more to get people to acknowledge the forces inside every white American than just about any other entertainer with his reach. Ford's movies built a vision of America and it is good that people like Lee are at hand to point out its architectural flaws. Our myths *must* be questioned and challenged and Lee used some of the most ingratiating, nervy form to do so.

James Gray has become something of a beautiful anomaly since his debut *Little Odessa* in 1994. Like Peter Bogdanovich his public persona is intrinsically tied to his voracious cinematic appetite. He appears to have seen every American movie made before 1990, can do spot-on impressions of every one of his influences and collaborators, and makes movies that showcase his love for classic cinema. He borrows heavily from directors with heavy brush strokes like Francis Ford Coppola and Michael Cimino, and thus even if he wasn't a Ford fan, he'd still be drawing from his playbook because they were. Gray's studies of immigrant families and the many genres in which these characters find themselves (from *Mogambo*-style jungle adventures to explorations of urban political machinations out of *The Last Hurrah*) simply conform to meet the stylistic and character choices to which Gray feels closest. Ford's idealized regiments of cultural custom and social intimacy between men finds purchase in every Gray film, as does his love of allowing room for individual gesture, something modern film doesn't usually leave breathing room for. Just as Ford doesn't cut away from Ward Bond in *The Searchers* as he silently spies Dorothy Jordan and John Wayne's loving farewell, Gray makes room for surprising and shocking gestures from his cast, as when he allows us to see Joaquin Phoenix's awkward return to his family's home in *Two Lovers* after he vows to leave. He sits where he knows his mother can see him before making his way across the room to propose to the woman we know was his second choice, but where the room can see the embrace, only the camera can see the ambiguousness of his expression as she accepts his proposal. A similar gesture right out of Ford in a movie with otherwise little in common with his work is Michael Almereyda's exquisite and generous *Experimenter* where in the final shot we see Stanley Milgram (Peter Sarsgaard) look at his wife (Winona Ryder) through the mirror that he's been conducting his life's work through, finally allowing them a moment of clarity of each other's image that their domestic life didn't offer them. Moments lightly underlined like that become rarer all the time.

Terence Davies, the poet of the British Cinema, always had Ford's complex family dynamic in his movies because it so mirrored his own. The difficult, dismissive fathers of *Rio Grande, How Green Was My Valley, The*

*Wings of Eagles*, *When Willie Comes Marching Home*, and *My Darling Clementine* are present in Davies' movies *Distant Voices, Still Lives*, *The Neon Bible*, *Sunset Song*, and *Benediction*, because that was how he knew his own father. Distance and obscurity was the language spoken in his house, so when husbands and wives are estranged in *The Deep Blue Sea* and *Sunset Song* it's both truth to the texts and things Davies understood in his bones. Like Ford Davies was after an impressionistic kind of cinema but, unlike Ford, Davies wasn't trapped by custom or the market. Sadly he's too unique to fit into the trends of his own national cinema and so isn't the kind of artist they cut blank checks for, but he's managed to build one of the greatest and most true bodies of work since Ford himself, films of staggering passion and horrible, quaking loss and confusion, of artists dying without having learned the lessons their own art would impart to others.

It wasn't all serious business paying homage to Ford. The Coen Brothers (whose screenwriter character *Barton Fink* is asked to write Ford's *Flesh* while the William Faulkner stand-in kills himself with drink) manage to shine their light on his work in comedies and tragedies alike. *O Brother, Where Art Thou?* is like a comic take on *The Grapes of Wrath* or perhaps an actually funny *Tobacco Road*. Their western omnibus *The Ballad of Buster Scruggs* reconfigures Ford's landscapes and wandering heroes in both elegiac vignettes of lonesome discovery and in uproarious riffs on western heroes. The uproarious red-baiting fantasia *Hail Caesar!* takes place during the blacklist, which saw Ford on the run from all sides trying to keep his allegiances, his paycheck, and his dignity all at once. The Irish gangsters of *Miller's Crossing* and the bloviating cowboys of their *True Grit* remake alike look backwards at Ford's character types. The Road Runner and Wile E. Coyote cartoons of Chuck Jones' *Looney Tunes* stable used Monument Valley as their perpetual, self-replicating backdrop. The writers room at *The Simpsons* seemed to harbor a few not-so-secret Ford scholars as details from his movies and his very warped sense of humor would appear all the time, down to a Stutz Bearcat (Ford's car, mentioned in a letter one of his lovers wrote to him) being driven by Mr. Burns. Similarly there's a lot of the idea of a Ford movie in the *Jackass* movies, from their fearless leader and his ubiquitous naval officer's cap (Johnny Knoxville) to the crew's changing fortunes and roles throughout many different, frequently bone-breaking adventures. Ford loved stuntmen and there are no more high profile stuntmen than the boys of Jackass, who are now getting as old as Wayne and Stewart were in *The Man Who Shot Liberty*

*Valance*. It sometimes pays to remember what a gross out, sophomoric sense of humor Ford had. Joseph McBride pointed out that for some people, the first time they ever heard the expression "Go Fuck Yourself," it was out of the mouth of John Ford. Add to that the famously violent on-set antics of Ford and his cast, like the time John Wayne woke Ward Bond up from a hangover-induced deep sleep by pouring vodka on him and lighting him on fire and their similarities grow by the minute. An unfortunate parallel between the Jackass crew and the Ford Stock Company can be found in the health issues they gave themselves in the line of duty and the deaths related specifically to their lifestyles. Ford was never the same after filming the death of stuntman Fred Kennedy just as the death of unparalleled actor, stunt performer and comedian Ryan Dunn fundamentally changed the *Jackass* cast's relationship to each other and to their lives on and off screen.

Analogues for Wayne heroes like Wayne can be found in Guillermo Del Toro's *Hellboy* movies starring a never more acerbic Ron Perlman. Harrison Ford plays another Wayne analogue as an Irish American cop in Alan J. Pakula's final film *The Devil's Own*, in which a not-convincingly brogued Brad Pitt comes over from the old country to bring guns on a boat back to Ireland, just as Ford had in the 20s. And conversely if you'd ever wished for a movie that only takes place in the red twilight that preempts the arrival of Henry Brandon's villainous Scar in *The Searchers*, look no further than Alex Proyas' *The Crow*, in which Brandon Lee becomes an avenging angel in full face paint. Caroline Link's *Nowhere in Africa* tells the story of *Mogambo* but goes looking harder for the truth of white emigres trying to insinuate themselves into Kenyan culture. Nicolas Cage plays the Wayne figure in John Woo's *Windtalkers* which incorporates the kind of footage of the war Ford himself shot. Unusually for a war film his foil is Adam Beach, who plays a Navajo code talker. The two men, as Western heroes must, learn to understand each other to survive in hostile territory. Frank "Spig" Wead's story gets an impressionistic overhaul in Julian Schnabel's *The Diving Bell and the Butterfly*, another true tale based on the life of Jean-Dominique Bauby. The late Icelandic filmmaker Solveig Anspach, who I had the immense privilege to know for a brief period of time, re-wired Ford's tales of island outcasts with *The Rebel, Louise Michelle,* starring the great Sylvie Testud, as did the legendary Chantal Akerman with her 2011 film *Almayer's Folly*, based on Joseph Conrad. Kelly Reichardt's westerns *Meek's Cutoff* and *First Cow* can be attributed to no one particular source of inspiration (Reichardt is one of the great American artists) but it's perhaps fair to say those particular Westerns, so unlike most others of the genre, owe their calm tone and simple framing to Ford's domestic qualities, which followed him even to the frontier in movies like *Rio Grande* and *Wagon Master*.

M. Night Shyamalan is one of the few directors to fully reach for the big, goofy moments of humor with which Ford so often attempted to fill his otherwise serious work. *Signs*, a kind of reverse American Bible story, and *The Village*, have tons of the kinds of earnest jokes Ford would ladle onto his cavalry films, as well as the pictorial pulchritude of the best of Ford. America looks beautiful, of course, in both Shyamalan and Ford's movies, which helps us care a little more about its destruction. Xavier Beauvois took a similar but more subdued approach, leaving out the humor of his Ford tributes and going for a more quiet and heart-string pulling integrity. *Of Gods and Men*, his all-male remake of *7 Women*, and *The Guardians*, his take on *The Grapes of Wrath*, both stare unblinking at the people who have agreed that their lot in life comes with suffering and they will simply bear it. At its best this strategy is enormously moving. Tim Burton adopted Ford's landscapes almost ironically. After abandoning suburbia and metropolitan settings from his early works (though in fairness he does make a pitstop in Ford's desert, George Stevens' Texas, and John Wayne's *The Alamo*, in *Pee-Wee's Big Adventure*) he began to use Ford's beautiful z-axis reliant portraits of communities, both built for him and on backlots, as a way to hint at creeping unease in close knit places in movies like *Ed Wood* (which features an appearance by Ford's friend and champion Orson Welles, played by Vincent D'Onofrio and voiced by Maurice LaMarche, presaging Lynch's turn as John Ford) *Sleepy Hollow, Big Fish, Dark Shadows,* and finally *Dumbo*, his best synthesis of Ford. In *Dumbo* Burton's sense of the Fordian landscape and the male heroic arc is combined with Ford's business partner Merian C. Cooper's love of the carnival, where *Dumbo* is set (incidentally the lightly Fordian romance *Water For Elephants* is also set in a traveling carnival). That our hero is a man without the use of his arm, as 'Spig' Wead lost the use of his legs, further endears him to Burton. Ford's movies themselves were sporadically carnivalesque but more importantly the sets themselves were like traveling carnivals, and so that feeling to a director with a set crew of collaborators always brings to mind Ford and his company and their weeks of partying in the desert or at the farm Ford bought for them.

Stories of Francis Ford Coppola, one of America's great cinematic artists, preparing for movies on his vineyard have a similar character to those of Ford's party-heavy working method. His temper on sets is reportedly just shy of Ford-esque but the stories of the ways he kept his filmmaking family and blood family afloat can't help but tap the heartstrings. Taking Carey Elwes, Billy Campbell, and Richard E. Grant up in a hot air balloon to bond them before they acted together in *Dracula*, allowing young screenwriters James DeMonaco and Gary Nadeau to live at his estate for months while they workshopped the script for what would become *Jack*, the movie that helped push Coppola out of debt, allowing Tom Waits and Crystal Gayle to brainstorm the score for *One From the Heart* on his grounds. It was very much like the stories of the non-stop party atmosphere of otherwise tempestuous Ford sets. Like Ford, Coppola hired his relatives or got them jobs elsewhere in the film industry, used a stock company that included Waits, Laurence Fishburne, Frederic Forrest, James Caan, and Robert Duvall. His children would spend time on set and so sometimes would his wife, who turned her documentation of the making of *Apocalypse Now* into the highly regarded movie *Hearts of Darkness*. And then there are the Fordisms lying all over Coppola's filmography. *Tucker: The Man and his Dream* has the same indefatigable spirit and occasional touches of melancholy as Ford's biopics *Young Mr. Lincoln* and *The Wings of Eagles*. His Irish musical *Finian's Rainbow* is born of the same outsized romanticism of the Irish that led to Ford's own Irish films, most of them at least partly musical. The overt, expressionism of *Dracula, Apocalypse Now, The Outsiders, Rumble Fish,* and *Youth Without Youth* are all rooted in the crossover of German technique brought here when Ford's hero Murnau and his peers' movies came to America and were paid homage in such Ford films as *The Informer, The Fugitive,* and *Four Sons*. *Gardens of Stone*, which was to star Coppola's son before his tragic death in an accident Coppola would illustrate in his movie *Twixt*, was very consciously a modern-day Ford cavalry movie. Coppola's own family history, like Ford's, was all plot in waiting. *The Rainmaker* is about a young man learning about the law through its application as in *Young Mr. Lincoln* and *Sergeant Rutledge*. And of course in his *Godfather* saga are utopian depictions of family units/military units getting together to celebrate through song, dance, and ritual.

Takashi Miike, the joyously provocative polymath of Japanese cinema, got close to Ford's treatment of honor in the line of duty with his terrifically exciting police movie *Shield of Straw*, in which a man refuses to give a fugitive to an angry mob like Judge Priest before him. Similarly holding off chaotic hordes are the heroes of a handful of dirty New York Movies, like the tributarily named *Fort Apache, The Bronx* by Daniel Petrie and Abel Ferrara's grimy *Fear City*, in which a cop and a pimp have to join forces to catch a serial killer. Sidney J. Furie & Robert Butler's *Night of the Juggler* condenses *The Searchers* into one sweaty day in Manhattan. Walter Hill's *The Warriors* plays like a comic book Cavalry picture and *Streets of Fire* is a musical in the Ford mold, where music is everywhere but not quite centralized as it would be in a more traditional artist's form. Hill always toed the line that *The Searchers* was not Ford's masterpiece as was often claimed, which explains why his own Westerns only fleetingly seemed like the work of a man working in Ford's sandbox. His 2022 comeback western *Dead for a Dollar* has the shape of a movie by Ford's friend Budd Boetticher, though there's no denying that his 1993 *Geronimo* is very nearly a remake of *Cheyenne Autumn*. *Wild Bill* (1995) is far more experimental than Ford ever got a chance to be, but the cockeyed sense of humor and the fatalist attitude recall both *She Wore a Yellow Ribbon* and *The Informer*. *Southern Comfort* has the same plot as *The Lost Patrol* except the villains do ultimately have Hill's sympathy more than most of his un-friendly soldiers. Hill more often paid tribute to Ford acolyte Sam Peckinpah than Ford outright. When he directed the pilot for David Milch's unspeakably beautiful TV show *Deadwood* he didn't quite the feel of Milch's Shakespearian language; he always relied on images over words. Milch's show had its share of icons in it, from Wild Bill Hickock to Calamity Jane to Wyatt Earp, who was one of Ford's favorites. By the time the show got its own movie treatment in 2019 director Daniel Minahan gave it the romantic tone of Ford's best westerns, with coarse whoremonger Al Swearengen (Ian McShane) passing gently into legend with his minders and admirers at his side like Judge Priest at the end of *The Sun Shines Bright*. *Deadwood the Movie* has one of the most faithful Ford structures of any modern film, and like a lot of late Ford the appearance of the characters (and the actors playing them) we recognize from the show has the feeling of seeing old friends. Milch understands the value of faces like Ford does and knows that just as we'll be happy to see Ben Johnson return to Ford's cinema in *Cheyenne Autumn*, it is a pleasure to see Al Swearengen one more time.

Rowdy Harrington's study of fighting men (*Road House, Gladiator*) have an awful lot of Ford's two fisted confidence and admiration. *Sopranos* creator David Chase's feature film debut *Not Fade Away* restages *How Green is My Valley* with rock and roll standing in for the end of the valley and freedom with it. Hungarian director Miklós Jancsó's roving camera studies of crowds of soldiers not infrequently calls to mind the Ford of the Cavalry and Civil War movies. To list the complete works of Ford disciples would take a full book unto itself but suffice it to say I've found echoes of Ford's strong, stoic heroes in movies as disparate as Kaneto Shindô's final film *Postcard*, Jim Mickle's *Stake Land*, Gavin O'Connor's *The Way Back* and *Warrior*, Hirokazu Kore-eda's *The Third Murder*, Joe Carnahan's *The Grey*, Werner Herzog's *Queen of the Desert*, Curtis Hanson's *The River Wild*, Craig Gillespie's *The Finest Hours*, Jeff Nichols' *Loving*, David Gordon Green's *Stronger*, Bong Joon-Ho's *Okja*, Richard Linklater's *Last Flag Flying*, Debra Granik's *Leave No Trace*, and Baltasar Kormákur's *Beast*. In the documentaries of Fred Wiseman I see dissections of the communities Ford's movies were attempting to invent an image of that only existed in un-voiced memory of a half-told truth.

When we look at John Ford's movies we see America as if for the first time and to some people it was the first time they'd had a look at the way stories work, the way they carry, the way we imagine ourselves; as heroes but not without sin, as messy people in a vicious place that nevertheless can cruelly allow for grace. John Ford may not be the most important director in America, but there would be no America to regard, to contemplate, to imagine, to see without him. Not the one we imagine, not the one we had to re-imagine, not the one we still have yet to build out of stories not yet told and images undreamt.

The only way to take stock of a country's artistic heritage, the painted image of its massacres rendered in heroic shapes and bold colors, is to never lose sight of the shape shifting simulacra. My editor Jon Nix reminds me that Jean Baudrillard saw Monument Valley as the essence of American culture – unnatural formations rising from nothingness in areas condemned to poverty by the usurping religious elite who wished for nothing so much as the whole world for themselves, but settled for country that was the birthright of the vanquished.

"America is neither dream nor reality." Baudrillard wrote in his book, *America*, in 1986. "It is a hyperreality because it is a Utopia which has behaved from the very beginning as though it were already achieved. Everything here is real and pragmatic, and yet it is all the stuff of dreams too. It may be that the truth of America can only be seen by a European, since he alone will discover here the perfect simulacrum - that of the immanence and material transcription of all values. The Americans, for their part, have no sense of simulation. They are themselves simulation in its most developed state, but they have no language in which to describe it, since they themselves are the model. As a result, they are the ideal material for an analysis of all the possible variants of the modern world. No more and no less in fact than were primitive societies in their day. The same mythical and analytic excitement that made us look towards those earlier societies today impels us to look in the direction of America. With the same passion and the same prejudices."

We will always have a craven pastiche of our grandfather's crimes, our grandmother's being cheated out of a life of free emotion and painless growth. The truth of what we lost to spare us the gilded rendering of what we believed but never earned. Ford's films recount the death of a country as much as its birth and rebirth in someone else's uterine blood. The birth of America as an idea was only ever the death of its first history, something that, despite the new America's best efforts, could never be erased. We tell stories now to remember what we can no longer reach. We watch Ford movies to know what audiences once treasured, believed, hoped to rise to, hoped to escape from and into. John Ford's America was at once never real and the only thing that was real in its indescribably heavenly falseness. His America was hell and heaven. And it's our America now. To forget what he gave us, a negative and positive example, to write off the bad men of history and their paeans to cleansing destruction and the pitiless morality of the conqueror, means we cannot ever describe ourselves anew. American artists cannot create something better for a people finally able to live in the truth of history without acknowledging everything on which they're building their foundations. A painting cannot be absent a subject or idea, a new work, a new law, a new role model revises the work of an old one, and a ghost must once have lived.

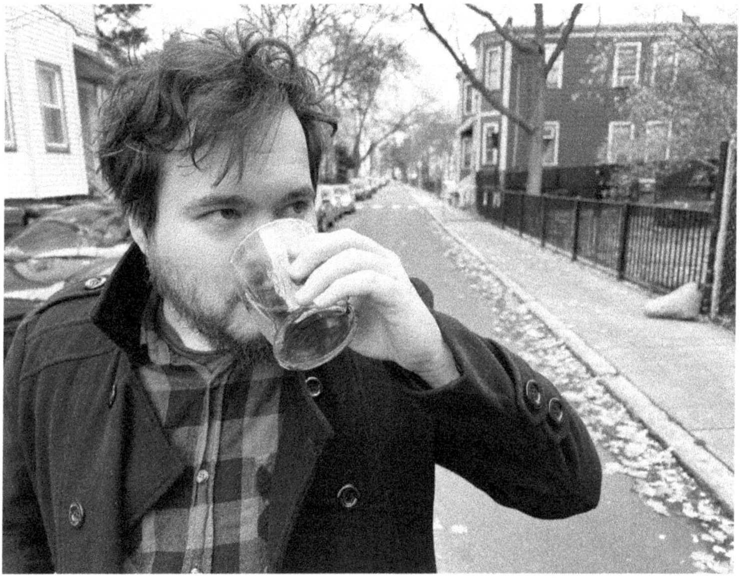

Photo Credit: Tucker Johnson

## *About the Author*

Scout Tafoya is a filmmaker, critic, and author from Doylestown, PA. His writing has been featured in The Village Voice, Film Comment, and The Los Angeles Review of Books among many other publications. He's the creator of *The Unloved* at RogerEbert.com, the longest running continuous video essay series on film. His movies include *Eyam*, *House of Little Deaths*, and *Hang The Pale Bastard*, and his first book is *Cinemaphagy: On the Psychedelic Classical Form of Tobe Hooper*, the first book length analytical study of the director of *Poltergeist* and *The Texas Chain Saw Massacre*.

Milton Keynes UK
Ingram Content Group UK Ltd.
UKHW040627151024
2185UKWH00032B/129

9 798987 478714